FRANCE
AND THE EIGHTEENTH-CENTURY
CORSICAN QUESTION

France
and the Eighteenth-Century
Corsican Question

Thadd E. Hall

New York: New York University Press
1971

To Patricia

Acknowledgments

I began this study as a doctoral dissertation at the University of Minnesota. In a sense, therefore, all of the professors under whom I studied at that institution have contributed, at least indirectly, to it. I am especially grateful to my mentor, Professor Paul W. Bamford, for his constant encouragement and constructive criticism. I remember clearly the first seminar paper that I wrote under his direction and how his advice helped me to resolve problems of structure, logic, evidence, and clarity of expression. The training that he gave me in reading eighteenth-century manuscripts saved me a great amount of time when I started research in French archives and had manuscript materials thrown at me in profusion. Moreover, before I entered archival repositories in France I had fixed in my mind their general physical plan and the mechanics for using them. This too I owe to Professor Bamford's counsel and direction; he has been truly a *directeur des recherches*.

I have also benefited from various kinds of assistance given to me by a number of other individuals. Dr. Gerard L. Buckout revealed to me the challenges of historical research and teaching while I was still an undergraduate. Professors John Turner and John B. Wolf read and commented on an earlier draft of the manuscript. Professor Wolf also graciously took time off from his research on his recent biography of Louis XIV to introduce me to the Archives du Ministère de la Guerre. Professor Norman Cantor commented on a later version of the manuscript and recommended it to New York University Press. Of course, no one but myself is in any way responsible for errors of omission or commission that this study may contain.

I acknowledge with thanks the receipt of several grants that facilitated the research for this study. They include a Fulbright Grant for study in Paris during the academic year 1963-1964, a University of Minnesota Graduate School Grant, and summer research support from Southern Illinois University. I would be remiss if I did not mention receipt of an American Philosophical Society Summer Research Grant for 1969. Although actually awarded for research on another subject, this grant facilitated my return to Paris during the summer of 1969, and I was therefore able to recheck a few of the citations for this study. These grants made possible research in the following archives and libraries: The Archives Nationales; the Archives du Ministère de la Guerre; the Archives du Ministère des Affaires Étrangères; the Archives du Ministère de la Marine; the Archives départementales des Bouches-du-Rhône (manuscripts loaned to the Archives Nationales for use in Paris); the Archives départementales de la Corse; and the Bibliothèque Nationale. I am grateful to the conservators, archivists, and librarians of these repositories for their many acts of kindness and their generous helpfulness. The "Research and Projects" division of the Graduate School of Southern Illinois University provided funds for typing the manuscript.

The Fulbright Grant also made possible a five-week sojourn on the island of Corsica that was both professionally rewarding and personally enjoyable. I am happy to second the observations about the Corsican peoples' hospitality that James Boswell made when he visited Corsica during the period covered by this study. I will long remember my experiences in Corsica, especially in Ajaccio, and the warmth of the Corsican people.

viii

The staffs of various libraries in the United States have facilitated the research for this study by making their resources available and by helping me to locate rare sources to which access was difficult. Included among these libraries are those of the University of Minnesota, the Ohio State University, Southern Illinois University, and the Weidener Library of Harvard University. On two different occasions the Weidener Library staff opened to me their magnificent collection of eighteenth-century French and Italian sources. Finally, I owe much to my wife Patricia for her encouragement, for the many times she read various drafts of this study, and for listening to me talk out problems of organization, logic, and evidence. Her task was the more difficult because during much of the time the manuscript was being prepared she was either carrying, bearing, or raising our first child.

Contents

LIST OF MAPS AND ILLUSTRATIONS

ABBREVIATIONS

AE	Archives du Ministère des Affaires Étrangères
AE–CP	Archives du Ministère des Affaires Étrangères, Correspondance Politique
AG	Archives du Ministère de la Guerre
AM	Archives du Ministère de la Marine
AN	Archives Nationales
AdBR	Archives départementales des Bouches-du-Rhône
BN	Bibliothèque Nationale, MSS Division
ASI	*Archivio Storico Italiano*
BSHNC	*Bulletin de la Société des Sciences historiques et naturelles de la Corse*
RC	*Revue de la Corse, ancienne et moderne, historique, littéraire et bibliographique*

Introduction

The years 1968 and 1969 marked the bicentenary of two major events in French and Corsican history: the acquisition of Corsica by the French monarchy and the birth of Napoleon Bonaparte. This book is about the former of those events, which explains why the latter is celebrated in French history; for it was the incorporation of the island of Corsica into the kingdom of France that made Napoleon a Frenchman and provided him with the military education and training that he used so ably first as a general in the French army and later as the Emperor of the French.

Bicentenary celebrations invariably result in an outpouring of printed materials. Of course, the majority of the books and articles published as a result of these bicentenary observances concentrated on Napoleon. But Corsica also received significant attention either as a result of the fact that it was Napoleon's birthplace or for its own sake. One of the simplest yet most profound statements about Corsican history to come out of this bicentenary literature appears, oddly enough, on the jacket of René Sédillot's study of *La Grande aventure des Corses:* [1] ". . . Corsica, the history of Corsica, are not as simple as is often believed." This statement is particularly striking when it is compared with the remark of a noted French journalist who in 1934 observed that "the entire history of Corsica is only an endless chain of wars and murders." [2] The journalist quoted here had a great deal to say about the island's natural beauty, the Corsican vendetta and funeral customs, and the modern "vice" of *fonctionnairisme*. Yet he was content to dismiss the island's history with a flourish of the pen.

Although other authors are more scholarly and write with less distortion, even a survey of the secondary literature on Corsica reveals pervasive partisanship. Corsica has its moralists [3] and its adulators of the past who condemn progress and yearn for the good old days.[4] The island has its anticapitalists [5] and its religious bigots, the latter applauding the Corsicans' "good sense" in keeping Protestants out of the island.[6] It has more than its share of tragedians.[7] Above all, Corsica has its nationalistic partisans, some with Corsican, some with French, and some with Italian leanings or antipathies.[8] In "Italo-Corsican" historiography, nearly everything written in the 1920s and 1930s is suspect as one or another aspect of the fascist irredentist argument that Corsica should be reconstituted as part of Italy.[9]

Partisan writing can be found on any subject, yet the frequency and extremity of such writing on Corsican history makes the subject a maze of strong feelings, legends, and oft-repeated fallacies. All but one of the writers cited as examples could have profited from the warning sounded by Colonna de Cesari-Rocca in 1907:

> There is no country in Europe whose history is more badly known than that of Corsica; no French department whose monuments have been more neglected, whose archives are more dispersed. The past has been treated with a stupefying levity. The modern works, quite as much as the older, abound in inexact citations. Moreover, in all these works, having been copied one from the other, without the authors having brought together

xviii

the traditions of the monuments and original texts, the errors have only grown in number and in importance. The concise monographs of the great modern collections ([such as]) Larousse, *Grande Encyclopédie*, etc.) have echoed these errors and have scattered them throughout the entire world.[10]

Colonna de Cesari-Rocca did much to help stop the propagation of errors. But new fallacies have been created and old ones have been dispersed more widely since Cesari-Rocca wrote his lines. Thus an incidental purpose of this study has been to help curtail, by non-partisan attention to original sources, their further propagation.

The first chapter of this study evaluates the nature of the eighteenth-century Corsican problem. At the root of that problem lay the fact that the republican government of Genoa governed its island possession badly. To make matters worse, Genoa did not have the military and economic strength to enforce its mismanaged rule. The result was a rebellion in the island, which Genoa could not suppress by itself. Essentially, the situation created was that of a power vacuum in the middle of the Mediterranean. Into that vacuum several great and small powers attempted to move, for whichever power could control the waters around Corsica was in a favorable strategic position within the Mediterranean. But more than Corsica was involved. When the treaty of Utrecht ended the War of the Spanish Succession, one of the unresolved problems was the balance of power in Italy. Although technically a neutral state, Genoa was nonetheless one aspect of the broader Italian problem. Therefore, the effect of the Corsican rebellion on Genoa had ramifications on the entire unresolved Italian settlement. This was particularly the case if, as frequently happened, Italy became a theater of war pitting the great powers against each other.

Whereas the central theme of this study is the Corsican question, it does not deal merely with Corsica. Neither does it presume to be a thorough examination of all the powers interested in that question. Such a work would require years of research in the archives of England, Spain, Austria, France, and the several Italian states that existed during the eighteenth century. This study is not that ambitious. Its focus is upon the politico-diplomatic history of French concern with Corsica during the reign of Louis XV. At the same time, it recognizes, even if only in passing, that the Corsican problem was certainly not the most important problem Louis XV's government faced during the eighteenth century. Thus no effort is made here to further the pretentious claim of one scholar who argued that Versailles' "secret" policy regarding Corsica was "the pivot of Louis XV's foreign policy." [11]

It has now been many years since Édouard Driault published *Florence, Modène, Gênes,* Volume XIX in the series *Recueil des instructions données aux ambassadeurs et ministres de France.*[12] This book established what has become the generally accepted interpretation of French diplomacy toward the Corsican question. Its thesis is that in the mid-1730s Versailles formulated a "secret plan" to acquire possession of Corsica from its sovereign, the republic of Genoa. Thereafter, Driault argued, one French minister of foreign affairs after another, and one envoy to Genoa after another, labored to implement the secret plan. French diplomacy achieved its objective and its triumph in 1768 when Corsica was ceded to the crown of France.

In the same year that his study appeared, Driault received support for his thesis from Louis Villat, whose studies on Corsican history have done much to enlighten many aspects of the island's past. The Corsican question, Villat wrote in a lengthy review essay on Driault's study,

> was to constitute . . . one of the "secrets" of French diplomacy in the eighteenth century; French diplomacy was to follow its course without weaknesses, without hesitations, throughout the ministerial crises which marked the reign of Louis XV. . . . There was in all this affair

a spirit of consistency and of decision, a logic and a versatility which determined its success.[13]

A year later, in 1913, Villat endorsed Driault's thesis in an article on "La Corse napoléonienne." Because of Driault's work, he argued, it was no longer possible to doubt that Versailles had a "véritable politique" toward Corsica. Noting the "remarkable continuity" from Cardinal Fleury to the Duc de Choiseul, Villat contended that the "secret" of the 1730s was the secret of all French ministers of foreign affairs up to and including Choiseul. Villat admitted that there were problems in implementing that secret; but "the government of Louis XV followed indefatigably the design to which it had attached itself. It triumphed in the end as a result of its long patience." [14]

From Driault and Villat, then, comes an intriguing and remarkable story of diplomatic perseverance. Somehow, over a period of thirty-three years and through the administrations of eight ministers of foreign affairs,[15] Versailles moved logically and unhesitatingly toward a definite diplomatic objective. This thesis has gone almost unchallenged. It appears nearly full-bodied in the most recent book on French-Genoese relations by René Boudard. He too refers to "the inevitable solution of the Corsican question, patiently prepared by Choiseul and anticipated by [the Marquis de] Chauvelin." Yet there lurked a doubt in Boudard's mind, a doubt that caused him to hint at a break in the continuity of the French plan. He was not entirely certain whether the fact that Chauvelin "anticipated" the "inevitable solution" to the Corsican question meant that the "secret plan" of the 1730s was followed from its formation until the ministry of Choiseul. He was also uncertain whether Choiseul followed that plan. "In 1762," Boudard wrote, "Choiseul had not fixed the modalities of the plan that was to give Corsica to France, but . . . he had resolved to precipitate the circumstances and to create an occasion." [16] In effect, Boudard implied that as early as 1762 Choiseul intended to acquire Corsica for France, but that he was not following the secret plan drawn up in the 1730s.

The first step toward resolving the problem of the French diplomatic approach to the eighteenth-century Corsican question is to recognize that it involves two different questions. One is, was there continuity in French diplomacy from 1735 to 1768, based upon the secret plan of 1735? So far as this question is concerned, the evidence for continuity, as presented by Driault, consists primarily of the "Instructions" sent to French representatives in Genoa. Although Louis Villat actually collected no new evidence, he has endorsed Driault's thesis.

As presented, the evidence needs frequent rhetorical questions and *sous-entendus* to demonstrate the thesis of continuity, logic, and unflinching pursuit of Corsica by French diplomats after 1735. Additional attention to the correspondence between Versailles and its diplomatic and military representatives in both Genoa and Corsica does not reveal continuity in Versailles' plan to acquire the island. Indeed, it reveals that the secret plan of 1735 was explicitly renounced shortly after it was formulated. It also reveals that one French minister to Genoa who continued to pursue acquisition of the island was dismissed and replaced by a representative more willing to carry out his government's instructions and that an officer in the French army who did not follow his instructions was placed under arrest before he left the island.

The reasons for this change in French policy must be sought in the shifting balance of power in the Mediterranean area, the conflict between France, Austria and England, and the role that Genoa played in that conflict. The change in French diplomacy was initially explored by Christian Ambrosi, who studied carefully the diplomatic correspondence for the period 1743 to 1753. Ambrosi's research led him to conclude that after 1735 Louis XV became not just indifferent but actually hostile to acquisition of Corsica. His ministers were certainly conscious of Corsica's importance and momentarily considered acquisition. They too, however, rejected this step; and they did not advise Louis XV to pursue a policy of acquisition.[17]

Chapters II, III, and IV of this study deal with the period from the formation of the "secret plan" of 1735 to the end of the Seven Years' War. They present additional evidence suggesting that Ambrosi's interpretation of French policy during the years 1743–1753 is substantially correct. These chapters also analyze the efforts that the French Government made to resolve the Corsican question before 1743 and after 1753, and they re-evaluate the evidence that Driault proposed in support of his thesis of continuity in French diplomatic relations with Corsica and Genoa.

The second question dealing with French diplomacy and the eighteenth-century Corsican question is more difficult than the first: Did Choiseul intend to acquire Corsica? Subsequent questions follow from this initial query. If he did so intend, when did he make this decision and by what means did he attempt to accomplish his objectives? Documents in the Archives of the Ministry of Foreign Affairs, the Ministries of War and the Marine, the *Archives Nationales,* and various printed documents do not suggest that possession of the island was Choiseul's initial objective. Instead, they suggest that Choiseul sought security in the Mediterranean through possession of certain strategic maritime places (*présides*) on the island of Corsica. He did not seek French sovereignty over the entire island until 1767, after he had failed to secure his initial objectives.

The lack of definite documentary evidence to support Choiseul's policy of full sovereignty over Corsica may or may not negate the thesis that such was indeed his policy. Certainly the diplomacy of Louis XV's France, with its *secret du roi,* is a vivid reminder that diplomatic documents do not always tell the whole story.[18] This is particularly true when a diplomat's motives are in question—and Choiseul's handling of the Corsican question is particularly difficult to evaluate precisely because the documents may not reveal his true motives and objectives.

Chapters V and VI of this study seek to evaluate two interpretations of Choiseul's approach to the Corsican question. The first interpretation is the story told by the documents, which suggests that until 1767 Choiseul was only interested in French possession of a limited number of strategic places on the island. The second interpretation is that Choiseul worked from the beginning of his ministry to secure possession of all the island. He may have adjusted his methods to circumstances, but French acquisition was his consistent objective. The latter interpretation may appear the more speculative because it cannot be documented by as much definite evidence. Yet for a variety of reasons it may be the easier to accept.

First, this interpretation leads to a form of reasoning about historical events especially prevalent among diplomatic historians. We know that France acquired Corsica in 1768; therefore, someone must have planned it. James MacGregor Burns has called this form of reasoning "the conspiracy theory of history." The notion that acquisition was Choiseul's first objective is enticing, secondly, because it seems to be consistent with a general interpretation of eighteenth-century diplomacy and with a more specific interpretation about the diplomacy of the Duc de Choiseul. Eighteenth-century diplomacy has a bad reputation; it is frequently pictured as the most amoral or immoral in the history of modern international relations. The thesis that French diplomats worked to aggrandize France by securing possession of Corsica, even at the expense of France's Genoese friend and sometimes ally, seems to fit nicely into this broader interpretation. More specifically, the widespread interpretation of Choiseul's ministry pictures him as the able and scheming minister anxiously seeking French "revenge" against England for losses suffered during the Seven Years' War. The thesis that from 1758 to 1768 he consistently worked for acquisition of Corsica accords well with this interpretation of his ministry.

But the conspiracy theory is questionable to anyone who has worked in the tangled web of international relations. The picture of eighteenth-century diplomacy certainly needs revision in the light of subsequent events, and Choiseul's ministry has yet to be studied in a critical, coherent, and comprehensive manner. In any case, neither the conspiracy theory of history nor the general and specific interpretations of eighteenth-century diplomacy should be permitted to obscure or otherwise premeditate against an objective appraisal of Choiseul's efforts to resolve the Corsican question.

Chapter VII is the concluding chapter of the politico-diplomatic aspect of the French approach to the eighteenth-century Corsican question. It deals with the actual conquest of Corsica during the two campaigns on the island in 1768 and 1769. The Conclusion evaluates some of the reactions among Frenchmen to the acquisition and conquest of the island. Though many Frenchmen of the period remained indifferent to Corsica's fate, there was considerable interest in the Corsican question among other Frenchmen of the eighteenth century.[19] It was an age when many admired courage, and certainly the Corsicans were courageous in their fight against Genoa. It was an age when many detested tyranny, and certainly Genoa's rule in the island was the worst form of tyranny—corrupt and inefficient. For these reasons many of Choiseul's countrymen criticized him for bringing to an end the saga of "the brave Corsicans." Moreover, by the end of the 1760s, Choiseul was deeply involved in a struggle with Madame du Barry's party at the court of Louis XV. Some of his enemies discovered that the minister's Corsican policy, which cost the king money, could be used against him. So the critics had their say, for one reason or another. Yet Choiseul's Corsican policy resolved a difficult and dangerous problem in a manner favorable to French interests, and for this he was applauded. Thus the acquisition and conquest of Corsica increased Choiseul's prestige at the very moment when, on December 24, 1770, Louis XV summarily dismissed his chief minister. Choiseul's ministry ended abruptly; but one of his final acts was to secure for France its last territorial acquisition under the government of the Old Regime.

It is tempting to point to the modernity of the issues involved in the eighteenth-century Corsican question: strategic interests and *raison d'état;* national pride; restive peoples stirred by new ideas and using them to protest real and imagined wrongs inflicted upon them by absentee (or, to use the modern term, "colonial") governments; the difficulties that "regular" armies had in dealing with guerrilla warfare; big powers versus small powers; and propaganda efforts and techniques adopted by every party involved in their efforts to picture their respective causes in the best possible light.

What seems most modern of all are the numerous frustrations of the French diplomats and military officers whose first duty was to carry out their king's orders and to protect French security and French national interests. These officials knew the form and the weaknesses of the Genoese republican government with which they had to deal. Yet as the years went by and the Corsican question remained unresolved, as the various negotiations with Genoa dragged on interminably, encountering one deadlock after another, the French officials on various occasions quite literally shook their heads in amazement and frustration. Anyone who reads their correspondence can sense their growing anger over unfruitful negotiations with a power they neither respected nor trusted. Then there were the frustrations of the Genoese—the governors and commissioners who dealt directly with the Corsicans and the doge, Senate, and Councils who correctly believed that Genoa's international position and security were being undermined by the growing success of the Corsican insurrection. They too were frustrated in their efforts to negotiate an end to the rebellion or to suppress it by force, as well as in their efforts to seek guarantees and assistance from the great powers which would not undermine their sovereignty over their island possession.

Finally, there were the frustrations of the Corsicans. For a time during the forty years that they were rebels, the Corsican frustrations were at least partially mitigated by hope—the hope that they might be able to free themselves from what they had come to consider the unbearable "yoke" of the republic of Genoa. But the hopes of the Corsican "national" or

xxvi

"patriot" leaders, as they came to be called, were eventually smothered by realities and then extinguished by force. There was the reality of internal divisions within Corsican society and among the leaders which at times seriously weakened the rebellion. There was the reality of Genoese interests and "honor" which would not allow the Genoese to end gracefully a bad business which they were not capable of resolving. And there was the reality of the international politics of the eighteenth century which led France to intervene militarily on the island four different times in the period from the 1730s to the 1760s. It was this last reality which led one of the great powers of the period to wage war upon one of the smallest powers, if Corsica can even be called a "power," and to dash forever the Corsicans' hopes for freedom and independence in two campaigns waged on the island in 1768 and 1769.

To this extent only will this study speculate about the modernity of the Corsican question, although this characteristic of the problem is evident on nearly every manuscript and page of printed material that constitute the sources upon which the study is based. Calling attention to it may help to support a principal purpose of this study, which is to demonstrate that the history of French approaches to the Corsican question, like Corsican history in general, is not as simple as is often believed.

NOTES

1. René Sédillot, *La Grande aventure des Corses* (Paris, 1969).
2. Albert Surier, *Notre Corse: Études et souvenirs* (Paris, 1934).
3. D. Fumarali, *Discourse sur l'histoire de la Corse, depuis son origine jusqu'à nos jours* (Marseille, 1930).
4. M. de Petti-Rossu, "Use Antichi," *U. Fucone: Revue de littérature et d'études corses*, 3e année (June 1928), 55–61.
5. Georges Maquard, *Mémoire sur la crise économique de la Corse. . . .* (Paris, 1908).
6. A. F. Bartoli, *Histoire de la Corse, des origines à la conquête romaine. Description, production, moeurs, curiosités* (Paris, 1898).
7. Pierre Bonardi, *L'Ile tragique* (Paris, 1937).

8. One of the most recent examples of Corsican nationalism appears in Jacques Grégori, *Nouvelle histoire de la Corse* (Paris, 1967). For an example of the French nationalist position, see A. Ambrosi-Rostino, *Corses et français; leur rapports à travers l'histoire* (Nîmes, 1940). The Italian nationalist position is ably stated in Sebastien Dalzeto, *La Corse et Gênes devant l'histoire, étude de critique historique* (Paris, 1950).

9. For a discussion of this subject, see Bertzardin Lusinchi, *La Corse et le problème des revendications italiennes* [Conférence faite le 4 janvier 1939 à Casablanca] (n.p., n.d.), and Pierre Andreani, *Le Fascisme et la Corse* (Marseille, 1939). Early in his book, which contains reprints of various newspaper articles published between 1929 and 1939, Andreani wrote: "Une folle espérance eniviait les campagnes du *Telegrafo:* régenter la Corse. Chaque semaine ce journal dirigeait de violentes attaques contre l'administration française et chantait des louanges du gouvernement fasciste" (p. 11).

10. Colonna de Cesari-Rocca, *Histoire de la Corse* (Paris, 1907), pp. i–ii.

11. Louis Villat, "La Question corse au xviiie siècle," *BSHNC* (Oct.–Dec. 1912), p. 371.

12. Édouard Driault, ed., *Recueil des instructions données aux ambassadeurs et ministres de France.* Vol. XIX, *Florence, Modène, Gênes* (Paris, 1912); hereafter cited as Driault, *Recueil.*

13. Louis Villat, "La Question corse," *op. cit.,* pp. 337, 349–350, 370.

14. Louis Villat, "La Corse napoléonienne," *Revue des Études Napoléoniennes,* III (1913), 438–439.

15. The eight ministers of foreign affairs were Germain-Louis de Chauvelin, 1727–1737; Jean-Jacques Amelot de Chaillou, 1737–1744; René-Louis de Voyer, marquis d'Argenson, 1744–1747; Louis-Philoxène Brulart, marquis de Puysieulx, 1747–1751; François-Dominique Barberie, marquis de Saint-Contest, 1751–1754; Antoine-Louis Rouillé, comte de Jouy, 1754–1757; François-Joachim de Pierre de Bernis, 1757–1758; and Étienne-François, duc de Choiseul, 1758–1761 and 1766–1770. Technically there was a ninth minister of foreign affairs, Choiseul's cousin, César-Gabriel, duc de Praslin, 1761–1766, but Choiseul had firm control over French policy during these years. Presumably André-Hercule, Cardinal de Fleury, also supported the "secret plan" for acquisition of Corsica, although Driault does not explicitly say this.

16. René Boudard, *Gênes et la France dans la deuxième moitié du xviiie siècle, 1748–1797* (Paris, 1962), p. 70.

17. Christian Ambrosi, *La Corse insurgée et la seconde intervention française au xviiie siècle, 1743–1753* (Paris, 1950), pp. 231–232.

18. Didier Ozanam and Michel Antoine, *Correspondance secrète du*

comte de Broglie avec Louis XV (1756–1774), 2 Vols. (Paris, 1956 and 1961).

19. On the subject of eighteenth-century interest in Corsica, see Gaston Courtillier, "La Corse et l'opinion publique au xviiie siècle," *BSHNC* (Oct.–Dec. 1911), 5–53, and my article on "The Development of Enlightenment Interest in Eighteenth-Century Corsica," *Studies on Voltaire and the Eighteenth Century*, LXIV (1968), 165–185.

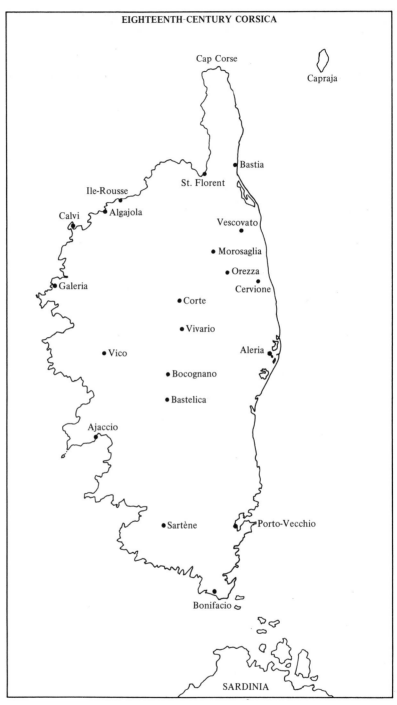

Cap Corse

Capraja

Bastia

St. Florent

Ile-Rousse

Calvi · Algajola

Vescovato

Morosaglia

Orezza

Galeria

Cervione

Corte

Vivario

Vico

Aleria

Bocognano

Bastelica

Ajaccio

Sartène

Porto-Vecchio

Bonifacio

SARDINIA

Eighteenth-Century Corsica: Principal Locations Mentioned in the Text.

CHAPTER I

Rebellion in the Mediterranean

The peoples who have dominated the island of Corsica at one time or another include the Etruscans, Greeks, Carthaginians, Romans, Vandals, Ostrogoths, Byzantines, Lombards, Saracens, Aragonese, Pisans, and the Papacy. None of these peoples imposed upon Corsica that effective authority that would have made their sovereignty more than a political or legal abstraction. None of them gave Corsica justice, without which their sovereignty was merely a label for pillage and oppression. The Genoese, who secured possession of Corsica in the fifteenth century, proved that they possessed rather average talents for mismanagement as compared to peoples who had earlier ruled the island.

Genoese authority in Corsica was derived from an agreement of 1447 whereby Pope Nicholas V gave the island in fief to Ludovico de Campo Fregoso, brother of the new doge, Giano de Campo Fregoso. When Ludovico became doge of Genoa in 1448, he ceded his rights to Corsica to his cousin Galeazzo. Internal unrest made it impossible for Galeazzo to execute his rights within the island, a situation that in 1453 led to the cession of those rights to the Bank of Saint-George. This institution, one

1

of the earliest manifestations of European capitalism, exploited Corsica economically for over a century. Its most important monopoly was salt, but it also had a monopoly on trade with Corsica in tobacco, coffee and *eaux-de-vie*. The Bank gave to the island a form of administration that provided for some institutions of local government and that had a great influence on the subsequent forms of Corsican governments, whether Genoese or native in origins. Yet the Bank had considerable difficulty in exploiting its rights. Its claims to the island were challenged by the kingdom of Aragon and by native Corsican leaders. For nearly twenty years after 1464 Corsica was partially governed by the family of Francesco Sforza, Duke of Milan, under whose protection Genoa had placed itself. During this time the Bank abandoned the island, only to return in the 1480s in another attempt to establish its authority on a solid basis. As one adversary of the Bank replaced another, war and internal conflict continued, and the Bank had to keep 3,000 soldiers on the island. Gradually and progressively during these troubled years, the Corsicans lost control over the internal administration of the island. Their authority increasingly fell into the hands of agents sent out from Genoa, and not until 1511 was the island peaceful again. It was a relative tranquillity that lasted for nearly forty years, only to be destroyed toward the end of the Hapsburg-Valois Wars.[1]

French interest in Corsica began in the mid-sixteenth century during the reign of Henry II. From the beginning of the century France faced the danger of encirclement by the extensive possessions of the Hapsburg family. Forced by this threat to think in strategic terms, French ministers realized that Corsica's location between the coasts of Italy and Spain might provide France with the opportunity to strike a decisive blow by cutting the communications between the two great blocks of the Hapsburgs' possessions. They pointed out that galleys based on Corsica could prohibit all navigation in the northern Mediterranean and, at the same time, the island could serve as a base for offensive operations in Italy and as a supply depot for troops used in the Italian campaigns. Moreover, such control of the Mediterranean that possession of Corsica would give to France would enable the French to bar the route from Spain via Italy to the Low Countries, a route used in both peace and war.

These considerations led to a proposal for French occupation of the island. The ministers and advisers responsible for the plan included Cardinal Jean du Bellay, the leaders of the Guise party (Charles, Cardinal of Lorraine, and his brother, François, duc de Lorraine), Nicolas Durand, chevalier de Villegagnon, and Maréchal Paule de Thermes. Villegagnon, a corsaire and explorer, drew up a memoir on August 28, 1552, which discussed the advantages to France of occupying Corsica. King Henry II accepted his proposals, and Maréchal Thermes became commander of the military action, a position he held until 1555 when he was replaced by Jordan Ursin. The invasion of Corsica was launched in August 1553, and it seemed the more appropriate because Genoa, Corsica's titular sovereign, was allied with Emperor Charles V against France. Within the island, the struggle pitted French troops against Genoese, Florentine, and German forces. The fighting was extremely destructive, ending with a French victory in 1556. The next year Henry II incorporated Corsica into the French kingdom and the French Government accepted the difficult task of devising a form of government for its new possession.[2]

Although the treaty of Cateau-Cambrésis (1559) gave Corsica back to Genoa, French influence in Genoese affairs did not end. The most vivid illustration of this influence occurred during the reign of Louis XIV. The radiance of the Sun King gradually grew dim as his constant wars exhausted France and Europe; but in the late 1670s and early 1680s he was at the height of his power. In 1684, France burned into the Genoese memory a proper respect for that power, and a lasting hatred for the country that wielded it. In the previous year, France, having gone to war against Spain, had become convinced that Genoa had rejected neutrality in favor of an alliance with Spain. Louis XIV ordered a fleet of ships at Toulon to arm for bombardment, and in May 1684 the fleet lay off the coast of

Genoa, prepared to back up any demands that France made against the republic. One of these demands was that Genoa surrender four galleys it had been building, which France feared would fall into Spanish hands. When the republic refused to obey, France began a devastating bombardment that lasted from May 18 to May 28.[3]

In addition to the fact that Louis XIV's display of power was long remembered and resented as Genoa sank into its former subservient position, the French bombardment had another important effect: the Corsicans took advantage of the republic's weakness and offered the island to Louis XIV. The French monarch probably refused the offer for a variety of reasons. An eighteenth-century explanation was that Louis XIV had no room in his "grand designs" for such a poor and barbarous kingdom as Corsica.[4] A modern scholar, rejecting this superficial explanation, has argued that Corsica would have been valuable in Colbert's and Louis XIV's plans for developing the Barbary and Levant trade and for any future designs on Egypt. Closer to the truth, he contended, is the fact that Louis XIV refused the island because it was not offered to him by any legitimate authority, and the principle of "legitimacy" was an important part of his conception of kingship. Louis was not the monarch to accept anything from the rebellious subjects of another ruler.[5]

Although Louis had this strong sense of legitimacy, a republican government like that of Genoa, in which the doge was elected, was not a "divine right" monarchy—nor was it treated as one.[6] Moreover, practical as well as theoretical issues were involved in the proposal to add Corsica to the French crown. In December 1682, the French envoy to Genoa, François Pidou de Saint-Olon, wrote a long memoir concerning the revenues and forces of the republic. This memoir reveals several significant aspects of the French Government's attitude toward Genoa and Corsica. Saint-Olon claimed that the French king had been the "true and legitimate" master of Genoa since 1528, "which was the year of the treason of Andrea Doria, who with those of his party first withdrew the city of Genoa and its

4

Estat from the obedience to the king." In a section of the memoir devoted to Corsica, Saint-Olon discussed the quality of its harbors, the nature of its government, and the kind of crops grown there. But he prefaced this discussion with the statement that the costs of administering the island were larger than its revenue.[7]

Louis XIV's legal advisers could easily have found French claims sufficiently well-founded to justify French annexation of Corsica; certainly French annexations in Alsace during the 1680s reveal that the strength and validity of French claims were not a matter of primary consideration. Yet there was no reason why Louis should make this particular acquisition. After 1685, when Genoa again sank back into a state of tutelage to France, Louis XIV could reap the advantages Corsica provided and let Genoa pay the costs of its administration and bear the grief caused by its rebellious people. In any case, what Louis XIV wanted was not possession of Corsica, but Genoa's neutrality in his conflicts with Spain, Austria, and Savoy. Every French envoy to Genoa in the years from 1685 to 1715 was instructed to use all his skills to attain this objective.[8]

French interest in Corsica did not cease when the Peace of Utrecht ended the long wars of Louis XIV in 1713. In part, this continued interest resulted from the fact that Corsica was a strategic part of the Mediterranean balance of power, which was altered considerably by the Utrecht settlement. By that treaty England received Gibraltar and Minorca from Spain, acquisitions that were useful in war against Spain and France and as protection for English commerce. The Spanish king, Philip V, lost a great deal by the treaty; but in 1716 he gained a new wife, Elizabeth Farnese of Parma. Elizabeth had most of the qualities Philip V lacked, and she ambitiously devoted her life to providing Italian thrones for her sons. Her ambitions, however, brought Spain into direct conflict with Emperor Charles VI, who acquired Milan, Naples, and Sardinia from Spain and who continued to believe that he was the rightful Spanish king. It was precisely because the Mediter-

5

ranean became the scene of these dynastic and territorial aspirations that Corsica played such a large role in eighteenth-century French diplomacy. But French interest in and ultimate acquisition of the island can be explained only when the great-power rivalry is added to the weakness of Genoa and the anarchy of Corsica.

Genoa did not make the administrative and political reforms that would have enabled it to govern Corsica efficiently, nor did it make the military and financial reforms necessary to suppress rebellion. Consequently, its possession of the island was constantly threatened. The fact that the Genoese desperately sought to maintain their troublesome possession was yet another symptom of the republic's decline, for possession of Corsica was one of Genoa's few symbols of prestige. The Corsicans, however, did not easily forget *how* Genoa ruled. Uninspired, inefficient, and oppressive, Genoese officials thought of Corsica only as a colony and did not attempt to make the island part of the republic. They were not totally insensitive to the island's potential, but they proved incapable of exploiting it, partly because the ideas and institutions of a relatively efficient, centralized administration that began to develop in Louis XIV's France had little effect on Genoa.

The Genoese republican government was oligarchical, dominated by the great Genoese families whose interest in public affairs extended only to the point of furthering their private aims. As René Boudard stated, "the political structure had remained several centuries behind the times, [and] tradition prevented any renovation." [9] The Genoese patrician families exercised their control and furthered their personal objectives through two Councils: the *Maggior Consiglio* (Great Council) and the *Minor Consiglio* (Petit Council). The latter included two hundred members drawn from the families of the Genoese oligarchy; it chose the numerous Genoese magistrates and decided on issues of peace and war. The Great Council included the two hundred members of the Petit Council, plus other patricians elected or confirmed each year; it constituted the general assembly or principal legislative body. Only the

Great Council could modify the constitution and levy taxes. It elected the doge through an extremely complicated process whereby the Great Council chose fifteen of its members as candidates for doge, the Petit Council selected six of the fifteen, and then the Great Council met again to select one of the six.

Genoese governmental institutions also included two Colleges. There was a Senate of twelve members drawn from the Great Council and rotated on the schedule of four new members every six months. Its duties were executive in nature. The other College was the *Camera,* a commission of eight members responsible for financial affairs. Together the two Colleges decided foreign policy, received the representatives of foreign governments, sent instructions to Genoese representatives, and controlled the military. The principal executive official was the doge, whose authority was extremely limited by the process of his election, by the fact that he served for only two years, and by numerous customs, traditions, and precautions against effective exercise of power. During the second half of the eighteenth century the importance of the doge increased, largely because the position was occupied by some very able men. Throughout the first part of the century, however, when the republic was faced by so many serious crises, especially the Corsican rebellion, the doge was not in a position to give effective and energetic leadership.

The Genoese political system was admirably conceived to prevent personal despotism; but its archaic institutions resulted in paralysis and impotence both internally and in foreign affairs. "The decadence," Boudard commented, "was fatal, inevitable. . . ." [10] It was especially fatal for Genoese-Corsican relations. Lacking strong leadership, the republic was not able to control the officials to whom it delegated the island's administration. The result was that even when the Genoese Senate or doge did propose ways to develop Corsica, they encountered the indifference and the self-interest of the agents who were required to put those plans into practice.[11]

The system through which Genoa governed its island possession was extremely vulnerable to indifferent and irresponsible officials. The highest Genoese official on the island was the governor, who was elected by the Genoese Senate for a two-year term and who held absolute power over the islanders. Assisting the governor were a fiscal agent and several vice-regents, the latter located at Calvi, Saint-Florent, Corte, Vico, Cervione, Sartène, Bonifacio, and Algajola. The system's principal administrative problem was the short term of the governor. Because the governors served only two years and because they often came from the poorer Genoese nobility, they had to be diligent if they were to profit in office. Because they had absolute power on the island, the governors could be diligent with impunity. Naturally not all the officials sent to Corsica were tyrants and thieves, but there were too many governors and vice-regents who had only one goal, to pillage the island and enrich themselves, which they often accomplished by selling pardons to criminals.[12] More than anything else, Corsica needed an efficient administration of justice and a local hierarchy of authority.

As late as the eighteenth century, the most characteristic social grouping on the island was the clan. What local power existed was held by local clan chiefs, who distinguished themselves by knowledge, wealth, and eloquence. A second potentially authoritative group of men were the *pères du commune,* who were local magistrates elected by their communities. They, too, generally owed their position to family or clan backing. Although the *pères du commune* sometimes opposed the chiefs, they were more frequently subservient to them. At times, therefore, Corsica was racked by internal war between the communities and the local chiefs. At other times the chiefs and *pères du commune* banded together against the Genoese, for the chiefs found they could gain additional distinction by leading rebellions. The Genoese officials aggravated this potentially explosive situation by not granting local leaders the "privileges" and prestige of noble status. Instead, they protected their own local authority by using titles of nobility to separate the Genoese from the Corsicans. As early as the sixteenth century, the Genoese began to destroy the titled nobility by issuing no new titles and by recognizing no differences among the islanders.[13]

Genoa also prevented effective Corsican participation in government. It is true that institutions for such participation did exist, but they were mere formalities. The villages and towns of each parish elected two *podestats* or judges. Under Genoese rule these officials merely carried out the judgments of their masters. In addition, the governor was required to consult the *syndicate,* an advisory body composed of ten magistrates, of whom eight were Corsicans and two were Genoese. "But in the deliberations the voices of the eight Corsicans were only equivalent to those of the two Genoese magistrates." [14]

To alienate the island's leadership was dangerous enough; but the Genoese officials alienated almost the entire population by their corrupt administration of justice. Corsican "justice" was too often administered through an institution known as the vendetta.[15] Rather than curb this widespread anarchical practice, the Genoese actually encouraged it by licensing guns as a revenue measure. More significant, however, was the fact that the Corsicans' inability to depend on Genoese justice forced them to rely on the vendetta—the only justice they knew.[16] Genoese judges were easily impressed by influence and money, either of which could determine the judgment given even in cases of murder. As Voltaire noted with amazement, Genoese judges frequently condemned criminals to death or the galleys on secret information, without questioning the accused and without any formalities. Technically, the process was called *ex informata conscience.* Voltaire suggested that the following formula was used: "Being informed by my conscience that so and so are guilty, I condemn them to death." If Voltaire's reporting was not quite correct, his conclusion was: "These islanders assassinate each other continually, and their judge follows by assassinating the survivors on the information of his conscience. On both sides it is the ultimate degree of barbarism." [17]

The preceding discussion does not exhaust the catalogue

of Genoa's mistakes in Corsica, but it is enough to indicate that the republic was primarily responsible for the constant problems it faced within the island. Greedy and inefficient officials, a restive native leadership, decadent absolutism, and corrupt administration of justice—in one way or another these grievances provided the basis for frequent revolts within Corsica. They were the fundamental causes of the most serious rebellion of all, which broke out in the island in 1729.

The incident that sparked the rebellion of 1729 occurred on the Genoese mainland in the province of Finale in Liguria. For some time the inhabitants of Finale had been increasingly restive under Genoese control. By October 1729 they were so recalcitrant that the republic decided to send troops, and Corsican troops were selected for the task of suppressing what threatened to become a major rebellion. While garrisoned in Finale, one of the Corsican soldiers was convicted of a minor infraction and by way of punishment was placed on the *cheval de bois,* or wooden horse, the purpose of which was similar to the English stocks. Soon a crowd of onlookers gathered. Irritated by the presence of the Corsican garrison in Finale, the crowd began to taunt the Corsican and in the process insulted the Corsican nation. A minor riot developed in which Corsican soldiers, answering insults with bayonets and gunfire, killed at least one member of the crowd and wounded several others.

This minor incident threatened to become a major problem for the republic. The inhabitants of Finale armed themselves, forced the Corsican soldiers to retreat to the Château, and then told the Genoese governor that they would set fire to the Château unless he turned over to them the guilty Corsicans. The governor ordered an Italian garrison to replace the Corsicans and proceeded to take legal steps against those Corsicans recognized as having killed or wounded members of the crowd. Several Corsican soldiers were convicted of murder and hanged.[18]

Had the Corsicans been accustomed to even a modicum of justice from their Genoese masters, this incident might not

10

have been so inflammatory. As it was, it became one of the last of numerous incidents that turned indignation and bitterness into open revolt.[19] While the Corsicans were mourning the death of their countrymen, they were also worried about possible famine for the harvests of 1729 had not been good. Moreover, at this time Genoa attempted to collect a hearth tax of two seini (40 centimes), which had recently been levied to recoup the financial losses the republic had suffered when it decided to stop licensing guns.[20] Toward the end of October 1729 Genoese officials, supported by troops, appeared in the village of Bozzio to collect the tax. Incidents of brutality further angered the inhabitants of that village who refused to pay.

The Genoese thus found themselves faced with a tax rebellion, which spread to other parts of the island as news of the events at Bozzio became more widely known. Even worse, the rebellion found a leader, in the person of Pompiliani de Poggio de Tavogna, "a fearsome enemy," according to the French officer Pommereul, "who had served a foreign power with distinction' and was as eloquent as he was an excellent soldier." Pompiliani had two lieutenants, both intrepid Corsican patriots, Andrea Colonna Ceccaldi and Luigi Giafferi. They spent the last weeks of 1729 and the first weeks of 1730 gathering a motley band of 3,000 to 5,000 men, and late in February 1730 they marched on Bastia, the Genoese stronghold on the northeast coast of the island.[21] There they presented their demands to the Genoese governor, Felice Pinello. They asked the right to keep arms; a reduction in the price of salt, permission for Corsicans to produce salt rather than buy it from Genoa; a maximum time limit of six months on the duration of judicial cases; and suppression of the hearth tax. Governor Pinello refused these demands, and at that point only the intervention of Mgr. Mari, Bishop of Aleria, stopped the patriots from storming Bastia. Bishop Mari persuaded them that Pinello did not have the power to grant their requests, promised reforms, and indicated that the Corsicans' grievances would be brought to the attention of the Genoese

Senate. Agreeing to wait three weeks for a reply, the rebels withdrew to the mountainous interior of the island, which was to be their stronghold for many years.[22]

The Genoese grew increasingly uneasy as news of the Corsican sedition reached the mainland. By the end of February reports placed the number of rebels at 6,000, and the republic took the precaution of sending to Corsica five ships loaded with troops and supplies; it also began to load two additional galleys. Yet Genoa at this time had no accurate knowledge about the state of the Corsican rebellion, and Governor Pinello simply added to the confusion by informing the Great Council at Genoa that the rebels were a band of thieves and that the Corsican nation remained loyal to the republic. Pinello's deceit was of course prompted by his desire to protect his own position and reputation, for if a major revolt occurred while he was governor he would be disgraced. But Pinello had already proven his incompetence, and the Great Council gave the unhappy task of pacifying the rebels to Gerolamo Veneroso, who was designated "general commissioner." When Veneroso arrived in Corsica in April 1730, the rebels had already moved toward Bastia, and reports reaching the mainland put their numbers at 14,000.[23]

Veneroso's mission began well. He invited the rebel leaders to discuss their grievances with him, promised a general pardon if they laid down their arms, and held out the hope that the republic would make major concessions. Veneroso gained time by these tactics, for the Corsicans withdrew from Bastia and began to discuss their grievances and requests for reform with him. Genoa, in fact, was willing to make some concessions, in part because Mgr. Agostino Saluzzo, Bishop of Mariana, had given the Senate a more accurate description of the revolt than Pinello had given the Great Council. In June the Senate sent two commissioners, Camillo Doria and Salvatore Squarciafico, to the island to aid in the task of pacification. Unfortunately for both the Genoese and the Corsicans, the Senate took too long discussing what concessions it would make. Not until the beginning of August did it arrive at a decision. By then the Corsicans were convinced that there was no substance to Veneroso's promises. Moreover, serious dissensions developed between Veneroso, who favored conciliation, and Doria, who advised rigorous repression of the rebellion. The latter found support from Francesco Gropallo, who succeeded Pinello as governor early in June. These delays and the rigorous policies of Doria and Gropallo provoked the Corsican rebels to make further demands, including the stipulation that Genoese troops be withdrawn from the island.[24] To meet such a demand was tantamount to granting virtual independence to Corsica, and that Genoa was absolutely unwilling to do.

Throughout its early bargaining with the rebels, Genoa grossly underestimated both the extent of their dissatisfaction and their strength. Veneroso realized this mistake soon after he arrived in Corsica, and when he saw how determined the rebels were, he wondered if they were receiving help from another power. But he was unable to hasten his government's reply to the Corsican's demands for reform, and thus his mission of pacification failed. Conciliatory talks with the rebels ended in July; thereafter the rebels withdrew into the mountains, burning a few Genoese houses on the way. They gave their erstwhile masters six weeks to meet their demands. Failing that, they declared, they would put everything in the island "to fire and sword." Veneroso asked to be recalled and late in August was replaced as commissioner by Camillo Doria.[25]

During the last months of 1730 and the first months of 1731, most of the island belonged to the rebels. They won significant military victories near Ajaccio and Bastia and published circulars in an effort to unite the Corsicans and to justify their rebellion. The intervention of Bishop Saluzzo led to a four month truce, starting December 25, 1730, which the Corsicans used to organize their resistance under the leadership of two generals, Andrea Colonna Ceccaldi and Luigi Giafferi. The generals were ably assisted by Mgr. Carlo Francesco Raffaelli, a pious and popular priest from Orezza.

The clergy, in fact, contributed a great deal to the rebellion. Although many lacked education and spiritual dedication, as a group they were intensely patriotic. As individuals they were important figures in their communities and some of them were important rebel leaders.[26] The Corsican clergy also helped the rebellion in another way. On April 20, 1731, a council of eighteen ecclesiastics met at the convent of Orezza and sanctioned sedition by declaring the rebellion "just," especially if Genoa violated the truce.[27] Georges Marie d'Angelo, the French vice-consul at Bastia, described the situation in Corsica as follows:

> All Corsica is united with one accord and in a submissive manner the likes of which has never been seen in the past. The other side of the mountains is completely in revolt, in the same way as Balagne and Nebbio. The rebels count on Cap Corse being in the same condition if God does not intervene there.[28]

Thus the first year of the rebellion proved particularly embarrassing to the republic because its military weakness allowed the rebels to organize and wage their war more effectively. It was more embarrassing and even dangerous because the general state of affairs in Italy and Europe boded ill for the republic's continued sovereignty over the island. The danger of foreign intervention increased as each month went by, and the courts of Europe were filled with ominous rumors. One rumor was that Elizabeth Farnese of Spain coveted Tuscany for her son Don Carlos, and that Corsica was too close to Tuscany not to be included in her designs. Another rumor had it that the court of Vienna was thinking of giving Corsica to the *Infant* Emmanuel of Portugal.[29] Even more serious was a third rumor that the Corsicans were seeking aid and protection from some foreign power. This was more than rumor; it was fact. As early as April 1730 the republic had learned that the Corsicans had sent four deputies to seek help from some European power. During the next year Canon Erasmo

Orticoni undertook a special mission to Pope Clement XII to offer Corsican sovereignty to the Papacy. When Clement XII refused, the Corsicans requested that he mediate between them and Genoa.[30] Truly, the "honor" of the republic was at stake.

Genoa momentarily escaped this dilemma by appealing to Emperor Charles VI who was technically the republic's feudal lord. The arrangement was enticing for the Emperor because he was interested in extending his power in Italy and was disturbed by Spanish pretensions to Tuscany. He therefore agreed to send troops to Corsica if Genoa would pay the military costs. Under this agreement, the first contingent of troops, numbering 4,000, arrived at Bastia in July and August of 1731. This force was not sufficient, however, for although the Corsicans could not match the Imperial forces, neither could the Emperor's army drive the rebels out of the mountains. In fact, the rebels resisted so fiercely that a second contingent of 2,000 troops was sent to Corsica in March 1732. With the reinforcements came a new commander, Prince Ludwig von Württemberg. He soon realized that the rebels could not be totally defeated for his forces were fighting more than an army; they were fighting an aroused people. To wipe out the rebel forces required a guerrilla type of warfare, which was unknown to the European armies of that time.[31]

Therefore, Prince Württemberg, who had been ordered to hold his troops on the defensive, adopted a policy of *la douceur* instead of force. On April 17, 1732, he granted a general pardon to the rebels; he also met with the rebel leaders and treated for peace. On May 13, by the Peace of Corte, the first Corsican rebellion officially ended. According to its terms, Genoa proclaimed a general amnesty and promised to release the Corsican chiefs, Ceccaldi and Giafferi, who had been seized at an earlier meeting between rebel leaders and Prince Württemberg. Other provisions promised the Corsicans greater participation in the government (re-establishment of two councils, the *Dodici* and the *Sei*), access to military and civil offices, cancellation of unpaid taxes, re-establishment of noble

View of Corte (R. Benson, *Sketches of Corsica.* London, 1825).

privileges, and foundation of a college. The most important part of the treaty, at least for the Corsicans, was that the Emperor guaranteed it. Under these terms the Imperial forces left the island in 1733.[32]

Throughout the first phase of the Corsican rebellion, French foreign policy had been confused, timid, and irresolute.[33] The person most closely connected with the Corsican situation was Jacques de Campredon, the French representative sent to Genoa in 1727 to deal with minor conflicts between France and the republic and with the succession problems in Tuscany. The Corsican revolt added two specific tasks to his normal duties of keeping Versailles informed about events in Italy and Genoa. First, he was to prevent Corsica from falling into the hands of a power "already too formidable." In view of persistent and increasing rumors about various powers' designs on Corsica, as well as the uneasy balance left in Italy after the Utrecht settlement, it was natural for Versailles to fear that some power might gain possession of Corsica at the expense of French Mediterranean interests. Campredon was

16

also directed to do what he could to prevent French ships coming from Leghorn from taking munitions to the Corsican rebels.

Actually both of these tasks proved to be beyond Campredon's capabilities, and there was little that he could do except keep his government informed about the threatening rumors. In March 1730 he reported to Versailles that the Genoese were anxious about the interest that the Emperor and the king of Spain were showing in their island possession, although they considered France and England *trop éloingés* to be dangerous. Two years later, after Imperial troops had been sent to Corsica, Campredon reported the rumor that Vienna was acting in concert with Spain to make the marriage of an archduchess with the *Infant* Don Carlos more attractive by procuring the crown of Sardinia or Corsica for Don Carlos. In May 1732 this rumor was embellished slightly. A person "of very good judgment" told Campredon that a marriage was being negotiated between Don Carlos and a sister of the Duc de Lorraine. The Duc would then give Corsica and the title of king to Don Carlos and would personally support him in every way possible in order to prevent "the prince who would become king of Spain" from establishing his power in Italy.[34]

The French Government's action was only slightly more vigorous in relation to the Imperial intervention in the Corsican rebellion. This intervention was particularly disturbing in view of the potentially explosive Italian scene. From 1729 to 1731 there was continual threat of war in Italy, which resulted from French, English, and Spanish efforts to introduce Spanish troops into the duchies of Parma and Piacenza. After 1731, when Charles VI agreed to major changes in Italy, the danger of war diminished, but the Italian situation remained tense. In these circumstances, the Emperor's assistance to Genoa meant an extension of Austrian influence and power in Italy, and a body of Imperial troops on Corsica posed an added threat if the question of the Italian duchies should develop into war. Versailles quite naturally viewed the Emperor's aid to Genoa as something more than a desire to help a needy state. Such suspicions were clearly revealed in the reply Campredon was instructed to make when the Senate at Genoa informed the French that it had asked for Imperial assistance against the Corsican rebels. Campredon was instructed to adopt a wounded attitude because Genoa had asked for Imperial help before consulting France. He was to tell Genoa that it ran great risks by inviting Austrian intervention, for the Austrians might stay in both Corsica and Genoa after the rebels were repressed; and even if the Imperial forces did leave when their mission ended, Genoa would pay dearly for such assistance.[35]

The reasons for Versailles' inactivity during the first phase of the Corsican rebellion are not difficult to determine. André-Hercule, Cardinal de Fleury, minister of state and chief adviser to Louis XV after June 1726, had adopted a policy directed at conciliating the great powers and avoiding French involvement in a war that might be of no benefit to France. It was a policy that brought France a secondary role in the international relations of the period and, at the same time, brought it so many pressing problems that it could not be actively involved in the Corsican rebellion. At the beginning of the Corsican revolt, France became a signatory to the Treaty of Seville (November 9, 1729) that isolated Austria and led to the introduction of 6,000 Spanish troops into Italy to guarantee Don Carlos' succession to Parma and Tuscany. The first introduction of Austrian troops into Corsica came immediately after Britain and Holland had signed a treaty with Austria (March 1731) and Spain had momentarily settled its difficulties with Emperor Charles VI (July 1731). Cardinal Fleury has been criticized for letting England take the initiative in the latter settlements; [36] but it is certain that he was too wise a statesman to risk letting the Corsican rebellion upset European agreements that had been so difficult to achieve.

Nonetheless, the fact that the Corsican rebellion did not appreciably affect Versailles' influence in the Mediterranean or in Italy resulted as much from the actions of other powers as from design on Fleury's part. Neither England nor Spain interfered in the Corsican rebellion; and the Emperor did not stay in Corsica or Genoa after an agreement had been reached with the rebels. Yet the Corsican revolt had posed a major question for French diplomats. The decadence of Genoese rule in the island had caused a major rebellion, which in turn had created a power vacuum in the Mediterranean. A foreign power had been called in to restore order. No one could be certain that further rebellions would be avoided. Nor could France be certain that a foreign power, invited or uninvited, stepping in at the pretense of disorder, would not remain, thus endangering French Mediterranean interests. Versailles' concern with the events in the island was not exaggerated, for French inactivity during the first phase of the Corsican rebellion was certainly dangerous. Subsequent events in Corsica were to underscore that fact more than once.

NOTES

1. The best scholarly discussion of these events is found in Ambroise Ambrosi-Rostino, "La Banque Saint-Georges et la Corse de 1453 à 1562," *BSHNC* (April–June 1912), *passim*. See also F. Girolami-Cortona, *Histoire de la Corse* (Bastia, 1906), pp. 165–172.
2. French interest in Corsica during the time of Henry II is treated in Henry Joly, *La Corse française au* xvie *siècle: La 1ère occupation, 1553–1559* (Lyon, 1942). Girolami-Cortona discusses a memoir written by the Cardinal du Bellay on the advantages of invading Corsica (*op. cit.*, p. 174).
3. Felix de Bréguigny, *Histoire des révolutions de Gênes, depuis son établissement jusqu'à la conclusion de la paix de 1748*, 2nd ed., 2 Vols. (Paris, 1752), II, 319–322; Cesare Cantù, *Storia degli Italiana*, 15 Vols. (Turin, 1877), XII, 75–76. Cantù prints two accounts from archives in Paris and Genoa that illustrate the confusion caused by this bombardment (pp. 77–81).
4. François-René-Jean Pommereul, *Histoire de l'isle de Corse*, 2 Vols. (Berne, 1779), I, 123.
5. Louis Villat, *La Corse de 1768 à 1789*, 2 Vols. (Besançon, 1924–1925), I, 9.
6. Bréguigny, *op. cit.*, II, 342–352.
7. Driault, *Recueil*, pp. 185–199.
8. See the instructions to Auberville, Pré, Ratabon, Louciennes, Iber-

ville, and Anneville, all of whom were French envoys to Genoa during this period, in *ibid.*, pp. 205–240.

9. René Boudard, *Gênes et la France*, p. 30. The subsequent discussion of Genoese political institutions is based largely on Boudard's excellent chapter on "L'État gênois, sa constitution politique," pp. 29–42. See also Vito Vitale, *Breviario della storia de Genova*, 2 Vols. (Genoa, 1955), *passim.*

10. Boudard, *op. cit.*, p. 30.

11. Christian Ambrosi, *La Corse insurgée*, pp. 19–20. Girolami-Cortona commented that the rare and isolated acts of generosity on the part of Genoese officials "were like tastes of millet in an ocean of gall" (*op. cit.*, p. 219).

12. Bréguigny, *op. cit.*, II, 360, implies that all the Genoese governors lacked justice. His description of the administrative system is faulty (II, 360*n*). For a more accurate account, see Cantù, *op. cit.*, XII, 377. Cantù, however, is also too sweeping in his judgments about the governors; see Vitale, *op. cit.*, I, 365.

13. M. de Cany, Major and Commander of Antibes, stated that after the peace of Cateau-Cambrésis (1559) the Genoese destroyed 700 noblemen by one way or another ("Mémoire sur la Corse, septembre 1739," AG, *Mém. hist.*, 206³). A similar account is found in Guyot de Puymorin, "Mémoires historiques et critiques . . . ," BN, *Fonds français*, 14608. This memoir is a very personal account of the author's service in the regiment of Flanders, which served in Corsica in 1739.

14. Pommereul, *op. cit.*, II, 177, 183. For further evidence of the way Genoa controlled Corsican affairs and institutions, see the report on Bastia drawn up by François Marie Stefanini in June 1770 ("L'Administration municipale de Bastia sous la domination gênoise," *Corse Historique*, No. 1 [1953], 54–67).

15. This subject is admirably and exhaustively treated in J. Busquet, *Le Droit de la vendetta et les paci corses* (Paris, 1920). See especially the Introduction and pp. 265–322.

16. *Ibid.*, p. 119. M. de Cany claimed 27,000 assassinations in a fifteen-year period and noted with horror that the Corsicans were able to bargain with Genoese officials for the death of an enemy (*op. cit.*).

17. Voltaire, "Précis du siècle de Louis XV," *Oeuvres complètes de Voltaire*, Adrien Beuchot, ed. New ed. (Paris, 1878), XV, 408.

18. Bréguigny, *op. cit.*, II, 361; Pommereul, *op. cit.*, I, 144; Jacques Campredon (French ambassador to Genoa) to Jean-Frédéric Phélypeaux, comte de Maurepas (minister of the marine), Nov. 1, 1729, AE–CP, *Gênes*, Vol. 84, fols. 234–237; the Abbé L. Letteron, ed., "Osservazioni storiche sopra la Corsica dell'abbate Ambrogio Rossi," [1705–1810], *BSHNC* (numerous numbers, 1895–1909), Bk. VI, par. 15, pp. 27, 30; par. 30, pp. 55–57. Hereafter cited as Rossi and fol-

lowed by book, paragraph, and page number as appearing in Letteron's edition.

19. "Les parents des soldats qui avoient été pendus exagéroient ces griefs; on s'attroupoit, on mummuroit sans ménagement contre la république" (Bréguigny, *op. cit.*, II, 362).

20. This is the generally accepted interpretation of the reason for the new hearth tax. See Aylmer Vallance, *The Summer King: Variations by an Adventurer on an Eighteenth Century Air* (London, 1956), p. 42; Dom Jean-Baptiste Gaï, *La Tragique histoire des Corses*, 4th ed. (Paris, 1962), p. 168; and Paul Arrighi, *Histoire de la Corse* (Paris, 1966), pp. 61–62.

21. Pommereul, *op. cit.*, I, 145–147; See also J.-M. Jacobi, *Histoire générale de la Corse*, 2 Vols. (Paris, 1835), II, 37–41; and *Le Mercure de France*, August 1730, p. 1878.

22. Bréguigny, *op. cit.*, II, 362–363. For a description of the geography (and of modern economic problems) of Corsica, see Henri Hauser, "En Corse: une terre qui meurt," *Revue du Mois*, No. 47 (Nov. 1909), 539–569, especially 555–556.

23. Bréguigny, *op. cit.*, II, 366; Campredon's letters of Feb. 28, March 7, and April 11, 1730, AE–CP, *Gênes*, Vol. 85, fols. 48, 65–67, 133–134. On Pinello's character and actions, see the Abbé L. Letterson, ed., "Mémoires de Rostini," *BSHNC* (Feb. 1882), pp. 378–382; hereafter cited as Rostini, *BSHNC*, followed by month, year, and page.

24. G. Oreste, "La prima insurrezione còrsa del secolo XVIII (1730–1733)," *Archivio Storico di Corsica*, XVI (1940), 294–314, 394–399.

25. Bréguigny, *op. cit.*, II, 366–367; Rossi, Bk. VI, par. 31, pp. 55–57.

26. On the role of the clergy in the various Corsican revolts, see the evidence presented in S.-B. Casanova, *Histoire de l'église corse*, 2 Vols. (Ajaccio, 1931), *passim*.

27. Pommereul, *op. cit.*, I, 161; Cantù, *op. cit.*, XII, 328; Girolami-Cortona, *op. cit.*, p. 241; Rossi, Bk. VI, par. 43, pp. 79–81; Rostini, *BSHNC* (March 1882), p. 473.

28. D'Angelo to François Coutlet (French vice-consul at Genoa), March 7, 1731, AE–CP, *Corse*, Vol. IX, fols. 65–67.

29. Driault, *Recueil*, p. lxxix.

30. Bréguigny, *op. cit.*, II, 390; Rossi, Bk. VI, par. 70, pp. 157–160.

31. On the campaign of the Imperial troops, see the "Journal de la campagne de Mr le Baron de Vachtendonk en Corse, 24 juillet 1731 à mars 1732," dated March 1732, and the "Extrait du journal de Mr de Wattenchtdonk," no date, AG, *Mém. hist.*, 145.

32. A copy of the pardon that Württemberg offered to the rebels is in AE–CP, *Gênes*, Vol. 89, fols. 324–325. See also Jacobi, *op. cit.*, II, 70–73, for a complete list of the treaty's terms, including some dealing with war costs, education, and justice. Genoa's official printed text of

the accommodation dates from Jan. 23, 1733 (AE–CP, *Gênes*, Vol. 91, fol. 51) and bears the title "Concessioni graziose fatte della serenissima repubblica di Genova a'popoli e sudditi del regno di Corsica colla interposizione della Cesarea garanti." A manuscript copy, in Latin and bearing the date May 13, 1733, is in AE–CP, *Corse*, Vol. VII, fols. 270–279. This same volume contains pages of the *Gazette d'Amsterdam* that report on Corsican affairs for October and November 1732 (fols. 264–267). See also the Abbé L. Letteron, ed., "Mémoire sur l'expédition des troupes allemandes en 1731–1733," *BSHNC* (Jan.–Feb. 1884), pp. 243–283.

33. This judgment applies equally well to nearly all aspects of French foreign policy at the time. Arthur M. Wilson has made this quite clear in his admirable study, *French Foreign Policy during the Administration of Cardinal Fleury, 1726–1743; A Study in Diplomacy and Commercial Development* (Cambridge, Mass., 1936), pp. 210–241.

34. See Campredon's letters of March 14, Aug. 5, and Sept. 28, 1730; July 21, 1731; March 25 and May 20, 1732, in AE–CP, *Gênes*, Vol. 85, fols. 87–92; Vol. 86, fols. 36, 146–151; Vol. 88, fol. 13; and Vol. 89, fols. 246–250, 382–386.

35. Chauvelin to Campredon, May 8, 1731, *ibid.*, Vol. 87, fols. 213–214.

36. Pierre Rain, *La Diplomatie française d'Henri IV à Vergennes* (Paris, 1945), p. 168.

CHAPTER II

Versailles Formulates a Plan

The terms of the Peace of Corte (May 1732) suggest that the agreement was the product of very enlightened statesmanship, and that it marked a new beginning in Genoese-Corsican relations. The terms were especially favorable to the rebels, a fact in itself remarkable considering that at the time only a few individuals and no constituted authority recognized the right of rebellion as legitimate. The general amnesty and the release of the Corsican chiefs suggested that the islanders need not fear retribution. Provision for participation of Corsicans in the government on the island promised some basis for future cooperation between Corsicans and Genoese. Moreover, the Imperial guarantee seemed to assure the Corsicans that Genoa would honor the settlement.

A simple recapitulation of the terms of the settlement, however, does not reveal its central defect: namely, that the treaty had been forced on Genoa and was considered by the Genoese a shameful defeat. Europe already knew the military weakness of the republic—but obvious weakness had become humiliation; and in the eighteenth century the Genoese had little left but their pride. Added to Genoa's wounded ego was the financial drain occasioned by the costs of the Imperial army in Corsica. The fact that the treaty required the republic to give up some of the revenue from Corsica served to compound the damage to Genoese pocketbooks.[1]

The sense of defeat Genoa experienced over the settlement with Corsica increased the republic's insecurity as the power rivalry in Italy made its neutral position more and more precarious. These factors explain why, shortly after the settlement, Genoa began to act as if the treaty did not exist. Suspecting that the Corsicans had sympathizers in Genoa, the republic's officials attempted to arrest Marco Antonio Raffaelli. When their victim escaped into the mountains, they arrested four Corsican leaders instead: Simone Raffaelli, Andrea Colonna Ceccaldi, Luigi Giafferi, and a certain Aitelli. At the end of 1732, the republic transferred these prisoners from the island of Savona.[2] This action was an overt violation of the explicit terms of the Peace of Corte. Although Genoa released its prisoners in April 1733, it did so only under pressure from Louis XV and Prince Eugene of Savoy. The violation of the treaty confirmed the Corsican patriots in their suspicions of Genoa's bad faith. Despite the fact that Emperor Charles VI protested this violation of the peace,[3] the Corsicans learned, significantly, that they could not depend on the Imperial guarantee.

The actions of Genoa's new governor in Corsica, Paolo Pallavicino, reinforced these lessons in the minds of the islanders. Reflecting the insecurity felt by the Genoese Government, Pallavicino began to turn Corsica into a police state. He practiced summary justice and compiled lists of "suspects" to be jailed. Thus provoked anew, the Corsicans rebelled again in the spring of 1734. The chiefs met in a *Consulte* at Saint-Antoine de la Casabianca in April, established a "Magistrato Supremo del Regno," and named Gian Pietro Gaffori and Giacinto Paoli "generals" of the kingdom; the latter was the father of Pasquale Paoli who, twenty-one years later, was to lead Corsica's most determined struggle for independence. In September, at another *Consulte* held at the convent of Ornano, the Corsican leaders decided to treat personally with the Genoese. Their offer was refused, however, and a subsequent mission by the Corsican chief Gaffori to Bastia also ended in failure.[4] But the responsibility for the failure of the Peace of Corte was not all one-sided. Governor Pallavicino was justified in believing that hostility toward Genoa still existed and that many Corsican leaders had not accepted the Peace of Corte. As one modern Italian scholar argues, the first rebellion did not end with the peace settlement. A strong group of Corsicans continued to block all of Genoa's efforts toward reconciliation.[5]

The new rebellion in 1734 put the Corsican question back into a European setting by involving it in a war that had broken out the preceding year. Although the immediate cause of that war was the question of the Polish succession, Italy became one of the main theaters of conflict. The issue at stake was Austrian predominance in Italy and French-Spanish-Sardinian aspirations to upset that predominance. In addition to wanting compensation in Italy for Stanislas Leczinski's loss of the Polish throne, France feared any increase of Spanish power in that area. Both Spain and Sardinia wanted the Milanese, and during the course of the war almost fought each other over Mantua. France, therefore, had two allies who were not themselves effectively allied; and the French were suspicious of both of them. Added to this confusion was the possibility that England might enter the war on the side of Austria.[6]

In this state of international anarchy, France again feared that a strong state might exploit the situation and take Corsica from Genoa. It was already suspicious of Spanish designs, and recent events on the island suggested that the power to watch was indeed Spain. In January 1735 the Corsican leaders called a general assembly of the people at Corte. This assembly elected Giacinto Paoli chief of the new Corsican Government, burned the laws of Genoa, declared the island independent from Genoa, and dedicated the new nation to The Virgin. The assembly also declared that any Corsican who refused public employ was a "rebel against the fatherland" and could be condemned to loss of his possessions or even to death. The same penalties were to be imposed upon any "traitor" who even insinuated that it was necessary to treat with the republic. Moreover, the assembly set up the machinery for an independent Corsican Government which included: a general assembly, composed of one inhabitant from each city and village, with authority to establish taxes and to deliberate upon all important matters of state; an executive "junta" of six members, with supreme authority in civil and criminal affairs and the power to appoint all officers and subordinate ministers; a four-member council of war and a four-member council of finances; and a magistracy of *pères du commune* with jurisdiction over roads and the safety of travelers. A special magistracy of two secretaries of state was to protect against anything that might trouble the peace, notably "traitors against the fatherland" or those suspected of treason; it could conduct its investigations in secret and impose the death penalty. Meanwhile, Corsican agents were busy soliciting assistance from the courts of Europe. The venerable Canon Erasmo Orticoni, who had requested help from the Papacy in 1731, undertook the most important mission: a trip to the Spanish court of Philip V.[7] The growing strength of the Corsican national government made the islanders' appeal to Spain particularly dangerous; and the danger was increased by the fact that Spain seemed on the verge of becoming the arbiter of Italian affairs. By the end of 1734, Spanish forces had driven the Emperor out of Naples and Sicily.

The French Government did not know whether Spain constituted a real threat to Corsica at that time, but there were strong rumors to that effect, and no one knew when or if the island would catch Elizabeth Farnese's roving eye. What was clear was that France had neglected the Corsican question for too long a time. Versailles had long been aware of the dangers in Spanish expansion, and a policy of strong friendship had not yet developed between the two Bourbon powers. In 1725 and 1726, Cardinal Fleury had managed to avoid a threatened war pitting England and France against Spain and Austria.[8] The year of the Corsican rebellion, 1729, found some influential

French ministers contemplating a war against Spain.⁹ Yet France also had its conflicts with the Hapsburgs of Austria. Thus at the time of the Imperial intervention in Corsica in 1731, Versailles did not yet know whether France had more to fear from Spain or from Austria. Genoa's appeal to the Emperor had for a time suggested Austria; but by 1735 Austria had lost much of its strength in Italy and the Corsicans, disillusioned by the Emperor's ineffectual guarantee of the Peace of Corte, had turned to Spain.

Apparently the one person in the French diplomatic corps who had definite ideas about the Corsican question was Jacques Campredon. Having served as French minister at Stockholm (1701-1717 and 1719-1721) and envoy to Russia (1721-1726), Campredon was an experienced diplomat when he arrived in Genoa in 1727. After the revolt in Corsica began in 1729, Campredon reported faithfully on the course of the rebellion, the problems in Genoa that resulted from it, the progress made by Imperial troops, the negotiations that led to the Peace of Corte, and, as we have seen, the rumors about other powers' interests in the island. Then, pleading bad health, he asked for and received permission to return to France. He was gone from August 1732 until June 1733, and during his absence his secretary, Ally, and the French consul at Genoa, François Coutlet, kept Versailles informed about developments in Corsica and Genoa. Their uniformly optimistic reports expressed the hope and belief that the Imperial intervention and the Peace of Corte had finally resolved the Corsican problem.¹⁰

Campredon, however, was too experienced a diplomat to be misled by paper accommodations and paper guarantees. One of his first dispatches after his return to Genoa on June 6, 1733, sounded a different and more pessimistic note. On June 9 he wrote to the minister of the marine, Jean-Frédéric Phélypeaux, comte de Maurepas, saying that he doubted if Corsica would remain peaceful, for Corsican hostility to Genoa was too deeply seated. A few days later he reported that the people of Orezza, the most heavily populated part of the island, did not want to accept the accommodation with the Genoese; if such advantageous conditions are not accepted, he queried, what would happen in the future when the Genoese recovered their full powers in the island and did not enforce the accommodation? [11]

Campredon's pessimism failed to have an immediate effect upon his superiors. Maurepas thanked him for his information about Corsican affairs and told him to keep writing, but he suggested that the problems in Corsica ought to be considered at an end because the republic would take whatever measures were necessary to re-establish peaceful relations.[12] Undeterred, Campredon continued to report on the progress made by the Corsican rebels, on Genoa's growing difficulties and renewed efforts to obtain Imperial help, and on its fears that one of the great powers would intervene to the detriment of the republic's sovereignty over the island. Gradually Campredon began to form a plan which he thought would resolve the terribly frustrating and obviously dangerous deadlock between the republic and its island subjects.

Although Campredon did not elaborate upon his plan until the spring of 1735, by October 1733 he was convinced that a new policy was needed. At that time he wrote to Versailles saying that all around him it was evident that many Italians desired, with "empressement marqué," to see the French and Spanish return to Italy. His dispatch of June 29, 1734, contained a long coded section concerning Tuscany, Parma, and Corsica and the possibilities of exchanging these territories. Campredon said that he still did not believe the tales about Genoese negotiations for the cession of Corsica. Two months later Campredon observed that if the Genoese decided to give up Corsica to save face and prevent its seizure by a major power, they would favor the Spanish. Indeed, one of the most important figures in the Genoese Government had recently observed to one of Campredon's friends that if the court of Madrid or of Naples would give a reasonable equivalent "the sale [marché] would soon be concluded." Finally, early in January 1735 Campredon sent to Versailles a long dispatch in which he reported on rebel Corsican gains and Genoa's weakness. The republic, he said, had neither troops nor officers capable of commanding them, and each day the insurgents controlled a greater part of the island. "These difficulties in defending Corsica," Campredon concluded, "make the most sensible men believe that Corsica is lost to the republic, and they do not doubt that the revolt is being fomented by the Spanish." [13]

Having thus prepared the ground, Campredon boldly became the initiator of foreign policy rather than merely the executor of his government's instructions. On March 8, 1735, he sent to Versailles a long memoir, the purpose of which was to convince his government that it should work to prepare Genoa for the cession of Corsica to France. Campredon's reasoning was certainly persuasive, although his facts were not entirely correct. He suggested that occupation of Corsica would involve limited expenses because the island produced such products as oil, wine, animals, fish, minerals, and forest products especially suitable for ship construction. Possession of such a strategic post in the Mediterranean would increase French power and prestige markedly because "it would hold in respect those who would like to contest or attack the lands of the Spanish princes in Italy." [14] Campredon again pointed to the interest that other governments were showing in Corsica, as he had so often done in his earlier correspondence. And he emphasized that negotiations for cession of the island should be highly secret and should be accomplished before a general peace confirmed and consolidated the republic's possession of it. These, Campredon concluded, were his "foibles idées." If he were in error, he thought that the minister would consider his zeal for the king's service and forgive him, in which case the entire matter would simply be forgotten. But if the minister thought his plan worth considering, Versailles should negotiate with Genoa to acquire Corsica and should also begin to form "a French party" on the island in favor of French acquisition.

A month later Campredon suggested that if the Genoese

were reluctant to negotiate, a squadron of French ships in the port of Ajaccio might help them come to their senses. The Genoese, he observed, would cede Corsica only out of necessity and fear: "When they are near this point, it will be easy to make them see the advantages that the king can secure for them in exchange for Corsica." [15] At that time Versailles had no viable alternative for resolving the Corsican question, and it decided to follow Campredon's lead. Early in April the government asked Campredon for additional information; it wanted to know what revenues Genoa secured from the island, the number, location, and expenses of the republic's troops, and what form of government the rebels had recently established in Corsica. Campredon was warned to use great cirsumspection so that "it can never be imagined that France has any view in relation to the present situation of the island of Corsica." [16] He was also warned that he would suffer the consequences of any incorrect actions on his part.

Then, late in April, Versailles gave its qualified approval to Campredon's plan. In a dispatch to Campredon, dated April 26, Germain-Louis Chauvelin, secretary of state for foreign affairs (1727–1737), indicated that Louis XV approved of the idea of acquisition of Corsica as a measure for protecting the French Levant trade, although he had no intention of occupying Corsica as a usurpation on Genoese sovereignty. However, France could not directly propose acquisition to the Genoese Senate, for French interest in the island would at once be known and all of Europe would be alarmed. Chauvelin therefore directed Campredon to begin the formation of a French party on Corsica and to use all of his ability in persuading the Genoese Senators that the island was only "a burden" to them. What Genoa needed, Campredon was to suggest, was the assistance of "some power which was only interested in protecting the Genoese." [17]

Thus by the middle of 1735, Versailles had finally developed a plan of action. Campredon was directed to work on both sides. He was to build up the French party in Corsica, so that the Corsicans would request French protection. France would then send troops to Corsica, an action Campredon would explain to Genoa by asserting that France's only interest lay in keeping other powers out of the island. France would help Genoa re-establish its authority—that is, unless the republic preferred to cede the island to France. If and when such an occasion arose, Campredon would receive money with which he could bribe enough Senators to agree. Meanwhile, he was to guard this secret plan carefully. As Chauvelin admitted, it had "l'air d'une injustice" and would bring dishonor to France if anyone discovered it.[18] It is this "dishonorable secret" that has lurked in the background of the French approach to the Corsican question and that has constituted the basis for the Driault-Villat thesis: namely, that from 1735 until 1768 Versailles followed a "secret plan" to acquire the island.

Soon after the French Government decided what course to follow in its relations with Genoa and Corsica, several events occurred that emphasized the necessity of resolute action. The new "independent" Corsican Government began to fall apart. Though united against Genoa at first, the Corsican chiefs soon began to quarrel among themselves. When Genoa attempted to reach a settlement with the rebels, the latter demanded too much, for many of them had caught the spirit of independence and would not trade that spirit for servitude, no matter how light a yoke Genoa offered them. The republic therefore decided to use force again. It increased the number of Genoese troops on the island and established a coastal blockade.[19]

Meanwhile, the rebels enjoyed good fortune in the arrival of two small English ships, laden with supplies, that offered temporary respite. But by February 1736, they were desperate. Divided among themselves and lacking even the barest necessities, they finally had to send an envoy to Genoa. Yet even in defeat they offered terms that meant Genoa's virtual exclusion from the island. The republic naturally refused.

Again the rebels were momentarily rescued from their desperate situation when, on March 12, a ship appeared off Aleria on the eastern coast of the island. On board was Baron Theodore von Neuhoff, a German adventurer whose shady career had led him into many European courts. But the Corsicans were desperate and Neuhoff's colorful appearance and attractive promises, and the supplies he brought, caused the islanders to elect him their king. Angelo, the French vice-consul at Bastia, reported that Neuhoff was elected only because the Corsicans believed they would not be disturbed by foreign powers if they had their own king.[20] He called Neuhoff "un Roy de Carnaval," and like a carnival, Corsica's first and only king came and went. He lasted only until October 1736, when he left the island under the pretense of securing additional arms and supplies. Although he had no appreciable influence on Corsican history, he provides a delightful subject for intrigue and romance.[21]

Baron von Neuhoff's brief kingship also had effects on French foreign policy. France had heretofore feared Spanish interference in the island and had discounted the seriousness behind Austrian intervention. The Neuhoff episode increased French suspicions of the Spanish intentions, for at the time there was a rumor in France that Spain was helping Neuhoff in order to work its way into the island through him.[22] More important, by 1736 it had become clear that the maritime powers were also becoming interested in the island. Two English ships brought the supplies received by the Corsicans in the summer of 1735 and an English ship brought Neuhoff the following year. In addition, the munitions that Neuhoff brought with him were purchased through loans made in Holland, a state that France considered the dupe of England. Finally, when Neuhoff left the island later in 1736, his journey ended in Holland, where he was imprisoned for debt. The Bank of Amsterdam obtained his release, in return for which he promised that institution a monopoly on Corsican commerce.[23]

The increased danger of Spanish or English intervention in the troubled island demanded from Versailles cautious, astute diplomacy. Campredon wanted to see his plan to acquire Corsica put into action, and for some time he had been pressing Versailles to act upon it. In October 1735, he wrote informing the ministry that the crisis that would allow Ver-

Baron Theodore von Neuhoff (Bibliothèque Nationale).

sailles to make its offers to the republic was near. By the end of November, he was disturbed about Versailles' inaction and wrote asking the king's intentions. If the plan displeased Louis XV, Campredon wanted to disengage his contacts in Corsica while there was still time.[24]

Apparently Louis XV did not believe he had enough knowledge of the situation to act immediately. He talked to his advisers and had them send off to Campredon for additional information, but he made no decisions until the spring of 1737. During that time, Campredon had been hopeful, despite the difficult position in which Versailles' inactivity had placed him, but his hopes were shattered when on March 5, 1737, the new secretary of state for foreign affairs, Jean-Jacques Amelot de Chaillou, informed Campredon of Louis XV's decision. Although the king favored action if the republic should be disposed to sell the island, he had no views upon it so long as it remained in Genoa's possession. Until now he had not even considered it suitable to take any part in the Genoese-Corsican dispute. If the republic was actually thinking of selling the island, however, French interests demanded that no other power should acquire it.[25]

The question of selling the island to France was never officially broached, although the Genoese had strong suspicions that Versailles had some interest in Corsica. From 1737 until the island was lost in 1768, the Genoese believed that Versailles had plans of its own and was not chiefly concerned with Genoa's interests. For the moment, however, Campredon was authorized only to insinuate that "France would not view it with tranquillity if another power wanted to become the master of this island." He was also authorized to publish a memoir suggesting that François, duc de Lorraine, had some designs on the island, a memoir designed to instill in Genoa the fear of losing its island possession.[26]

Campredon was personally mortified by his government's decision to hold back. He informed the ministry that he would conform to that policy, but took the opportunity to point out

that he and his principal contact on the island had been compromised:

> . . . after having ordered me to follow the project of the
> acquisition of Corsica, which was unanimously approved
> in the king's council, and which M. Magnasco [Campre-
> don's contact in Corsica] was on the verge of making
> succeed, I have been commanded to think about it no
> longer, without doing anything for this good subject, who
> has died of chagrin from it.[27]

Later, however, even Campredon seemed to realize the difficulties of his plan. On May 2, 1737, he informed the ministry
that he was now convinced that the Genoese would not agree
voluntarily to cession of the island, which meant that French
acquisition would have to come through force; unfortunately,
he admitted, pretexts for such action were not at hand.[28]

Despite the threat of French designs on Corsica, the republic
sought French support when it learned that Neuhoff was sending military supplies to his Corsican supporters. Although by
this time Neuhoff's support on the island was withering rapidly,
his actions were sufficient to frighten the Genoese Senate into
making new overtures for French assistance, the news of which
leaked out quickly. By June 12 the Genoese public was in a
ferment over the news of an agreement between the republic
and Versailles whereby Louis XV would send troops to Corsica.
There were such heated disputes over this issue in the Petit
Council, Campredon said, that Tommaso Centurione and
Gerolamo Pallavicino, the latter a declared enemy of France,
challenged each other to a duel. Unofficially, Versailles and
the Senate agreed upon the terms for French support in July,
although the formal convention dated from November 1737.[29]
A separate and secret article to this agreement assured the
republic that Louis XV would never allow its sovereignty over
Corsica to be injured in any manner whatever, and that all

French actions and regulations would be carried out in the name of the republic.[30]

The fact that only France agreed to intervene was not at all satisfactory to the republic, which had requested a joint intervention by France and the Emperor. The Turks were again threatening central Europe, however, and the Emperor was in no position to offer military support to Genoese power in Corsica. Genoa accepted what help it could get, but it must have been with some tribulation that the Genoese saw the first six battalions of French troops, under the command of Alphonse, comte de Boissieux, land at Saint-Florent on February 8, 1738.[31]

Boissieux quickly established French forces at Bastia and Saint-Florent, but he did not immediately attempt to suppress the rebels. As Maurepas observed, "certainly it will not be by sieges and battles that one will reduce the rebels." The French plan was gradually to deprive the Corsicans of the land where they gathered for their ambushes and from which they derived their sustenance. At the same time, Versailles intended to consider the Corsicans' grievances. Maurepas was pleased to note "that most of the rebels are disposed to submit to the equitable conditions that France will impose upon them; the king's intention is not to make them submit to any other." [32] These same principles appeared in Boissieux's orders from Cardinal Fleury. The French commander was directed to use moderation in preference to force and was authorized to negotiate with the Corsican leaders and listen to their grievances.[33]

The arrival of French forces in Corsica in 1738 set off new speculations in the European courts concerning Versailles' designs in the Mediterranean. At Turin the prevailing opinion was that the French sought to extricate themselves from their *faux pas* without damaging their prestige. France, it was believed, would try to make some arrangements with the Corsicans and would then leave the island. The Corsicans, for their part, would be pleased because Genoa had not, by itself, been able to compel them to submit.[34] Other courts were more suspicious than Turin. Lord James Waldegrave, the English ambassador at Paris, believed that French aid to Genoa regarding its restive island possession was designed to allow Fleury a major voice in Genoese affairs. Sir Horace Mann, who was even more suspicious, believed that Versailles wanted Corsica for itself or for Don Philippe of Spain. Genoa would receive something in return for its cession of the island, perhaps La Lunegiane.[35] Finally, Jean de Chambrier, the Prussian minister at Paris, speculated in a dispatch to Frederick II, dated June 17, 1740, that the French intended to stay in Corsica for a long time to come.[36]

There was also a great deal of speculation, questioning, and even criticism among the French people concerning the reasons why France sent troops to Corsica in 1738. The lawyer Barbier, picking up gossip and rumors, reported that many Frenchmen believed France received nothing and that only the republic profited. The usual explanation, he said, was that France wanted to make certain the island did not fall into another power's possession.[37] There was good reason to believe that this might indeed happen. One after another, rumors about pretensions to Corsica swept through France. One possibility was that the Spanish *Infant,* Don Philippe, would be given Corsica and some other lands. Another story suggested that Elizabeth Farnese had designs on the island and was secretly giving aid to former king Neuhoff, whose brief return to the island in September 1738 seemed to confirm this rumor. Still another rumor was that Corsica would be given to Sardinia, which would in return give some territory to France.[38]

If foreign courts and the French people were excited by French intervention in 1738, so too were the Corsicans, but for different reasons. Boissieux's conciliatory action led the Corsican leaders to believe that perhaps France was sympathetic to their cause. Moreover, Versailles had given them an additional reason to hope for French support. In November 1737, Versailles sent a special agent, the Sieur A.-M. Pignon, to Leghorn to meet with a Corsican, the Abbé Gregoire Salvini, and to listen to the Corsican peace proposals. This step was taken in great secrecy. Pignon was given a code and special instructions which told him that once he had determined the sincerity of the Corsicans' proposals, he should inform Salvini of the king's intentions. Louis XV had no intention of destroying the Corsicans or of making them submit to an oppressive government. His only interest was in ending the troubles in Corsica, and he would not condemn the islanders without listening to their proposals for peace. If they accepted his mediation, he would seek to obtain for them "reasonable conditions." [39]

Thus deserted by the Emperor and by their own king, with little hope for assistance from Spain, and encouraged by Boissieux and Pignon, the Corsicans appealed directly to Versailles. In May 1738, Canon Erasmo Orticoni and Gian Pietro Gaffori addressed a letter to Cardinal Fleury. After praising Fleury's virtues, the Corsicans pleaded the "justice" of their cause. They eulogized "the diligence and patience" of Boissieux, whom they had requested to inform Louis XV of their needs. Finally, they solicited the king's "good offices" in removing Genoa's yoke from them, for they had no voice with which to make their protests known.[40]

Fleury's reply to the Corsicans' request for assistance was respectful but firm. "You were born subjects of the republic of Genoa," he wrote, "and they are your legitimate masters." This sentence seemed to sum up Fleury's position, for he refused to assist the Corsicans against Genoa. However, Fleury tried to say nothing that would definitely turn the islanders against France. Although he reminded them that their faith did not permit rebellion against their legitimate masters, he indicated that he was not their judge and would neither condemn nor justify their acts of resistance. Finally, Fleury wrote that Genoa proposed to proclaim a general peace and, under the guarantee of Louis XV and the Emperor, to promise amnesty for hostilities committed by Corsicans.[41] Fleury's reply followed closely the instructions sent to Campredon. France would be a mediator, but that was all. The secret plan of 1735 for acquisition of Corsica was no longer considered seriously by the ministry.

Reinforcing this judgment is a letter that Fleury wrote early in June 1738, in which he asked Boissieux to convey his reply to the leaders of the Corsican rebels. Then he observed: "His Majesty cannot, without being dishonorable and without breaking his word, treat otherwise with [the Corsicans] than on the condition that they re-place themselves under the legitimate obedience of their sovereigns." In order to secure peace and tranquillity in Corsica, Fleury continued, it may be necessary "to speak strongly" to the Genoese; but until then Boissieux should be particularly careful not to prejudice their sovereignty, "upon which we have no right to infringe. . . ." [42]

Additional evidence that Versailles was not pursuing a policy of acquisition is found in Pignon's instructions, of which there are at least three different versions. One instruction seems to be an abbreviated and incomplete early draft.[43] A second seems to be a nearly completed draft with minor corrections.[44] The third instruction is apparently the one actually sent to Pignon; it is dated November 13, 1737.[45] There are minor but significant differences between the second and third instructions. In the second copy, Pignon was told that if the Corsicans should "by chance" offer the island to France he should leave them "no hope that His Majesty is able to abandon his plan for that reason." This statement did not appear in the third copy of the instructions; but in both the second and third copies Pignon was directed to tell the Corsicans that "it is expedient to them, as much as to all of Europe, to remain under the domination of the Genoese." On January 24, 1738, Pignon informed his superiors that he had had several interviews with the Corsican Salvini, who "realized that the people of Corsica could not dispense with remaining under Genoese domination since the king wished it. . . ." [46] A month later Pignon was told that "the course of submission is . . . the only one which is most expedient to these peoples, by which they will be able to count on the guarantee of the king who is in a better position than the Emperor to oblige the republic of Genoa to respect the conditions of the accommodation." [47]

Fleury's chief concern, therefore, was not acquisition of Corsica; it was, rather, the restoration of tranquillity to the island so that no other power would have a pretext for intervention. An attempt to gain this tranquillity was made in a declaration of pacification signed at Fontainebleau on October 18, 1738, and guaranteed by both Louis XV and the Emperor. This was the general peace promised by Fleury in his letter to Orticoni and Gaffori. The pacification granted a general pardon for disorders since 1733; forgave *tailles* and impositions not collected up to the month of September 1738; promised that four noble families, with right of primogeniture, would be created each year; installed at Bastia a supreme tribunal with three foreign *auditeurs;* and promised both strict justice and closer supervision of Genoese officials. These regulations were to be enforced after the Corsicans put down their arms.[48] The terms of the pacification were better than the Corsicans could have expected, but they still feared being returned to Genoese control. Demonstrations against Genoa continued and Boissieux had to suppress them by force, in the process suffering a humiliating defeat at Borgo. Then, in February 1739, Boissieux died.

Boissieux's death came at a decisive moment, for Versailles was in the process of re-evaluating its policies toward the Corsican question. Beginning in January 1739, the government was disturbed over the course of the rebellion and irresolute about how to deal with it. In effect, the court was divided between two policies. Some favored abandoning the enterprise, even though such action would give the impression of weakness and inconstancy. Others favored resolute maintenance of the engagements already made with Genoa to submit the island to Genoese sovereignty, a policy that might entail rigorous methods, considerable sacrifices, and even devastation of the island.[49]

For the moment Versailles decided to honor its commitments to the republic, and in March 1739 Boissieux's replacement, Nicolas Desmarets, marquis de Maillebois, landed in

Corsica. At the time there were ten battalions of French troops on the island, for early in 1739 Boissieux's initial six battalions had been reinforced by four more. Yet Maillebois did not immediately attempt forced pacification of the island. He believed that the troops under his command were still insufficient for that task. Moreover, he received instructions from Versailles in April indicating that Cardinal Fleury still hoped to avoid hostilities against the Corsicans.[50] The use of force would make the rebels hate France as they hated Genoa, a situation that Versailles wanted to avoid if it could.

The French Government's hope for peaceful resolution of Corsica's problems was not realized. On the island, Maillebois was constantly troubled by Genoese officials, who preferred a forced pacification to a negotiated peace, and who feared that the French were winning the confidence of the Corsican peoples. In addition, the submission imposed upon the Corsicans by the Convention of Fontainebleau (October 1738) did not eliminate the islanders' internal divisions and personal feuds or the hatred they felt toward Genoa.[51] Consequently, Maillebois had to use force in disarming the rebels. The arrival of six more French battalions in May 1739 brought his effective forces to nearly 8,000 troops, part of which were set in motion throughout the island early in June. Although both Corsicans and French fought vigorously, the French troops were superior in number, discipline, equipment, and tactics. By October Maillebois had restored a tense peace to the island and French troops were in control of most of the coastal area and the principal towns. Scattered rebel forces still held parts of the mountainous interior, but they were of minor consequence.[52]

Maillebois' difficulties with Genoese officials led to a further reassessment of French policy. By now it was clear that Versailles must accomplish two goals. First, it must calm the republic's fears that France was getting ready to take the island for itself. Second, it must pacify the island in order to avoid the danger that another great power would use the troubles on Corsica to increase its strength in the Mediterranean.

The first step toward accomplishing this double objective

was to find a suitable replacement for Campredon, whose activities and independence had not pleased his superiors. In January 1739, after having been told to forget his secret plan, Campredon was still pressing for its adoption. If the king undertook considerable expense to help Genoa, he suggested, "would it not be natural that he keep this island until their reimbursement; and if, according to all appearances, the republic will never be in the condition to do it, will this not be a quite natural means to engage it to make the cession of the island to France . . . ?" [53] Campredon's persistence caused his dismissal. In February he was told to devote more of his time to the subject of commerce, which was a fairly strong hint that the ministry thought he was too deeply involved in political affairs which did not concern him. Then, in April, he was dismissed on the grounds that his age and infirmities did not allow him to pursue Corsican affairs with the vigor required. Louis XV was not discontented with his service, Campredon was informed, so he should not consider himself disgraced if the king replaced him with a subject better able by his *activité* to execute the king's orders.[54] Reading between the lines, Campredon realized that, in fact, he was being disgraced, and he took dismissal as a criticism of all his past services. He pleaded his diligence and his forty years of service. He asked what would happen to his family, for he had only his pension and a small income of 1,800 livres.[55] It was all in vain.

Campredon's replacement, François Chaillon de Jonville, had been the French minister at Brussels, but he was a young man, without a great deal of diplomatic experience. Argenson reported that he was the son of a *fermier général* and that he had received his position through Cardinal Fleury's *valet de chambre*.[56] However that may be, Jonville's character, background and instructions make it clear that his presence in Genoa was designed to calm the republic's fears about French intentions. Indeed, his instructions, dated June 24, 1739 (which, incidentally, contain only slight mention of Corsica), told him to drop suggestions during the course of his conversations with Genoese Senators, indicating "that the republic has much more to fear from other powers than from France." [57]

In his discussion of these instructions, Driault stated: "The instructions of M. de Jonville are entirely harmless [*toute anodine*]; there is scarcely a question of Corsica; one would not believe while reading them that he could be charged with an important negotiation; it happens that the instructions present less interest than the correspondence." Driault then commented that Jonville replaced Campredon because the latter was not capable of making the Genoese understand that "the positive interest of the republic was to rid themselves of Corsica at the best price." [58] Yet careful reading of Jonville's instructions reveals that this was not his assignment; and careful reading of his correspondence reveals a great deal of gossip and speculation but little else of major interest, except some coded dispatches reporting on English interests in Corsica. Jonville was certainly not charged with important negotiations; on the contrary, he repeatedly asked to be reassigned. "Je m'ennuye de ne faire ici que le gazeteer," Jonville remarked, and then added: "I dare flatter myself that I could do something better. . . ." [59]

The new instructions that Jonville received on January 12, 1740, were even more specific. Louis XV pledged his royal word, and he was even willing to accept the Emperor's guarantee, to restore Genoese sovereignty over its island possession. Amelot emphasized that the republic was extremely sensitive about its sovereignty over Corsica and that Jonville should be cautious never to give the Genoese cause for suspecting France of "infidelity." [60]

Along with these instructions came a "Mémoire sur la Corse" which clearly reveals that, at the time, Versailles had no intention of purchasing the island from Genoa. The French Government was not at all worried about the adventurer and pretender Neuhoff, according to the new secretary of state for foreign affairs, Jean-Jacques Amelot de Chaillou, because he lacked both funds and support in the island. It was concerned, however, that Neuhoff might receive help from outside, know-

ing that he had already asked for such assistance. If he did
not succeed in getting outside help, then the Corsicans might
decide to offer the island to a power capable of delivering
them from the Genoese. Jonville's task, therefore, was to calm
Genoese fears that France had some designs on Corsica and,
at the same time, convince the republic that it should fear the
intentions of other powers. Amelot defined Versailles' position
quite candidly:

> The king has stated and today again states to [the republic]
> that he has not the slightest intention of acquiring the
> ownership of this kingdom, but it is at the same time in
> his interest that, his estates being so near to Corsica, it
> does not fall into hands other than those of the republic.
> Also, it would not be just that, having made such great
> expense to conserve it to [the republic], some other power
> receives the fruit of it.[61]

Once Versailles had begun to calm Genoese fears, it still
needed to pacify the island. By the end of 1739, Cardinal Fleury
and Amelot had begun to work out a plan to accomplish this
second goal. In November the ministry acknowledged Jonville's reports that the Corsicans had laid down their arms,
adding that "c'est à quoi le Roy s'estoit engagé." The king
realized, however, that the Corsicans were still alienated from
their sovereigns and the republic still had reason to fear "their
ferocity." Thus, on the king's orders, Jonville was to present
to the Genoese Senate an attached memoir emphasizing these
points. Jonville was to use extreme caution in keeping knowledge of the memoir from the Corsicans and other powers. Louis
XV expected a prompt answer from the republic.[62]

The memoir to be submitted to Genoa was quite short and
to the point. It reiterated the problems mentioned in the letter
cited above and then stated that "the perfect submission of this
island is the work of time, and of a moderate and equitable
administration." Only after the Corsicans had become accustomed to "un joug doux" and had experienced "the blessing

44

of a tranquil condition" would their confidence in Genoa be renewed. The memoir ended with the statement that Louis XV believed it necessary to make these observations to the Genoese so that they could more easily decide what action to take and what proposals to make to France, in order "to consolidate and affirm the submission of these ferocious peoples, to civilize them by laws suitable to their character, and to make them disposed to obey those laws." [63]

Versailles waited in vain for a reply to this memoir throughout the last two months of 1739 and January 1740. Jonville informed his superiors of the evasive tactics undertaken by the Genoese officials in their efforts to avoid his representations and queries. Versailles finally pressed the matter by sending a letter to Jonville from Amelot on January 12, indicating that Louis XV was willing to police and govern the island of Corsica and make its inhabitants respect the laws. In doing so, however, the republic must place its complete confidence in Louis XV and trust him without reservation. The Genoese must give "absolute and unlimited power to the commander of the French troops," must allow the French king to do everything in his own name, must remove Genoese forces from the island, and contribute to the king's expenses. For his part, the king would give his royal word to return Corsica to Genoa within a fixed time and would accept the Emperor's guarantee. If the republic did not accept these conditions, then, Amelot thought, a threat might make them see the correct course of action. If Genoa "believes its sovereignty harmed when one seeks only to conserve it, Genoa ought no longer to count on French help *on any occasion*." [64] [Italics added.]

The two commissioners appointed by Genoa to negotiate the terms of French occupation, Gian Battista Grimaldi and Carlo-Emmanuele Durazzo, were naturally suspicious when they saw the conditions that Versailles demanded before it granted its aid, for those conditions amounted to virtual sovereignty over the island. The republic had the king's word and perhaps an Imperial guarantee (which, however, might prove worthless) that sovereignty would be restored to it after the

45

rebellion ended. Yet it was not at all pleased. To safeguard its own interests, Genoa expressed its desire to modify some of the terms and again requested a joint Austrian-French occupation of the island. Versailles agreed to a joint intervention, and for a time it appeared that the Emperor would send a force of 4,800 men to Corsica in support of Genoese sovereignty.[65] But fate intervened before such an agreement could be made—Charles VI died and Europe went to war. In consequence, there was no Austrian-French occupation.

France was therefore obliged to resolve the Corsican problem by itself. On February 7, 1741, Amelot proposed a new plan of action to Agostino Lomellini, the Genoese minister to France. Although the rebellion seemed to be over, Amelot said, the republic apparently did not want the king to withdraw his troops suddenly. Louis XV would therefore agree to leave six battalions on Corsica as long as the republic considered it necessary, but he specified two conditions. First, Genoa must give France some "places de sûreté," including the ports and citadels of Ajaccio and Calvi. Second, Genoa was to furnish the French troops with beds, wood, lights, benches, tables, and utensils. If the republic accepted these conditions, it should inform Maillebois who had instructions to withdraw all French troops except the six battalions subject to the above conditions.[66]

Once again Versailles waited in vain for a definite reply to its proposals. Finally, it acted. In April 1741, Maillebois received orders to withdraw the French troops from Corsica. He returned to the continent in May, and in September the Marquis de Villemur took the last French contingent off the island.[67] The Corsicans and the Genoese again found themselves facing each other without the pacifying presence of an outside military force.

It is quite certain that Versailles sought some advantage from the aid that it offered so generously to Genoa, although not the kind of advantage Campredon had envisioned in his secret plan of 1735. The proposal to leave six battalions of French troops on Corsica resulted from Versailles' realistic appraisal of Corsican-Genoese relations. The French ministers knew that the only way to overcome Corsican antipathy toward Genoa and to make certain that the republic respected agreements made with the rebels was to leave a mediating force on the island. Jonville frequently stressed this point in his correspondence. On July 23, 1739, he sent two dispatches to his superiors; one of them stated that although Corsica had nearly submitted to the occupying forces, real peace in the island could only be established by the formation of a new political administration. This new administration must be supported by an authority respected by the Corsicans and able to assure them that Genoa would not use its rights of sovereignty to undermine the new form of government. The second dispatch emphasized that there were two irreconcilable factors involved in the Genoese-Corsican conflict: "the constant determination of His Majesty [the king of France] to re-establish the sovereignty of the republic of Genoa over Corsica," and the "repugnance" of the Corsicans for Genoa. These irreconcilables would only be overcome by leaving some troops on the island and by establishing a new form of civil government. In return for its assistance in re-establishing Genoese sovereignty, France should hold certain strategic coastal places.[68]

Nicolas-Prosper Bauyn, seigneur d'Angervilliers, secretary of state for war from 1728 to 1740, emphasized the same points in a memoir that he wrote, apparently, at Cardinal Fleury's request. Angervilliers observed that new laws alone would not insure peace in Corsica. Its sovereign should have a body of troops on the island to enforce these laws, to build forts in the interior, and to open roads; ten years would scarcely be enough for these tasks. But the Genoese were too weak to accomplish them, and it did not appear that Louis XV would use his troops and his money as a free gift to the republic. Still, if French troops were withdrawn, the revolt would begin again and France would lose everything it had invested. Moreover, "in the present circumstances [of Europe]," Angervilliers stressed, "we have more interest than ever that no other foreign power put their feet in Corsica." He therefore proposed that Maillebois hold the ports of Bastia, Calvi, and Ajaccio, and let the Genoese control the citadels as well as the interior of the island. If convenient, the Genoese could be informed that it was in their interest to give France the citadels as well as legislative power, which it would use for a few years and then return to the republic. Then Angervillier added: "For a long time it has been considered sufficient for us to have some bases on the Corsican coasts as the Europeans have on the coasts of America, regarding the Corsicans of the interior of the country as one does the savages in the Indies." He also advised against continuing to support the sixteen French battalions in Corsica at a cost of more than 200,000 livres per month, and he recommended withdrawal of eight battalions in order to diminish expenses.[69]

The French proposal to leave troops on Corsica in return for certain strategic coastal places (*présides*) was thus not directed at establishing French sovereignty over the island. It was instead an effort to resolve the Genoese-Corsican conflict and, at the same time, gain security in the Mediterranean at a time when European affairs were approaching a crisis. Moreover, on the eve of the War of the Austrian Succession there was a growing sentiment at Versailles in favor of cultivating the republic's friendship by actively supporting it against the Corsican rebels.

This broader rationale for Versailles' generosity toward the Genoese can be found in the shifting balance of power in Italy, which was the crucial question in the Mediterranean during the 1730s. This balance was changed considerably by the Treaty of Vienna (November 13, 1738) which ended the War of the Polish Succession (the preliminaries having been signed in February 1737). By the terms of this treaty the Emperor gave Naples and Sicily to Don Carlos and in return received Parma and Piacenza. Tuscany was given to François, duc de Lorraine, who was betrothed to the Arch-duchess Maria Theresa. The Duchy of Lorraine was first given to Stanislas Lesczinski as compensation for losing the Polish throne; upon his death it was to revert to French sovereignty.

48

This complicated settlement eventually added the important territory of Lorraine to France, but it had a definite disadvantage. It placed Imperial power in the duchies and in Tuscany. Furthermore, it located the Spanish Bourbon line in the southern part of Italy, which meant that northern Italy, the route through which France might attack Austria from the south, was closed to the French. France had, in fact, been squeezed out of Italy. Only two openings through Italy into the heartland of Europe remained. One was through the lands of King Charles-Emmanuel III of Piedmont-Sardinia, an opening of doubtful value because of Charles-Emmanuel's doubtful allegiance. The second opening was the neutral republic of Genoa, and that opening had to be kept accessible at all costs. The secret plan of 1735 was diametrically opposed to the policy of friendship toward the republic that developing international conditions seemed to require.

Early in 1738, René-Louis de Voyer, marquis d'Argenson, acutely summarized both the short-term and long-run objectives of French policy toward Corsica and Genoa. At the time he was a *conseiller d'état;* later, from November 1744 to January 1747, he was the secretary of state for foreign affairs. The entry in Argenson's journal for February 1738, the month Boissieux landed in Corsica, includes an extremely interesting commentary on the Corsican question and its relationship to the Italian balance of power. Argenson did not see any "mystery" in the reasons why French troops were sent to the island, although he thought it odd that France should send such a small force when the Emperor could not suppress the 1731 revolt with 10,000 troops. He believed that French forces should hold certain of the island's key positions for Genoa. They should not encourage the revolt, for the "honor" of France must be protected. But France should not force the rebels into submission to Genoese sovereignty. France, Argenson felt, should plan to stay in Corsica for a long time, because the island offered a vantage point from which to watch Spain, it would benefit French commerce in the Levant, and it might even become a great warehouse for French goods.

Argenson's most important discovery, however, only indirectly concerned Corsica. French aid to Genoa, he thought, would make those "poor people" dependent on France and thereby give France a solid hold on the republic. French influence in Genoese affairs would thus give France a "foothold" in Italy or a "doorway" to Italy. As a result, Versailles would no longer have to depend on Sardinia, which always sold its support of French policy at an extremely high price. This policy of French aid to Genoa, Argenson said, was preferable to full ownership of Corsica, which would be difficult to maintain.[70]

In one sense, Argenson merely reiterated, with special emphasis on the Italian situation, what constituted the fundamental reason for the Corsican problem of the eighteenth century. Whatever might be said of Corsica's economic potential, its strategic position was its principal value. Without the dynastic and territorial conflicts of the eighteenth century, the Corsican rebels probably would still have been rebels; but there would not have been an eighteenth-century Corsican question.

In another sense, however, Argenson's comments on the Italian situation are of critical importance for considering the development of French foreign policy toward the Corsican question. In essence, Argenson suggested that, whereas Corsica was of strategic importance, France's chief interest was in conserving the allegiance of Genoa, which was France's principal entry into Italy and, if the need should arise, its principal avenue of attack against the Austrians. His astute observations on the Mediterranean and Italian scene appeared just as a major change in the direction of French policy was taking place. One part of the secret plan formed in 1735 involved an offer to purchase Corsica from Genoa. But from 1737 on the French Government dropped this part of the plan and directed its attention toward keeping Genoa within the French alliance system. In other words, Versailles went back to the main policy of Louis XIV.[71]

Finally, the most conclusive evidence that French policy

toward Corsica underwent a change after 1737 is the fact that for at least the next twenty-one years (and perhaps for the next thirty years) Versailles followed substantially the policy recommended by Cardinal Fleury, Amelot, Jonville, Maurepas, Angervilliers, and Argenson. It was not the policy of the so-called "secret plan" of 1735, a plan which in fact was discarded two years later. It was, rather, the policy of pacifying the rebellion in Corsica in order to prevent other powers from establishing themselves there and of keeping Genoa within the French sphere of influence. Events in Corsica and Italy after 1740 served to convince the French Government that the policy it had decided on by 1740 was both wise and "politique."

NOTES

1. Genoa calculated the cost of Imperial aid at 30 million livres. See Aylmer Vallance, *The Summer King*, p. 46.
2. Felix de Bréguigny, *Histoire des révolutions*. . . . , II, 430–431. G. Oreste, "La prima insurrezione corsa," *Archivio Storico di Corsica, XVII* (1941), 173–182.
3. Pierre Lamotte, ed., "L'intervention de l'Empereur en Corse en 1731–1732," *Corse Historique*, No. 3 (1953), 16–19.
4. Rossi, Bk. VII, par. 18, pp. 66–68; par. 30, pp. 93–95; par. 35–37, pp. 108–114.
5. Vito Vitali, *Breviario della storia de Genova*, I, 377. See also Bréguigny, *op. cit.*, II, 429, and P. Caraffa, ed., "Memorie per servire alla storia delle rivoluzioni di Corsica dal 1729 al 1764, del Padre Bonfiglio Guelfucci, di Belgordere," *BSHNC* (June and Aug. 1882), 55. Hereafter cited as Guelfucci, "Memorie."
6. Arthur W. Wilson, *French Foreign Policy*, pp. 252–257. For the military history of this war, see Charles-Pierre-Victor, comte de Pajol, *Les guerres sous Louis XV*, 7 Vols. (Paris, 1888), I, Chapters V-XII.
7. "Résolution des rebelles de Corse en 22 articles" (Jan. 29, 1735), AE–CP, *Gênes*, Vol. 95, fols. 97–100; Rossi, Bk. VII, par. 41, pp. 121–124; François-René-Jean Pommereul, *Histoire de l'isle de Corse*, I, 197–198; Vitale, *op. cit.*, I, 378; Driault, *Recueil*, p. lxxxii.
8. Penfield Roberts, *The Quest for Security, 1715–1740* (New York, 1963), pp. 247–248.
9. Wilson, *op. cit.*, pp. 210–241.
10. AE–CP, *Gênes*, Vols. 89–91, *passim*.

11. Campredon to Maurepas, June 9 and 16, 1733, *ibid.*, Vol. 91, fols. 395, 403.

12. Maurepas to Campredon, July 25, 1733, *ibid.*, Vol. 92, fol. 21.

13. See Campredon's letters of Oct. 13, 1733, June 29 and Aug. 24, 1734, and Jan. 13, 1735, in *ibid.*, Vol. 92, fols. 139–145; Vol. 93, fols. 371–380; Vol. 94, fols. 105–107; and Vol. 95, fols. 22–28.

14. Campredon to .... [Chauvelin], March 8, 1735, *ibid.*, Vol. 95, fols. 157–168. Letters from French ambassadors to the ministry were not always addressed to a specific person. Ordinarily, however, they were sent to the secretary of state for foreign affairs.

15. Campredon to .... [Chauvelin] [secret], April 6, 1735, *ibid.*, Vol. 95, fols. 242–251.

16. "Eclaircissements à demander à M. de Campredon" April 12, 1735, *ibid.*, Vol. 95, fols. 222–223.

17. .... [Chauvelin] to Campredon, April 26, 1735, Vol. 95, fols. 280–281. See also Driault, *Recueil*, pp. 282–283.

18. AE–CP, *Gênes*, Vol. 95, fols. 280–281, and Driault, *Recueil*, pp. 282–283.

19. Pommereul, *op. cit.*, I, 201–202.

20. Angelo to Campredon, April 12, 1736, AE–CP, *Gênes*, Vol. 97, fols. 203–204.

21. Vallance's biography of King Theodore, cited above, is popular but based on some primary sources. Valerie Pirie, *His Majesty of Corsica: The True Story of the Adventurous Life of Theodore Ist* (New York, 1959), is, as the title suggests, popular. The only scholarly biography is by André Le Glay, *Théodore de Neuhoff, roi de Corse* (Paris, 1907). For a light, literary interpretation of Neuhoff while he was king of Corsica, see Raymond Dumay, "Quand Figero 1er régnait sur la Corse," *Les Oeuvres Libres*, CLXVIII (1960), 77–102. See also Rossi, Bk. VII, par. 58, pp. 160ff; Guelfucci, "Memorie," pp. 65–69; and Rostini, *BSHNC* (April-May 1882), *passim.*

22. Edmond-Jean-François Barbier, *Chronique de la régence et du règne de Louis XV (1718–1763), ou Journal de Barbier*, 8 Vols. (Paris, 1857), III, 56, 145. By 1734 there was also a Spanish party on the island, led by Canon Orticoni. See Christian Ambrosi, *La Corse insurgée*, p. 44.

23. J. C. L. Simone de Sismondi, *Histoire des français*, 31 Vols. (Paris, 1842), XXVIII, 207. An anonymous memoir entitled simply "Mémoire sur l'Isle de Corse," dated March 1737, forcefully called the minister of the marine's attention to the English threat. Pointing out how extremely important it was to French commerce in Italy and the Levant that Corsica did not fall under the domination of a power with a navy, the author first described the island's advantageous location. Then he suggested that the power that possessed Corsica needed only some armed frigates and corsairs to keep French ships out of Italy

during a war. He further suggested that commerce with the Levant would be seriously disrupted by such a power, for ships coming from there had to reconnoiter Corsica before sailing to the ports of Provence. AM, B¹ 60, fols. 38–40.

24. Campredon to .... [Chauvelin], Oct. 6, 1735, and Campredon to Maurepas, Nov. 24, 1735, AE–CP, *Gênes*, Vol. 96, fols. 246–249.

25. .... [Amelot] to Campredon, March 5, 1737, *ibid.*, Vol. 99, fols. 74–75.

26. Campredon to .... [Amelot], March 14, 1737, *ibid.*, Vol. 99, fols. 95–98.

27. Campredon to .... [Amelot], April 25, 1737, *ibid.*, Vol. 99, fols. 164–167.

28. Campredon to .... [Amelot], May 2, 1737, *ibid.*, Vol. 99, fols. 184–186.

29. Campredon to .... [Amelot], June 20, 1737, *ibid.*, Vol. 99, fols. 261–266; .... [Amelot] to Campredon, Nov. 19, 1737, *ibid.*, Vol. 100, fol. 212; Baron Cervoni, ed., "La première intervention française en Corse, en 1738," *BSHNC* (Feb. 1882), 367–369.

30. "Article séparé et secret dont la copie a été remise à M. Sorba, le 15 septembre 1737," AE–CP, *Gênes*, Vol. 100, fol. 111. Volumes 100 and 101 of this series contain a great deal of information regarding the Franco-Genoese agreement.

31. Charles-Pierre-Victor, comte de Pajol, *Les guerres sous Louis XV*, VI, 37. In addition, the French navy armed a frigate, a barque, and four galleys, assigning them to Corsican duty for four months at a projected cost of 186,694 livres. AM, B¹ 60, fols. 78–79.

32. Maurepas to Campredon, Nov. 26, 1737, AE–CP, *Gênes*, Vol. 100, fols. 233–234.

33. "Mémoire historique de ce qui s'est passé en Corse pendant le commandement de M. de Boissieux, en 1738," AG, *Mém. hist.*, 145; Pajol, *op. cit.* VI, 39–40; Driault, *Recueil*, p. lxxxiv; Sismondi, *op. cit.*, XXVIII, 209.

34. See Arthur Villette's correspondence with the Duke of Newcastle for February, March, and April, 1739. *Public Record Office. State Papers Foreign, Savoy and Sardinia*, Vol. 42, analyzed by André Le Glay in *Histoire de la conquête de la Corse par la françaises: La Corse pendant la guerre de la succession d'Autriche* (Paris, 1912), p. 11.

35. *Ibid.*, p. 13.

36. Jules F. Flammermont, *Les correspondances des agents diplomatiques étrangères en France avant la Révolution* (Paris, 1896), pp. 6–8.

37. Barbier, *op. cit.*, III (April 1739), 166, and III (July 1739), 208. Barbier was a lawyer and consultant who had an agency established in Paris. Nearly all his information is secondhand, but he is particularly

valuable as a source who listened to others and who kept up on news in gazettes. He talked very little about himself, but he reported a great deal about others, about the rumors circulating in Paris, and about the general temper of his times. One careful student of eighteenth-century journals stated that there were two kinds of memoirs during that period, passionate and curious. Barbier's memoirs were only curious: "Il fait le Journal de tout le monde, excepté le sien." See Charles Aubertin, *L'Esprit publique au* xviiie *siècle: Étude sur les mémoires et les correspondances politiques des contemporains, 1715 à 1789* (Paris, 1873), p. 172.

38. Barbier, *op. cit.* III (April 1739), 167; III (Aug. 1739), 185; and III (Feb. 1739), 159.
39. For Pignon's mission to Leghorn (and later to Corsica), see AE–CP, *Corse*, Vols. I, VII, and Rostini, *BSHNC* (Feb. 1883), 291.
40. Orticoni and Gaffori to Fleury, May 18, 1738, in Driault, *Recueil*, p. 284; and AE–CP, *Gênes*, Vol. 101, fol. 170.
41. Fleury to Orticoni and Gaffori, June 6, 1738, *ibid.*, Vol. 101, fols. 182–185; and Driault, *Recueil*, pp. 285–286. Fleury promised the Corsicans that the French monarch would mediate between them and Genoa and would listen to their grievances. For his troubles, Louis XV asked no payment other "than that of having contributed to the happiness of a country that has always been dear to him as well as to his glorious ancestors." Oddly enough, Campredon believed Fleury's reply was "une très belle homélie, mais beaucoup trop flatteuse et courtoise pour des gens dignes du gibet." Campredon to Maurepas, July 24, 1738, AE–CP, *Gênes*, Vol. 101, fol. 214.
42. Fleury to Boissieux, June 7, 1738, *ibid.*, Vol. 101, fol. 186.
43. AE–CP, *Corse*, Vol. I, fols. 69–70.
44. *Ibid.*, Vol. VII, fols. 282–284.
45. *Ibid.*, Vol. I, fols. 71–74.
46. *Ibid.*, Vol. I, fols. 130–133.
47. *Ibid.*, Vol. I, fol. 170.
48. A copy of the treaty, which was signed by the Prince of Lichtenstein for the Emperor, Jean-Jacques Amelot de Chaillou for France, and François-Marie Brignole for Genoa, is in AE–CP, *Gênes*, Vol. 101, fols. 339ff.
49. René-Louis Voyer, marquis d'Argenson, *Journal et mémoires du marquis d'Argenson*, ed. E. J. Rathery, 9 Vols. (Paris, 1859), II, 78; Le Glay, *Conquête de la Corse, op. cit.*, pp. 9–10.
50. Pajol, *op. cit.*, VI, 44.
51. General de Vault, Directeur du Depôt de la Guerre, "Mémoire ou extrait de la correspondance de la cour et des généraux pendant les campagnes de 1738 et 1739," AG, *Mém. hist.*, 145.
52. *Ibid.*; Pajol, *op. cit.*, VI, 45–61; Louis-Joseph-Charles-Amable d'Albert,

duc de Luynes, *Mémoires du duc de Luynes sur la cour de Louis XV (1735–1785)*, eds. L. Dussieux and E. Soulie, 17 Vols. (Paris, 1860–1865), III, 65; Driault, *Recueil*, pp. lxxxv–lxxxvi. Maillebois' reasons for using force are found in a letter and memoir that he sent to Cardinal Fleury on April 3, 1739 (AE–CP, *Gênes*, Vol. 102, fols. 142ff.). In describing the success of his military plans on June 6, 1737, Maillebois observed: "J'ai été assez heureux pour faire beaucoup de peur et peu de mal . . . ," (*ibid.*, Vol. 102, fols. 253–259).

53. Campredon to Maurepas, Jan. 1, 1739, *ibid.*, Vol. 102, fols. 6–10.
54. See the ministry's letters to Campredon, dated Feb. 21 and April 7, 1739, *ibid.*, Vol. 101, fol. 18, and Vol. 102, fol. 135.
55. Campredon to .... [Amelot], April 16, 1739, *ibid.*, Vol. 102, fols. 166–167.
56. Argenson, *op. cit.*, III, 116.
57. Jean-Jacques Amelot de Chaillou became secretary of state for foreign affairs in February 1737. Jonville's instructions are in AE–CP, *Gênes*, Vol. 102, fols. 312ff. See also Driault, *Recueil*, pp. 288–292.
58. Driault, *Recueil*, p. lxxxvi.
59. Jonville to Amelot, April 24, 1743, AE–CP, *Gênes*, Vol. 112, fols. 250–251. Gaston E. Broche has demonstrated beyond any doubt that Jonville was not given important negotiations. See his important study, *La république de Gênes et la France pendant la guerre de la succession d'Autriche (1740–1748)*, 3 Vols. (Paris, 1935), II, 9–11, 58.
60. Amelot to Jonville, Jan. 12, 1740, AE–CP, *Gênes*, Vol. 104, fols. 18–19.
61. Amelot, "Mémoire sur la Corse," *ibid.*, Vol. 104, fols. 25–29.
62. *Ibid.*, Vol. 103, fol. 332.
63. *Ibid.*, Vol. 103, fol. 333.
64. Amelot to Jonville, Jan. 12, 1740, *ibid.*, Vol. 104, fols. 18–19. The French demands in return for their help are found in Amelot's "Mémoire sur la Corse," sent to Jonville with this letter and located in Vol. 104, fols. 25–29.
65. See the extensive correspondence regarding the possibility of Imperial intervention in Corsica in AE–CP, *Corse*, Vol. II. At one time the Emperor talked about sending 8,000 men to Corsica, but in May 1740 he agreed to send a 4,800 man force if Genoa transported them and paid half their expenses. Maillebois thought that the Emperor was planning to place a small body of troops in Corsica in order to have his flag on the island. See his letter of April 21, 1740, *ibid.*, Vol. II, fols. 132–133.
66. AE–CP, *Gênes*, Vol. 106, fols. 47–48.
67. Amelot to Jonville, April 11, 1741, *ibid.*, Vol. 106, fols. 147–148; DuPont to Amelot, Sept. 13, 1741, *ibid.*, Vol. 108, fols. 21–23. Driault incorrectly stated that a regiment remained at Calvi under the command of M. de Cursay (*Recueil*, p. lxxxviii). Military action undertaken

by Boissieux and Maillebois is described in Baron Cervoni, ed., "Extrait de la relation des campagnes de 1738 et 1739, dans l'ile de Corse . . . ," *BSHNC* (Feb. 1882), 376–412.

68. AE–CP, *Génes.*, Vol. 103, fols. 56–84 and 85–87.

69. "Mémoire de M. D'Angervilliers sur les affaires presentes de la Corse," *ibid.*, Vol. 108, fols. 299ff. This memoir has been dated "1741," which is clearly an error. Angervilliers died on February 15, 1740. Internal evidence suggests that it was written sometime after May 1739.

70. Argenson, *op. cit.*, I, 288–289 (February, 1738). Argenson was convinced that Corsica would be an "excellent guarantee" for French commerce in the Levant and would assure France a preferred place in Genoa's commerce (II, 25 and 204, Oct. 1738 and July 25, 1739). But he believed that the greatest advantage of French troops' being on Corsica was the foothold that it gave France in Italy (II, 203–204, 243–244, July 25 and Aug. 22, 1739). M. de Cany (AG, *Mém. hist.*, 206 [3]) also doubted whether "ownership" of the island would benefit France. He stressed the unending expense involved in making the country flourish and in fortifying it.

71. Argenson's conception of Genoa as a "foothold" in Italy or a "doorway" to Italy suggests that the "gateway" thesis of French foreign policy during the seventeenth century was an important part of French policy during the eighteenth century also, and that it applied to areas other than French borders. In any case, the subject warrants further investigation. The French policy of establishing "doorways" or "footholds" goes back at least to Armand-Jean du Plessis, Cardinal de Richelieu, who recommended it to Louis XIII in 1629. See J.L.M. Avenel, ed., *Lettres, instructions diplomatiques et papiers d'état du Cardinal Richelieu*, 8 Vols. (Paris, 1853–1877), III, 179–183. John B. Wolf has recently argued that Richelieu, Mazarin, and Louis XIV were all concerned with certain ". . . 'gates' on the frontiers that would swing open for the foreigner to invade or that might be openings for French military excursions beyond the frontiers" (*Louis XIV* [New York, 1968], pp. 189, 443). In his review of Wolf's book, Andrew Lossky argued that the "gates" thesis was "both interesting and tempting," but that ". . . further investigation is needed before we can accept the 'gates formula' as established. . . ." See *The Journal of Modern History*, XLII (March 1970), 102.

CHAPTER III

The Policy Affirmed: The Corsican Question and the War of the Austrian Succession

A small state surrounded by powerful neighbors may hope to maintain itself intact by adopting a position of neutrality. Yet even publicly affirmed neutrality may be of little protection in quarrels among the more powerful neighbors if the neutral state has any strategic importance. Such was Genoa's position when the war to divide Maria Theresa's inheritance began. The republic not only held the strategically important island of Corsica, but its own geographical position was of strategic value. As the alliances of the great powers developed, dividing Europe into two opposing camps, Genoa's position became increasingly significant and its neutrality increasingly tenuous. The dual factors of its location and its possession of Corsica eventually brought the republic into the war, and were no less important in confirming for the French their interest and policy on the Corsican question.

As early as 1740, the Genoese Senate, fearing French designs on Corsica, had instructed its ambassador to London, Gian

Battista Gastaldi, to try to secure an English guarantee for its continued possession of the island. From May to October Gastaldi worked vigorously, talking to a number of English ministers, the most important of whom was Thomas Pelham-Holles, the Duke of Newcastle. In the end, however, Gastaldi failed to achieve his objective. André Le Glay, who carefully analyzed the English, French, and Genoese documents of this tortuous and futile negotiation, concluded that the English Government refused its guarantee because it was contemplating conquest of Corsica for itself. "It kept its hands free in order to take, while giving itself the benefit of honesty." [1]

The English guarantee was particularly attractive to Genoa for a number of reasons. First, it seemed to afford some protection from the suspected machinations of Versailles. It was desirable, secondly, if there was any truth in the rumors that Spain was supporting the pretensions of Neuhoff. Thirdly, it would calm the republic concerning English intentions; for the Genoese remembered that it had been an English ship that brought Neuhoff to Corsica in March 1736, and three Dutch ships, laden with munitions, that had brought him back to the island in September 1738. Because the republic had already received guarantees of its sovereignty over Corsica from Louis XV and Emperor Charles VI, the quest for an English guarantee makes the nature of its policy clear. Genoa was seeking to embroil as many powers in the Corsican question as possible, in the hope that no one power would dare touch its island possession for fear of retaliation by the others.

The English guarantee was attractive from one other point of view: It would offer some protection from the designs of Charles-Emmanuel III, king of Piedmont-Sardinia. Just what those designs were in 1740–1741 is not entirely clear. Le Glay pictured Charles-Emmanuel as the precursor of nineteenth-century Italian unification, who had designs on Genoa and Corsica. Linked with Sardinia, Corsica would make him a real power in the Mediterranean. Charles-Emmanuel III, said Le Glay, "had a great appetite, and when he would sit down at table to eat Italy leaf by leaf, he would begin with Genoa. The possession of Corsica would facilitate things. This would be, in sum, the logical beginning of the conquest of the entire peninsula." [2]

This description of Charles-Emmanuel's intentions suggests the benefit of hindsight and the influence of events related to the unification of Italy in the nineteenth century. Elsewhere in the same study, Le Glay described the king of Sardinia's ambitions more modestly and accurately: "The king of Sardinia wanted an opening [un débouché] on the Mediterranean, and he was able to have it only by taking some Genoese territories." It was above all for this reason that Charles-Emmanuel became interested in Corsica and stirred up the troubles on the island. If he could establish a protectorate over it, perhaps even occupy it, he could use it as an exchange for certain lands on the continent in which he was interested. [3]

Charles-Emmanuel's position in Italy was of course a key position in any war between France and Austria. He controlled passes across the Alps and therefore access to northern and central Italy, as well as access to Austria through northern Italy. Thus when the War of the Austrian Succession broke out, France, Spain, and Austria (the latter backed by England), made concerted bids for his allegiance. Charles-Emmanuel played his domination of the Piedmont mountains for all it was worth, making his allegiance a costly proposition. Until he finally decided which side to join, he remained a thorn in the sides of all four powers. He also caused considerable dissension between France and Spain on the one hand, and Austria and England on the other.

Ever since the wars of the seventeenth century, French ministers had paid particular attention to the House of Savoy. Cardinal Fleury was no exception. Savoy had been a useful, if troublesome, ally in the War of the Polish Succession. Even after 1740, Fleury continued to argue that Piedmont-Sardinia was indispensable to France; and this fact must be kept in mind in order to understand French policy toward Genoa and Corsica. Yet Fleury had a difficult problem on his hands, a problem that eventually proved insoluble. All Fleury's bargaining powers with Charles-Emmanuel were handicapped by the fact that Spain's territorial ambitions in Italy conflicted with those of Charles-Emmanuel. Thus Fleury could meet the Spanish demands only by sacrificing all chance of winning the House of Savoy. By July 1742, Fleury had worked out a territorial division which he hoped would satisfy both Spain and Charles-Emmanuel and would therefore bring Sardinia into the war in support of the Bourbon powers.[4] But his planning was wasted effort, for he had by then already lost Charles-Emmanuel. In September 1741, under pressure from the Spanish court, Fleury promised protection from the French fleet at Toulon for Spanish troops going to Italy. The following December he agreed to grant passage through France for Spanish forces on their way to the Italian war.[5]

Charles-Emmanuel, naturally incensed and frightened by these actions, turned away from France. On February 1, 1742, he and Maria Theresa entered into a temporary convention that promised him the duchies of Milan, Parma, Plaisance, and Modena, allowed him to reserve all his claims to the Milanese, and required him only to give one month's notice if he should decide to break the convention.[6] The Spanish campaigns in Italy in 1742 and 1743 threatened Charles-Emmanuel's position further, leading him to confirm the choice of allies he had made. On September 13, 1743, casting his lot definitely with Maria Theresa and England, he signed the Treaty of Worms with those powers. This treaty bound England, Austria, and Piedmont-Sardinia into a triple alliance against the Bourbons of Spain, Naples, and presumably also France, which, up to this time, had been acting only as an auxiliary of Spain. By the terms of the treaty, England was to subsidize Sardinia and provide a Mediterranean fleet. Sardinia was to provide an army of 45,000 troops. Sardinia's reward would include all of Lombardy south of the Po River and on the right bank of the Ticino River, plus a part of Piacenza.[7]

As far as the French policy toward Corsica was concerned, the Treaty of Worms had two important consequences. It meant, first, that France had lost Piedmont-Sardinia, thus closing the Alpine passes to French forces and raising Genoa's strategic position to a new importance. Secondly, it pushed Genoa toward active participation in the war. The republic had remained neutral in the struggle until 1743, but its neutrality was gradually destroyed by a number of events, one of the most important of which was the Treaty of Worms. According to article X of that treaty, Maria Theresa ceded her rights on the marquisat de Finale to Charles-Emmanuel, declaring that "the public cause" required that the king of Sardinia be able to communicate by sea with the maritime powers. Genoa was asked to facilitate this article, which was indispensable for the liberty and security of Italy. The republic was far from being concerned about the Austro-Sardinia interpretation of the liberty and security of Italy. Genoa was, in fact, deeply mortified and justifiably angered by this treaty. Maria Theresa had no claim to the marquisat de Finale, which in 1713 had been sold to Genoa by Charles VI for the sum of 1,200,000 *piastres*.[8] The Treaty of Worms, with its explicit threat to Genoese possessions, pointed out the painful fact that the republic's neutrality was too tenuous to sustain for long. English designs on Corsica in 1743 merely seemed to emphasize that fact.

Ever since the War of the Austrian Succession there had been numerous incidents on Corsica that cast serious doubts on the republic's ability to retain possession of it. One of these occurred in January 1743, when former king Neuhoff reappeared once again, landing on the Ile Rousse in his last effort to recover his lost kingdom. Corsica had known some months of relative peace since the French troops left in September 1741, largely because the islanders were exhausted from fighting and because many of the Corsican leaders had left for the continent. In mid-1742, therefore, Genoa had attempted to establish a basis for continued tranquillity and had offered several concessions as a basis for an agreement. The Genoese would not, however, agree to establish a Corsican nobility or a university; and they would not grant Corsicans access to administrative and ecclesiastical posts. The islanders protested these omissions, claiming, in addition, that taxes were too high. The Genoese commissioner, Domenico Spinola, refused to take these protests seriously. He stalled for time, putting off the levy of new taxes until December 1742, and then failed to keep his word. When he began to levy the taxes in November, using for this purpose special tax collectors rather than the local *podestats,* the Corsicans again threatened more than verbal protests. Thus, at the beginning of 1743, the situation in the island was potentially explosive. It was precisely at this moment that Neuhoff decided to return.

Neuhoff's appearance at that time was particularly dangerous for yet another reason. Again it was an English ship, the *Revenger,* which brought Neuhoff to the island; and the pretender possessed a passport from Lord John Carteret, the English secretary of state for the Northern Department. England, too, was fishing troubled waters, scouting the situation in Corsica to discover how much support Neuhoff had among the people. Although Neuhoff's *crédit* had vanished by this time, illicit English support of his return[9] caused considerable alarm in Genoa. In February 1743, Gastaldi presented a memoir of protest to the English ministers, asking an explanation for the support given to Neuhoff. The reply he received was hardly satisfying, although the Genoese Senate pretended to be content with it in order not to give the islanders further hope of English assistance. The Duke of Newcastle explained that the English passport given to Neuhoff had been to Lisbon, and that the captains of the ships had exceeded their instructions, out of personal sympathy for Neuhoff, in taking him to the island and in supplying him with arms.[10]

Because the republic feared that French or English interests in the island might lead to more active intervention in case of further rebellion, it decided to send to Corsica someone capable of restoring tranquillity. For this task, following the death of Spinola on February 21, 1743, the Senate chose Pietro Maria Giustiniani. The new commissioner was an amiable moderate who was reputed to have "a cool head" and who was respected by the Corsicans. Unfortunately, the republic again acted sensibly too late. The islanders, now convinced that Neuhoff would not return again, believed that they were left to their own resources. At a *Consulte* held at Bozzio in March, they decided to establish a permanent government in the form of a regency, led by two generals named Gian Tommaso Giuliani and Brandone. Thus by the time Giustiniani arrived in June, they were united behind their national leaders.

Despite the fact that Giustiniani offered the Corsicans even more significant concessions in the months following, nothing he proposed satisfied the Corsicans' regency government. Already, at a *Consulte* held at Corte on April 27, this regency government had demanded so much that only the governorship remained to the republic. It was truly "une declaration indirecte d'indépendance." [11] With the help of a special emissary from Pope Benedict XIV, Father Leonardo da Porto Maurizio, Giustiniani used moderation and the promise of concessions to obtain relative peace on the island.[12] Yet even while the discussions went on, the authority and power of the regency increased and Genoese influence declined.

After the regency government was established, England's interest in Genoa's island possession seemed even more dangerous. The republic's response to this growing danger was to increase the pressure on English ministers for a guarantee of Genoa's sovereignty over the island. Like the attempted pacification under Giustiniani, however, Genoa's quest for an English guarantee was not successful. Renewing his efforts at London, Gastaldi had an interview with the Duke of Newcastle on June 12, 1743, during which he threatened that it is wise for a state to get rid of what it cannot peacefully hold. In effect, that meant that if England did not help with an official guarantee, there might be some undesirable consequences. Newcastle complained about rumors that the republic was getting ready to cede Corsica to Spain, and he told Gastaldi that England would never permit the cession of Corsica, especially to the House of Bourbon. In the end, however, still protesting Genoa's excessive favor for Spain, Newcastle promised support for the project of an English guarantee. Gastaldi appeared to have won—but it was a hollow victory. A short time later William Pulteney, the Earl of Bath, told him that a general peace must be established before England would put its guarantee in writing. In effect, Gastaldi had only promises, which were held out to him as bait for several more months. By October it was clear that the promises were empty and that the English guarantee would not be made.[13]

Following its failure to reach an accord with England, Genoa turned to Vienna and Turin. Apparently it hoped to exchange Corsica for a territory on the continent that could be controlled more easily. Perhaps in return for Corsica, Genoa could acquire from Turin Montferrat, Les Langhes, and the provinces of Tortone and Novare. Or, if the republic negotiated with Austria, perhaps it could obtain part of Tuscany, including Leghorn, and part of the Milanese.[14] The republic's speculations were understandable in view of its desperate efforts to hold Corsica at all. Nonetheless, they were idle and fruitless speculations. They are important because they clearly reveal the republic's fear that Corsica would soon be lost.

Thus, by 1743 the republic had discovered that its continental possessions were threatened by Vienna and it had failed to secure an English guarantee for its possession of Corsica. Moreover, its efforts at Vienna and Turin to exchange the island had been rebuffed. The next year it received an additional shock. As the Italian war broadened, Charles-Emmanuel took an active interest in Corsica. His renewed attention to the island was particularly dangerous because he too, like Neuhoff and the English, was fishing troubled waters. In the summer of 1744, just when the Corsicans' regency government was making great progress toward controlling the interior of the island, Charles-Emmanuel announced his intention to levy a regiment of Corsican troops for service in his army. In July, the capitulation for a levy of a Corsican infantry regiment was signed, with both the English and the Austrians heartily approving this overt infringement on Genoese sovereignty.[15]

This last indignity caused the republic to reject neutrality. Threatened on the continent by the Treaty of Worms, rebuffed diplomatically at London, Turin, and Vienna, threatened in Corsica by English and Sardinian intervention coupled with a reviving independence movement, the republic decided to cast its lot with the Bourbon powers. Supporting the Bourbon powers was probably a wise choice for the republic; certainly the enemies of the republic were the enemies of Spain and France. Moreover, Genoa had on record French support for its sovereignty over Corsica. If any more persuasion were needed, there had been some significant Bourbon victories in Italy which seemed to be producing the expulsion of Austrian armies from Naples and an attack by a strong Franco-Spanish army in Piedmont. If the republic continued its tenuous neutrality, it certainly risked losing Corsica or some holdings on the continent. If, on the other hand, it adopted the Bourbon cause, it could at least hope to maintain its possessions through Bourbon victories, and it might even add to those possessions.

In some respects, Madrid's view of the developing Italian scene was more realistic than Versailles'. In particular, Madrid more quickly realized that once Charles-Emmanuel had been lost to the Bourbon powers, Genoa would become the key to northern Italy. As early as March 1742, Elizabeth Farnese, who justly believed Charles-Emmanuel would not approve Spanish plans for Italy, began to speak of the need to negotiate with the Genoese for passage through their lands. The French minister Amelot accepted the principle of negotiating a treaty with Genoa a year later, but the French had two reservations. First, French ministers persisted in pointing out the logistic difficulties of military action in the republic's lands. Second, Versailles held some hope that Charles-Emmanuel could be enticed back into the Bourbon camp, a hope that would be forever destroyed if Genoa's demands for Alexandria and Tortone were met, as they would have to be, at Charles-Emmanuel's expense.[16]

Though agreeable to negotiation in principle, Versailles

hung back where an actual treaty was concerned.[17] In August 1744, when the Bishop of Rennes, Louis-Guy Guérapin de Vauréal, was authorized to meet with Spanish ministers to secure a treaty with Genoa, he was to let it be understood that nothing would result.[18]

Not until the death of Emperor Charles VII on January 20, 1745, were the French convinced that "the general state of affairs" necessitated the signing of a treaty with the republic. Thereafter Versailles decided on definite intervention in Italy and gave in to Madrid's urgings that Genoa become the base for combined Italian operations. The period from January through April was spent by France, Spain, and Genoa in working out the details. Finally, on May 1, 1745, the Treaty of Aranjuez was signed, and that same day all officers of the French *État-Major* were ordered to be at Aix to begin the new campaign in Italy.[19]

The most important article of the Treaty of Aranjuez, so far as this study is concerned, was article XII by which the Bourbon rulers, their heirs and successors, guaranteed to Genoa the possession of all its states, including the kingdom of Corsica and all new acquisitions stipulated in the treaty, and promised support for their protection. It was a perpetual guarantee, effective in peace and war.[20]

Genoa's decision to abandon its neutrality put it in a dangerous position if the Austro-Sardinian forces should be victorious in Italy, but at the time the Treaty of Aranjuez was signed there seemed little danger of such an eventuality. Indeed, Genoa seemed to have made a wise choice. In the last months of 1743, the Bourbon forces had been victorious in Piedmont, Parma, Plaisance, and Pavi; by December 1745, they were investing Milan under the command of the Spanish general, Don Juan, comte de Gages.

The Treaty of Aranjuez did not, however, bring the republic immediate assistance in Corsica. Conditions there went from bad to worse as the national government gained strength. Charles-Emmanuel further complicated the situation by continuing to exploit Corsican opposition to the republic. By mid-1745, the Corsican regency government had made so much progress that the Genoese influence in the island was confined to the citadel of Corte and the walled cities of Bastia, Ajaccio, Calvi, and Bonifacio. Encouraged by their successes within the island and discouraged by the lack of attention the republic gave to their propositions for a settlement, the Corsican leaders held another general assembly at Orezza on August 29 and 30, 1745. There a new government was established in the form of a Consulate. For the moment, its purpose was to establish order and to enforce justice within the island. The Abbé Ignazio Venturini was named President of the Consulate. He was assisted by Alerio Francesco Matra and Gian Pietro Gaffori, who were given the title "Protectors."

Venturini was a priest who drank excessively and who owed his election to his strong clan backing. Matra had been in the regiment *Royal-Corse,* a regiment of Corsican soldiers in the service of France,[21] but he had left it to join the Corsican revolt as a means of gaining personal power. Gaffori soon became the real leader of the group. He had a reputation as a Corsican nationalist, having been involved in the revolt against Genoa since 1734 and active in Neuhoff's short-lived government. Then, when Boissieux arrived on the island in 1738, he had become a supporter of the French. Now he rapidly became the outstanding leader of the Consulate. His enforcement of justice, suppression of brigandage, and equitable collection of taxes attracted considerable support for the Corsican national movement.[22]

The Genoese Senate returned to a policy of repression when it saw the rapid success of Gaffori's leadership. Giustiniani was replaced by a new commissioner, Stefano di Mari, in October 1745. Mari immediately banned the nationals from the *présides* and then began to confiscate objects of value from the churches of Cap Corse in an effort to find money for the Genoese troops. His actions further offended the Corsicans' national and religious sentiment and confirmed them in their hatred for the republic's tyranny. It was a volatile situation, the more explosive because the Corsicans were now convinced that their nominal masters were a weak, distant power.[23]

It was just this volatile situation that Charles-Emmanuel continued to exploit. By September 1745, the Sardinian king discovered a Corsican who would carry out his Corsican plans in the person of Domenico Rivarola, a man who much resembled the *condottiere* type of the Italian Renaissance. Rivarola had worked for Spain as its consul at Bastia and later joined Neuhoff's government as secretary of state for war. Eventually he became a colonel in Charles-Emmanuel's army, and in September he was ordered to go to Corsica to raise a regiment for Sardinia's service.[24]

Time and again Charles-Emmanuel professed that he had no personal interest in Corsica and that he did not seek to acquire any right, authority, or pre-eminence over the island. Instead, he asserted, he merely wanted to support the revolt against Genoese injustice and inhumanity.[25] Yet events toward the end of 1745 seemed to give the lie to his professions. Early in November, Rivarola appeared on the island and offered the Corsicans the protection of the king of Sardinia. Then, working in conjunction with an English fleet under Admiral Townshend, he forced capitulation of the city of Bastia on November 21 and moved on to seize Saint-Florent as well.[26] Only the failure of the English fleet, Sardinian troops, and Corsican rebels to work together saved Calvi and Ajaccio from a similar fate.

These events brought panic to Genoa. They also brought an immediate appeal to Genoa's French ally for support.[27] At the moment, however, the French found their own coasts threatened, and could not send naval help; for the time being, the Genoese had to content themselves with moral support. In April 1746, late even with his moral support, Louis XV announced that he intended a prompt and effective contribution "to establish the tranquillity, the order, and the subordination of Corsica." [28]

Versailles could not send troops to Corsica early in 1746

because Louis XV's government was trying to pick up the pieces of a diplomatic and military blunder. Even before the Treaty of Aranjuez was signed, the Marquis d'Argenson, who had become French minister for foreign affairs in November 1744, had been working to gain Charles-Emmanuel's support for his Italian vision.[29] A partisan of the Sardinian alliance, Argenson began his approaches to Charles-Emmanuel as early as April 1745. Between April and December, two more attempts were made to secure a treaty with Sardinia, all behind the back of Spain and Genoa and all to the detriment of both Spanish and Genoese interests. By January 1746, Argenson saw some hope of success. He instructed the Marquis de Maillebois, commander of the French troops in Italy, to keep French forces in a defensive position until his secret treaty with Sardinia was signed. The result was that the Franco-Spanish gains of 1745 were lost in the campaign of 1746.[30] Early in 1746, Charles-Emmanuel was reinforced by Austrian troops released from service in Germany by the Peace of Dresden (December 24, 1745), after which Frederick II had withdrawn from the war. Using these additional forces, the Sardinian king struck hard in the early months of 1746.

Although the republic badly needed military support to resist Charles-Emmanuel both on the continent and in Corsica, all it got from Versailles was Pierre-Paul Guymont, *envoyé extraordinaire*. His mission to Genoa was a matter of formality occasioned by the Treaty of Aranjuez. His instructions, dated March 22, 1746, followed the standard form except for two specific items. He was urged to use all his zeal and vigilance in maintaining "these republicans in the principles of a wise and solid *politique*." That meant, in effect, the Bourbon alliance. He was also instructed to assure the republic that Louis XV favored all their interests, in particular "the re-establishment of order and tranquillity in Corsica, to reduce the peoples of this island under the obedience [owed to] their legitimate sovereigns." [31] These instructions essentially restated the program developed at Versailles nearly a decade earlier. That is, Versailles intended to keep the republic neutral (or, as the case then was, allied with France), in part through protecting Genoese sovereignty over Corsica.

Apart from this verbal encouragement, however, the republic received no help from its allies. Spanish forces retreated to French soil in July 1746. French forces followed them in August and September. Genoa was left alone to face the fury and revenge of Austro-Sardinian troops. On September 6, caught between the Austrian army on land and the English fleet at sea, the republic surrendered to Austro-Sardinian forces commanded by General Antoniotto Botta-Adorno, son of a Genoese immigrant to Austria who had been Imperial Commissioner in Italy since August 1754.

Both Louis XV and the Maréchal de Noailles were sorry to see the republic deserted by France. The king even went so far as to write a guarded protest to the new Spanish monarch, Ferdinand VI.[32] But French "grief" was small consolation to the Genoese, who suffered heavily from the forced requisitions, insults, and threats from the occupation forces. They suffered for a time, but finally were goaded to resist with arms. Provoked by new insults, they took matters into their own hands on December 5, 1746. Using any weapons available, they drove Botta-Adorno's occupying forces from the city, and by December 10 they had liberated themselves.

The courage of the Genoese people was the only admirable element in an otherwise disastrous year for the Bourbon powers. Such courage was the more noteworthy because it came from a people believed to be utterly decadent. By liberating themselves, the Genoese had done even more than earn praise for their personal valor; they had saved Provence from invasion. Having retreated to Puget in Provence, a short distance from Toulon, the French army gathered and anxiously awaited an attack by Austro-Piedmontese forces supported by English ships. Genoa's self-liberation caused the enemy enough consternation that the beleagered French troops had a momentary respite. By January 1747, Charles-Louis-Auguste Fouquet, maréchal de Belle-Isle, who had been placed above Maillebois as a commander of French forces in Italy, was again ready to take the offensive.

From the beginning of 1747 to the end of the war, Versailles took the initiative and gave increased attention to its Genoese ally. The Bourbon alliance with Genoa, plus the plans for the 1747 campaign in Italy, required additional assistance to the republic, which was still threatened by Austrian forces despite its self-achieved liberation. Concrete assistance came in the form of a 250,000 livres subsidy to assure Genoa's defense. In addition, from February to May 1747, Versailles sent to the republic engineers, supplies, and 6,000 French troops. The commander of the French forces was Joseph-Marie, duc de Boufflers, son of the more famous Maréchal de Boufflers.

Sent to Genoa in April 1747, Boufflers was assigned several tasks of which the first was to assure the defense of Genoa against the Austro-Sardinian troops. The latter, with the aid of an English subsidy, had put the city under siege earlier in April. He accomplished this with courage and skill and the siege was finally raised in June, when Austro-Sardinian forces were called from Liguria to defend Charles-Emmanuel's lands, then under the threat of invasion from Belle-Isle's army. At the same time, Louis XV became actively involved in the problem of how best to aid the republic. In a personal letter to Belle-Isle, the king expressed his fears for Genoa's fate and directed Belle-Isle to draw up a plan for marching to Genoa by the shortest possible route. He said that he was not only interested in protecting his troops and in acting offensively in Italy in order to find "a suitable establishment" for Don Philippe, but he was vitally concerned about his Genoese ally, which needed his help.[33]

In addition to the military defense of Genoa, Boufflers assumed some political functions. He was appointed *ministre plénipotentiaire,* making him the supreme political representative of France to the republic and thus giving him superiority over Guymont. His instructions were similar to those that Louis XV had given to Belle-Isle. "The essential objective at the

71

present time," Boufflers was informed, "is to encourage the Genoese and to tie them unalterably to the principles and the sentiments that bind them to the alliance of the king." [34] Although Boufflers's defense of Genoa brought him praise from Versailles and honorary nobility from the republic, he did not live long enough to complete his tasks. On July 2 he died of smallpox at Genoa. His replacement as *ministre plénipotentiaire* was a person of greater prestige: Armand de Vignerot du Plessis, duc de Richelieu. Richelieu's task involved the continued defense of Genoa. Politically, he was to continue Boufflers' efforts to hold Genoa faithful within the Bourbon alliance and to watch carefully any attempt the republic might make to deal independently with Vienna and Turin. He was cautioned that the techniques of dealing with republics were different from those employed in relations with monarchies, and he was told to cultivate friendships with all government members, particularly the nobility. [35]

Driault suggested that Richelieu's mission to Genoa was of little importance, for negotiations toward a general peace were begun soon after he arrived. [36] So far as Richelieu's defense of the republic was concerned, this judgment is certainly correct. Yet French policy toward the republic had to deal both with the position of Genoa in the Bourbon alliance and with the effect of the Corsican question on that position. Where the latter was concerned, Richelieu's mission was more significant, for he was in charge of the assistance Versailles finally gave Genoa on the island.

When Richelieu took charge of Franco-Genoese relations in September 1747, affairs in Corsica had reached a new low. The new Genoese commissioner, Mari, had used various expedients to hold the island for the republic after the news of Genoa's capitulation to Austro-Sardinian forces arrived in September 1746. He even managed to win back the population of Bastia by some well-timed concessions, his task being facilitated by internal divisions among the leaders. Gaffori and Rivarola were constantly at odds with each other; and in February 1747 a new *Consulte* was called at Vescovato de

Casinca in an attempt to prevent civil war by taking power away from the generals. This effort was abetted, naturally, by the Genoese who hoped to weaken the Corsican leaders through the spirit of national unity. Yet Mari's expedients would have been of little help if England had decided to intervene actively. Fortunately for the republic, the English were lax in exploiting these internal divisions. On the one hand, they feared for Belgium and Holland, which were threatened by French forces in February 1746. In additon, Philip V's death in July of that year raised the possibility of a separate peace between England and King Ferdinand VI of Spain. For these reasons, the English abandoned Corsica for the moment.[37]

If the English momentarily abandoned Corsica, Charles-Emmanuel did not. In July 1747, Rivarola again attacked with 200 men. Although his weak forces and lack of help from the English fleet doomed his efforts to failure, his action caused Genoa to renew its request for French assistance. In the same month that Richelieu went to Genoa to continue the work of Guymont and Boufflers (September 1747), Versailles finally sent more than moral support to Corsica. On September 4, a force of 500 Genoese, French, and Spanish troops under command of Colonel Choiseul-Beaupré landed in the island to relieve Bastia. Driving Rivarola back to Saint-Florent, Choiseul-Beaupré wanted to take that city also, but was deterred from this action by Mari, who feared that Corsicans led by Gaffori would attack them from the rear.[38]

From this point on, Louis XV and his ministers, especially Richelieu, took an active interest in the affairs of Corsica. Choiseul-Beaupré hazarded the personal opinion that now was a good time to suggest that Genoa should cede Corsica to France.[39] It was the wrong moment for such a suggestion, and Versailles paid no attention to it. In December Rivarola's forces were reinforced by 500 additional Sardinian troops, led by the Corsican general Gian Tommaso Giuliani. The reinforcements were supported by English ships, for England had returned to a policy of intervention.[40] Versailles, therefore, was concerned that the island should be kept out of English-Sardinian hands.

To accomplish this objective, French military strength on Corsica was increased during 1748. As early as March of that year, Richelieu sent to the island a captain of the regiment of Quercy, Jean-Baptiste-Antide Frévet, chevalier de Fontette, with instructions to determine the state of defenses and the necessity of reinforcements. Then, on April 3, Genoa and France signed a convention for the island's defense. The French forces were to direct the defense of the cities, but otherwise were not to interfere in civil affairs. In addition, France undertook to send 480 men to the island. The commander of these troops was M. de Varignon, who hurriedly left Genoa on April 5 in order to reach Corsica before the arrival of Austro-Sardinian forces.[41] On May 28, 400 more French troops, under the command of Marie Rioult de Douilly de Cursay, arrived at Bastia, bringing the total number of French troops on the island to around 1,000. Cursay's instructions were to be particularly attentive to all Corsicans who had not declared themselves against Genoa. Clearly this was a military venture designed to defend the island against France's enemies; it even carried clear delineation of the limits of French action. His Majesty, Cursay was informed, "desires perpetual peace, and considers as his enemies only those who support the Austro-Sardinian forces." The object of his mission was "to pacify Corsica and to seek to make a treaty between the inhabitants and the republic, of which the king is the mediator and the guarantor, and which is able to maintain forever tranquillity in this island." Because the Corsicans hated the name "Genoese" so fiercely, Cursay was told, he should never speak to them about submitting to the republic but always in the name of France and about the protection that the king would accord them.[42]

In another sense, however, the sending of French troops to Corsica constituted a political action. Versailles was gravely concerned about the effect of the loss of Corsica on its Genoese ally. In February 1748, Puysieulx wrote to Richelieu:

74

Since the fatal epoch when we were pushed out of Italy, I have always feared equally for all the states of the republic, and this fear will remain until the peace, especially [because] it is only by violent resources and the strength of money that we are sustaining the Genoese.

Turning to the Corsican question, Puysieulx pointed out the danger if England and Sardinia captured the island. "Once Corsica is lost," he wrote, "Genoa will not be slow in disappearing in its turn." To lose the republic, he continued, would be an unmitigated disaster, for Italy would thenceforth be closed to French troops. Two months later Puysieulx came back to this point: "The protection that the king accords to the Genoese is very expensive, but if their preservation is the result of our excessive expenses in men and money His Majesty will not have cause to regret it." [43]

In reality, Puysieulx was merely restating the French policy toward Corsica that had been developed from 1737 to 1740. France should aid in the pacification of the island to accomplish two objectives. The first was to prevent the island from falling into the hands of a power that might threaten Provence or French trade in the Levant. The second was to make Genoa dependent on France so that French forces would always have their "doorway" or "foothold" in Italy. Both objectives were critical for continued French power in the Mediterranean and Italy. The first, to be sure, could have been accomplished by taking Corsica rather than by supporting Genoese sovereignty in the island. Yet if this alternative had been selected, it would have meant sacrificing the second objective and closing the door to French influence in Italy. Considering the state of affairs in 1748, the sacrifice of the second objective would have been sheer folly. The events after February 1748 show definitely that French policy was no longer concerned with the plan designed to secure the possession of Corsica for France. They indicate, in addition, that Puysieulx's restatement of Cardinal Fleury's, Amelot's, Jonville's, and Argenson's ideas on the Corsican question was the policy definitely adopted by the French Government at the end of the War of the Austrian Succession.

Additional support for this judgment can be found in the reply that Versailles made to two of its officials, one of whom proposed alternative policies. In October 1747, Guymont suggested, in a coded dispatch, that it would be "advantageous" for France to acquire possession of Corsica. "If one has some designs along this line," he said, "it would be necessary from this moment on to act in such a way as to arouse neither the jealousy nor the suspicion of the Genoese, but only to lead them to the point where they will themselves make an arrangement with us on this subject." The closest thing to an answer that Guymont received to this proposal came in a letter from Puysieulx a month later. The minister told him that Genoa now had only one solution to its problems: It must come to an agreement with the rebels as soon as possible and at any price and then faithfully fulfill the terms of that agreement.[44]

Richelieu had different ideas. In a memoir on the "État actuel des affaires en Corse," August 3, 1748, Richelieu said that it was important to establish peace in Corsica in such a way that the king could "conserve a sort of influence and authority over these peoples." This matter should not be neglected, and we must receive "some orders and principles that should be followed." Richelieu personally favored leaving French troops on Corsica after the War of the Austrian Succession was over. But Puysieulx pointed out the dangers of such a policy. Would not Vienna and Turin feel justified in doing the same thing, he queried? And would not the Genoese, who already suspected France of wanting "to carry off the sovereignty of Corsica," be adamantly opposed? Moreover, could Versailles give the Genoese reason to complain that while the king gave back territories conquered from his enemies he was uninterested in the fate of his allies "and profits from their weakness and the confidence that they have had in him to despoil them of their rights or of their possessions?" Puysieulx then concluded: "It therefore appears to us indispensible that the troops of the king, as well as the Austrians and the Piedmontese, leave Corsica in the time that will be stipulated by the definitive treaty. . . ." [45]

Once the war on the continent was over, French military action on the island was also considered at an end. Louis XV wanted an end to the Corsican affair, a view supported by Belle-Isle, and the secretary of state for war, Marc-Pierre de Voyer de Paulmy, comte d' Argenson, who believed that France should avoid getting mixed up in the Corsican problem. Puysieulx stated the same position in a comment written on the margin of a letter from Richelieu (August 10, 1748): France "does not pretend in any way to second the resolutions that the republic believes it ought to take against the Corsicans, not having engaged itself to reduce these peoples to obedience." [46] At the time Versailles contended that the problem was Genoa's, for it had made no agreement with the republic to fight the latter's war against the Corsican people. The most it would do was to defend the republic's rights at the peace conference held at Aix-la-Chapelle. That conference and the treaty it produced in October 1748 formally ended the War of the Austrian Succession. The treaty contained an implicit guarantee of Genoa's sovereignty over Corsica.[47]

Any effort to read French designs on sovereignty over Corsica at the end of the War of the Austrian Succession neglects these continued attempts by France to support its Genoese ally. It also neglects the private and public assurances that Versailles had no interest in the island other than keeping it out of the hands of other powers. Puysieulx clearly expressed such an assurance in the letter that he wrote to Richelieu on September 14, 1748. The king, he observed, "does not wish to be master of Corsica, but neither does he wish any other power to be master of it." A short time later he expressed the same viewpoint in a comment written on the margin of a letter from François-Claude de Chauvelin, who was the *maréchal de camp* for French troops in Genoa: "It would be absurd to imagine that we would ever be able to have the least view on Corsica, which is totally useless to us; besides, we have ports in the neighborhood. But what is important to us, and ought to be even more important to the republic, is that this island does not pass into certain hands." [48]

These private statements by top-ranking French ministers substantiate the more public declarations made to Genoa, which revealed essentially the same attitude. It is therefore clear that by 1748 Versailles was not surreptitiously scheming to obtain possession of Corsica. Indeed, it had reaffirmed the proposals made between 1737 and 1740.

NOTES

1. André Le Glay, *Conquête de la Corse*, p. 34. For the evaluation of these negotiations and criticism of Genoese and English duplicity, see especially pp. 20–34.
2. *Ibid.*, pp. 45–46. It is significant that Charles-Emmanuel would not be enticed by just such a scheme when Argenson offered it to him in 1745. See Alfred Baudrillart, *Philippe V et la cour de France*, 5 Vols. (Paris, 1890–1901), V, 337–340.
3. Le Glay, *op. cit.*, p. 7. For a more balanced picture of Charles-Emmanuel's ambitions, see Giuseppi Roberti, "Carlo Emmanuele III e la Corsica al temps della guerre de successione Austriaca," *Rivista Storica Italiana*, VI (1889), 665–698, and Sir Richard Lodge, *Studies in Eighteenth Century Diplomacy, 1740–1748* (London, 1930), pp. 35, 40.
4. On the Spanish aspirations and Fleury's offers, see Baudrillart, *op. cit.*, V, 25–26, 53–54, 102.
5. *Ibid.*, pp. 65, 69, 74, 91.
6. *Ibid.*, p. 78; See also Louis Dimier, *Histoire de Savoie* (Paris, 1913), p. 252.
7. Walter L. Dorn, *Competition for Empire, 1740–1763* (New York, 1940), pp. 153–155; Dimier, *op. cit.*, p. 255; and the excellent chapter on the Treaty of Worms in Lodge, *op. cit.*, pp. 31–79.
8. For an analysis of the broader background and results of the Treaty of Worms, see Pierre Muret, *Peuples et civilisations*, Vol. XI, *La prépondérance anglaise (1715–1763)* (Paris, 1937), pp. 407–410. Lodge, *op. cit.*, p. 78, called article X the "most iniquitous provision" of the entire treaty.
9. On Neuhoff's tour of Corsica and lack of support, see André Le Glay, *Théodore de Neuhoff*, pp. 271–277.
10. "Mémoire présenté au roi d'Angleterre," Feb., 1743, AE–CP, *Gênes*, Vol. 112, fols. 142–144. See also Amelot to Jonville, April 23, 1743, in

ibid., fols. 176–178, and François-René-Jean Pommereul, *Histoire de l'isle de Corse,* I, 251.

11. J.-M. Jacobi, *Histoire générale de la Corse,* II, 195–196.

12. Felix de Bréguigny, *Révolutions,* II, 30; the Abbé L. Letteron, ed., "Diario delle missioni di S.L.," *BSHNC* (July–Oct. 1889), 517–575.

13. Le Glay, *Conquête de la Corse,* pp. 69–73, analyzes these futile negotiations. For a lengthy critique of Le Glay's analysis, see Rosalia Rispoli, "La seconda insurrezione còrsa del sec. xviii (1733–1737)," *Archivio Storico di Corsica,* XVII (1941), 289–330, 433–459; XVIII (1942), 37–48, 161–178, 257–277.

14. Jonville to Amelot, Aug. 21, 1743, AE–CP, *Gênes,* Vol. 113, cited by Le Glay, *Conquête de la Corse,* pp. 81–82.

15. *Ibid.,* pp. 90–93.

16. Baudrillart, *op. cit.,* V, 89–90, 206–208, 214, 236; Gaetan de Raxis de Flassan, *Histoire générale et raisonée de la diplomatie française,* 2nd ed., 7 Vols. (Paris, 1811), V, 238.

17. According to the Comte de Maurepas' *Mémoires,* Versailles sent the Duc de Boufflers to Genoa in 1744 to warn the republic against trusting Maria Theresa. Boufflers supposedly told the Genoese that their honor and liberty were much more important than their lives, and that they should never stop trusting in Providence, which always detests tyranny. Supposedly, also, Boufflers said to the Genoese that "the moments are precious; do not use them in vague declarations." *Mémoires du comte de Maurepas, ministre de la marine,* 4 Vols. (Paris, 1792), IV, 187–189. This account gives the impression that Versailles actively sought an alliance with the republic in 1744; but the speech cited dates from 1747. In any case, Maurepas' *Mémoires* are not to be trusted. See A. de Boislisle, ed., *Mémoires authentiques du maréchal de Richelieu (1725–1757)* (Paris, 1918), pp. xxvi and n. 2.

18. Baudrillart, *op. cit.,* V, 229.

19. *Ibid.,* pp. 266–267, 278–280.

20. Friedrich Schoell, *Archives historiques et politiques . . . relatifs à l'histoire des* xviiie *et* xixe *siècles. . . ,* 3 Vols. (Paris, 1819), II, 363.

21. French officers and agents began to recruit Corsicans for this regiment in 1739. For a brief description of its history, see Paul-Louis Albertini and Georges Rivollet, *La Corse militaire, ses généraux: Monarchie, Révolution, 1er Empire* (Paris, 1958), pp. 61–80.

22. On the assembly held at Orezza, see Rossi, Bk. VIII, par. 8, p. 123; on Gaffori, Bk. VII, par. 3, p. 36.

23. Christian Ambrosi, *La Corse insurgée,* p. 44.

24. *Ibid.,* pp. 60–61; N. Tommaseo, "Lettere di Pasquale de'Paoli," *ASI,* XI (1846), 3, n. 1 (hereafter cited as Tommaseo, *Lettere);* Alexandre Saluces, *Histoire militaire du Piémont,* 2nd ed., 5 Vols. (Turin, 1859), V, 339–400.

25. Charles-Emmanuel to Rivarola, Dec. 24, 1745, cited by F. Girolami-Cortona, *Histoire de la Corse*, p. 332; "Rivarola à magistrates de Bastia," Nov., 1745, AE–CP, *Gênes*, Vol. 119, fol. 347.

26. Le Glay, *Conquête de la Corse*, p. 107; Jacobi, *op. cit.*, II, 198–200. On Rivarola's expedition to Corsica and the internal resistance against him, see also Du Pont and Coutlet's correspondence with Argenson for the months of December 1745 and January and February 1746, in AE–CP, *Gênes*, Vols. 119, 120.

27. The Marquis d'Oria (Genoa's envoy at Paris) to Argenson, Jan. 8, 1746, *ibid.*, Vol. 120, fols. 30–31.

28. "Declaration du roi en faveur des Corses fidèles," AE–CP, *Corse*, Vol. VIII, fols. 76–77. See also AE–CP, *Gênes*, Vol. 120, fols. 222–223, 248–249. Genoa solicited this declaration and, once a project had been drawn up, made changes in the wording that it believed were "plus convenable à la dignité du Souverain."

29. For Argenson's views on Italy, see his *Journal et mémoires*, I, xxxv, and Charles Aubertin, *L'Esprit public au* xviiie *siècle*, pp. 210–211.

30. Baudrillart, *op. cit.*, V, 337–342, 387; Camille Rousset, ed., *Correspondance de Louis XV et maréchal de Noailles*, 2 Vols. (Paris, 1869), II, 259–260, 271–272; Lodge, *op. cit.*, pp. 100–120.

31. Driault, *Recueil*, pp. 299–304.

32. Noailles to Louis XV, Sept. 14, 1746, and Louis XV to Ferdinand VI, Oct. 31, 1746, in Rousset, *op. cit.*, II, 226, 246.

33. Louis XV to Belle-Isle, June 30, 1747, AE–CP, *Gênes*, Vol. 122, fols. 409–410.

34. "Mémoire . . . d'instruction au sieur duc de Boufflers," April 17, 1747, *ibid.*, Vol. 122, fols. 221–226, and AG, *Arch. hist.*, A¹ 3248.77.

35. "Mémoire . . . d'instruction au sieur duc de Richelieu," Sept. 8, 1747, AE–CP, *Gênes*, Vol. 123, fols. 193–198.

36. Driault, *Recueil*, p. 315.

37. Du Pont to .... [Argenson], Feb. 9, 1746, AE–CP, *Gênes*, Vol. 120, fol. 105; C. Ambrosi, *op. cit.*, pp. 75–79.

38. Guymont to Louis-Philogène Brûlart de Sillery, marquis de Puysieulx, Sept. 1, Sept. 4, and Oct. 8, 1747, AE–CP, *Gênes*, Vol. 123, fols. 167–169, 182, 286–289. The Marquis de Puysieulx became secretary of state for foreign affairs after the fall of Argenson in January 1747. See also C. Ambrosi, *op. cit.*, p. 82, and the Abbé L. Letteron, ed., "Pièces diverses concernant l'insurrection de Domenico Rivarola et le siège de Bastia en 1747," *BSHNC* (March 1883), 48–70.

39. Guymont to Puysieulx, Oct. 8, 1747, AE–CP, *Gênes*, Vol. 123, fols. 286–289.

40. The Abbé L. Letteron, ed., "Journal d'Antonio Buttafoco," *BSHNC* (July–Sept. 1913), p. 29.

41. The Austro-Sardinian forces, consisting of 1,200 troops commanded

by the Chevalier de Cumiana, left Savone on April 19, but because of unfavorable winds they only arrived before Bastia on May 15. See Guymont to Puysieulx, April 13 and 21, and June 1, 1748; Richelieu to Puysieulx, April 15; and "Extrait d'une lettre de Gênes" of May 28, 1748, in AE–CP, *Gênes,* Vol. 124, fols. 200–201, 235–237, 376–377, 212–218, 365–366.

42. "Instructions pour M. de Cursay," May 20, 1748, AG, *Arch. hist.,* A¹ 3305.33. C. Ambrosi, *op. cit.,* p. 98–99, contended that Cursay's accomplish with 1,020 men what Maillebois had not done with 8,000. This judgment, however, neglects the fact that the reinforcements venture was political rather than military, because Cursay could not were directed against the Austro-Piedmontese, not the Corsicans; and in this sense it was clearly a military venture.

43. Puysieulx to Richelieu, Feb. 20 and April 16, 1748, AE–CP, *Gênes,* Vol. 124, fols. 96–99, 223–224.

44. Guymont to Puysieulx, Oct. 8, 1747, *ibid.,* Vol. 123, fols. 286–289; Puysieulx to Guymont, Nov. 7, 1747, *ibid.,* Vol. 123, fols. not numbered.

45. *Ibid.,* Vol. 125, fols. 95–98; Puysieulx to Richelieu, Sept. 14, 1748, *ibid.,* Vol. 125, fols. 230–233.

46. Argenson to Belle-Isle, Sept. 3, 1748, AG, *Arch. hist.,* A¹ 3306.5; Richelieu to Puysieulx, Aug. 10, 1748, AE–CP, *Gênes,* Vol. 125, fols. 129–131.

47. A. de Clercq, *Recueil des traites de la France,* 15 Vols. (Paris, 1844–1888), I, 75; Jacobi, *op. cit.,* II, 209–210. The guarantee was implicit because article 14 stated that for the general peace, and especially for the tranquillity of Italy, all things would remain as they had been before the war.

48. Puysieulx to Richelieu, Sept. 14, 1748, and Chauvelin to Puysieulx, Jan. 3, 1749, AE–CP, *Gênes,* Vol. 125, fols. 230–233; Vol. 126, fols. 9–13.

CHAPTER IV

The Policy Affirmed: The Coriscan Question
and the Seven Years' War

Although the Peace of Aix-la-Chapelle has been described correctly as a mere truce, it nonetheless marked a significant turning point in European history by ending thirty-five years of disputes and wars over Italy. Yet the peace did not end the Corsican question. The Corsican rebels were still rebels, though at the time more subdued, and Genoa was still too weak to restore its sovereignty over the island unaided. So long as these conditions prevailed, the threat of great power intervention was still very real and potentially dangerous to French Mediterranean interests. During the brief peace and the Seven Years' War that followed Aix-la-Chapelle, these three aspects of the Corsican question combined to reconfirm the policy that Versailles had adopted from 1737 to 1740 and again in 1748.

Shortly before the final treaty of Aix-la-Chapelle was signed on October 28, 1748, the Maréchal de Richelieu wrote a letter to Puysieulx in which he summarized concisely the nature of the Corsican problem from the French perspective. At the same time he recommended to Versailles a plan of action:

. . . All of your reflections in regard to Corsica start from the principle that it is not convenient for the king to be the master of this island, but that it is even less convenient for him that any other prince is able to possess it. . . . If this principle is true it is certain that it is very important for us that the Genoese remain the possessors, and if it is of such great interest to us that they remain effectively the masters of it, we should not neglect the means [to accomplish this objective]. . . .

The "means" that Richelieu proposed involved delaying the departure of French troops from Corsica so that their presence would support negotiations between the Genoese and the Corsicans that were then under way.[1]

As we have seen, Puysieulx did not react favorably to the proposal that France should leave troops in Corsica when Richelieu advanced it two months earlier. But in mid-October 1748 a general European peace was about to be signed, leaving the Genoese-Corsican problem unresolved. Puysieulx therefore modified his earlier position. He observed that "the Corsicans are a people on whom there are absolutely no resources to spend." But he agreed to take the matter up in the king's Council and let Richelieu know what was decided. Meanwhile, the king approved the negotiations that Richelieu had undertaken to bring about a peaceful settlement between the republic and its island subjects, providing that certain conditions were met. The first was "to act only in concert with the republic of Genoa." Second, the matter of leaving French troops on Corsica must be treated in the most "inviolable" secrecy. Third, a very capable and wise man should be found to command any French forces left on the island, a man "capable by his talents and discretion of usefully fulfilling such a delicate commission."[2]

In the months that followed, whatever reluctance to intervene that remained among the members of the French Government was overcome by the fact that Genoa continued to press Versailles for aid. Throughout the fall of 1748 the republic repeatedly requested that French troops remain in Corsica until the end of the year, a request that was vigorously supported by Richelieu. On January 3, 1749, Louis XV agreed to these representations. Shortly thereafter, the Genoese proposed that French troops remain until the accommodation with Corsica was concluded, and prevailed upon France to send 250 more men to augment French forces already on the island. Then, on January 17, the Genoese asked Louis XV to send up to 2,000 troops and to prolong their sojourn until the republic was assured of the island's pacification.[3] These appeals for French support were occasioned by the republic's fear that the independence movement led by the Corsican Gaffori would be uncontrollable once French forces left the island. Versailles agreed that this would happen, and therefore decided to intervene, despite the king's reluctance, for French intervention was the only way to strengthen Genoa and thereby shore up the French foothold in Italy. As Guymont argued, Corsica's natural resources would greatly aid the republic, but they could be exploited only if peace were restored in the island.[4] Moreover, French intervention was the only way to make certain that none of the great powers seized the island; whoever is sovereign of Corsica, Richelieu had observed, "will be master of the commerce of the Mediterranean." [5]

Thus began the most intense peace offensive that Versailles had hitherto attempted. The higher French officials involved were the Marquis de Puysieulx, the Comte d'Argenson, the Maréchal de Belle-Isle, and the Maréchal de Richelieu. Two French representatives to Genoa were also involved: Guymont and, after April 1749, his replacement, François-Claude, marquis de Chauvelin. Versailles' peace efforts were too broadly based to be staged, too massive for their sincerity to be doubted. Certainly the French efforts were not foredoomed to failure, despite the wretched record that the Genoese and Corsicans had compiled for getting along together. Perhaps the problems that eventually developed could have been avoided if the superior French officials, especially Puysieulx, had supervised their subordinate officers more carefully, or at least had intervened more quickly when affairs began to go baldly. In any case, the vulnerable member of the peace team was the commander of the French forces on Corsica, Marie Rioult de Douilly de Cursay. His words and actions aggravated what was a difficult task from its inception.

Cursay was capable and wise, of that there was no doubt, and by background and temperament, he seemed highly qualified for the task of pacification. His family had come originally from Argentan and then from Poitou, and he was, to use his biographer's expression, "impregnated by the philosophic ideas beginning to circulate in France." [6] Cursay succeeded surprisingly well in his efforts to pacify the island, simply by consulting with the Corsican leaders and by introducing an equitable, if harsh, administration of justice. Yet in the process he exercised too great an authority, independent of the Genoese officials and apparently unconcerned about their sensitivities. He failed to take into account one of the cardinal principles that the king had established as a basis for French intervention: namely, that the French must act in concert with the Genoese at all times.

The fault was not entirely Cursay's. His dangerously vague instructions provided for great latitude of action and thus increased the chance of misinterpretation. As early as July 1, 1748, he complained of having neither authority in the island nor sufficient instructions and wrote to Richelieu asking advice on how to conduct himself.[7] He received new instructions early in September. He was told to avoid any action that might upset agreements made between Versailles and Turin for Corsica's evacuation, to increase the number of Corsicans attached to him, to avoid using force, and, if possible, to prevent the Corsicans from fighting among themselves. The government left to Cursay's prudence "the application of all that was told him, according to the circumstances and the situation of the country in which he finds himself." [8]

The vagueness of these instructions is not difficult to explain, for Versailles itself had not yet decided what action it would take. Yet by the end of October Cursay apparently knew in general terms what was expected of him. At that time he reported that no other power had as much influence in Corsica as France and that force would not be needed "to reduce" the islanders. Nonetheless, French influence was needed "to make them put up with Genoa's yoke." [9] Early in November he received more definite instructions, though they were still ambiguously phrased. Puysieulx told him that the king had approved the negotiations between Genoa and the Corsicans which the republic had requested Richelieu to undertake. Versailles had a great deal of confidence in Cursay's wisdom and intelligence and in his ability to make the Corsicans listen to reason, as well as to make the Genoese realize how important it was for them to remedy the causes of Corsica's revolutions "by treating its inhabitants as men, and not as slaves." [10]

Belle-Isle's instructions were slightly more specific. He told Cursay to assure the rebel chiefs that the king would act as mediator, that a new general amnesty would be granted, and that a new *règlement* would be issued which would both establish a new form of government in Corsica and prevent the Genoese from violating the settlement. For the moment, however, Cursay was not to enter into any detailed discussions with the rebel leaders. Above all, he was to avoid any action that might make Genoa suspicious of French intentions because "all that the king does is only for its good, and to conserve Corsica to it. The king has no idea of making himself master of it; but he does not want it to fall into the hands of any other power. One wishes to conserve it to the power of the republic, and that is the only object of all our troubles and of all our designs." [11]

Although Cursay had complained earlier about having no instructions, by mid-November 1748 he found himself abundantly endowed with them. They came from a number of sources—Puysieulx, Argenson, Belle-Isle, and Richelieu. Unfortunately for Cursay and the French pacification efforts, no one in the French Government coordinated those directives or critically analyzed what Cursay was supposed to accomplish.

87

Had someone done so, it might have been seen that Cursay had been given several impossible tasks. He was to persuade the rebel chiefs to rely on French mediation, yet he could not give them details about what France was doing. Moreover, Cursay was not to talk to the rebels about submitting to Genoa, an instruction that took into consideration the islanders' hatred for Genoa but was in direct conflict with Versailles' stated intention of preserving Genoa's sovereignty over the island and with Cursay's directives to avoid giving the republic cause to suspect French intentions. If the Genoese heard about Cursay's approaches to the rebel chiefs, as they undoubtedly would, they would justifiably suspect France. In short, Cursay's conflicting instructions, if carried out, were bound to create distrust on all sides—and trust was precisely the ingredient needed to makes Versailles' peace efforts succeed. The lack of coordination, supervision, and central direction from superior French officials made it impossible for Cursay to effect pacification, regardless of what he did and how much confidence Puysieulx placed in his intelligence and ability.

The fact was, however, that the French ministers did not entirely trust Cursay. They sent to Corsica Guisard de Rouveret, a *commissaire des guerres,* who had political as well as military duties. At first he was directed to act simply as an observer and help impart to the Corsicans "the wise and equitable principles upon which peace ought to be based." He was to work closely with Cursay and present any disagreements with Cursay's policies in writing. Later, after the republic began to complain about Cursay's actions, Guisard was directed to inform Versailles about the Corsicans' attitudes toward Cursay. All of his investigations were to be done in secret. Guisard became a kind of political commissar in military guise, whose chief task was to report on Cursay's activities rather than to support them.[12] Puysieulx also undertook a special correspondence with Colonel de Courcy, one of Cursay's subordinate officers. Courcy's task, like that of Guisard, was to send confidential reports on Cursay's activities to the government.[13]

The reports from these officers became more numerous and

lengthy as the months went by and Genoese complaints about Cursay's actions increased in frequency and vigor. Thus to a lack of central supervision and coordination at the top was added suspicion and spying at the bottom. An affair begun so badly and pursued so incompetently could hardly hope for striking success, no matter how able Cursay may have been. French officials all along the line lacked the unity of purpose and direction that might have supported him in his efforts to deal with the sensitivities of the Genoese and the inflated aspirations of the Corsicans.

The fact remains, however, that in interpreting his instructions Cursay assumed excessive powers and paid too much deference to the Corsican rebels. Eventually he brought down upon himself the wrath of the Genoese and the censure of his superiors. By April 1749, Puysieulx's confidence in Cursay had begun to falter. The Genoese, he noted at that time, were unhappy with Cursay's absolutism in Corsica and wanted to be informed in advance about his activities: "Nothing is more natural than this desire. . . . I am persuaded, Monsieur [de Chauvelin], that you will neglect nothing to end and to anticipate the legitimate causes of complaint that the republic may be able to form and that you will communicate to M. de Cursay the necessary instructions." A month later Puysieulx explicitly vetoed a proposal that Cursay had made to send three Corsican deputies to Versailles in order to present the islanders' grievances to the king. Such action, he said, was

> diametrically opposed to the principles with which we have undertaken, and which we presently follow, the negotiation in question. The king's intention has never been to exercise any act of sovereignty in Corsica, and His Majesty's only object has always been and still is only to employ his protection and his authority in order to restore tranquillity in the island by means of conciliation.[14]

While Cursay attempted to pacify the island from within, French ministers at Genoa tried to bring the islanders and their sovereigns together. Richelieu had begun this work toward a Genoese-Corsican agreement, but when he left Genoa at the end of 1748 his mission was not completed.[15] His successor was François-Claude, marquis de Chauvelin, who was named *ministre plénipotentiaire* to Genoa in January 1749 and lieutenant-general of the French forces in Italy and Corsica the following August. In April Guymont had been recalled from the republic, thus leaving Chauvelin in complete charge of Franco-Genoese relations. Chauvelin's instructions, dated October 14, 1749, are not very revealing, largely because he had been in Genoa since the beginning of the year. As Puysieulx reminded him, "you know our principles and our system with regard to the republic." Chauvelin was told to report regularly all news, both good and bad, concerning the courts of Italy and to treat Corsican affairs in special reports.[16]

By the time that Chauvelin received these instructions, he had already begun to consider the detailed *règlements* that Versailles hoped would bring peace to Corsica. His position as mediator was extremely delicate. Throughout 1749 and 1750, Cursay continued to go his own way. He issued French passports to ships coming from France, compromised himself by being too friendly with one of Baron von Neuhoff's relatives who was still on the island, and did not provide the support requested by Genoese financial officials. He even interfered with Genoese courts and set up a special court through which he personally exercised judicial authority.[17] At first Chauvelin supported Cursay against the increasingly hostile attacks that the Genoese made against these actions, and he pushed for a personal interview with Cursay to iron out obvious differences in their approaches to the Corsican problem. But before long Chauvelin became exasperated. Early in 1751 he informed Puysieulx that the animosity between the Genoese officials and the French commanders in Corsica was "an evil too inveterate" for him to remedy. Chauvelin had despaired of Cursay, and said that only the conclusion of the definitive *règlements* could restore order.[18]

Puysieulx also became exasperated with the French commander and frequently scolded him for giving the Genoese so many reasons to complain about his actions. The minister considered Cursay's activities a personal betrayal, and he voiced his frustrations to the Maréchal de Belle-Isle:

> It would seem to me that in proportion as one approaches the dénouement of the *règlement*, [Cursay] fears that he will be unable to maintain all that he has promised. It is, however, his promises that have engaged us to let him go ahead, although the republic does not cease to represent to us that M. de Cursay is throwing dust in our eyes. He began this affair; it is necessary that he finish it, or that it miscarry between his hands. We have always given to him a complete confidence; we have always listened favorably to him; we have left him the master of it. He has never had from us anything but the most reasonable insinuations, and rarely any orders. It seems to me that in his turn he should, out of respect for the intentions of the king, out of feeling and gratitude, conform to circumstances a little more submissively. . . .[19]

These words are a striking illustration of the weakness and indecision that characterized the French ministry at mid-century; they also indicate that Puysieulx deserves his reputation as an ineffective minister.

The lack of coordination, central direction, and decisive action among superior French officials was damaging enough for Versailles' mediating policy. What made success even more doubtful was the fact that the king's new favorite, Mme de Pompadour, decided to give Cursay some advice. The degree of her influence upon Versailles' policies and Louis XV continues to be debated, but the observations that she made to Cursay reveal that she was both a meddler and a shrewd and perceptive observer of the international relations of the period. For a long time now, Mme de Pompadour wrote to Cursay, the republic had been exhausting itself in its war against the Corsican rebels:

It is necessary to put an end to it. It is not a question of beating the Corsicans, but of giving them peace. They need [peace] as well as the Genoese, whom they (perhaps rightly) call tyrants. But it is feared here that your Genoese officers are spoiling everything; they are jealous that foreigners are mediators in this affair. The envy that is the weakness of Italians, and especially the Genoese, will often put your patience to the test, because they wish to have all the honors of a peace they are not capable of making. [But] disregard them, Monsieur, and do yourself honor while doing your duty.

The Corsicans, Mme de Pompadour continued, are now almost in the same position as the Dutch were when fighting Philip II:

After many battles and sieges, the rebels change their name. They are no longer subjects in revolt, but irreconcilable enemies. Thus force destroys right and puts everyone on a par. This is why the Corsicans demand much and the Genoese wish to accord them only a pardon. They speak like irritated masters against slaves in rebellion: but this tone will not be sustained. The important point is to conserve the sovereignty to the Republic and to make the Corsicans content. It is a very delicate business. One turns it over to your prudence and to that of M. de Chauvelin. The honor and the word of the king are involved. It is a motive more than sufficient to arouse your zeal.[20]

As Mme de Pompadour shrewdly observed, the task of making the Corsicans contented while, at the same time, conserving Genoese sovereignty over the island, was extremely delicate. Cursay had already learned just how delicate, and nearly impossible, the task really was; and it did not help for the king's favorite to tell him to disregard the Genoese officials at the same time that his superiors in the ministry were telling him to be more attentive to Genoese sensitivities. The Genoese interpreted Cursay's actions as an effort to destroy their sovereignty over the island and fumed that he was leading the Corsicans to disobey their legitimate masters. By March 1751 the republic had become so concerned that it solicited Cursay's recall. After that date the attacks against him became more frequent and more violent. The republic also expanded the demands that it made to Versailles. It wanted both Cursay and French troops removed from the island. In place of military support, the Genoese Senate wanted a subsidy that would facilitate the employment of Genoese instead of French forces. By March 1752, Agostino di Sorba, the republic's minister to Paris since 1749, had become emphatic and persistent in his requests for a French subsidy. If monetary support were not possible, he asked that French troops be withdrawn anyway.[21]

Puysieulx's worst fears were realized. Because Cursay paid too much deference to the Corsicans and ignored the Genoese, the republic began to suspect that Versailles was attempting to take possession of their territory. Having lost the basis for trust, French officials could not persuade the Genoese otherwise. In May 1751, Puysieulx told Sorba that Louis XV had decided to withdraw his troops and that in the future Sorba was to discuss only matters related to the evacuation. Then, in January 1752, the new secretary of state for foreign affairs, François-Dominique Barberie, marquis de Saint-Contest, submitted the *règlements* for the pacification of Corsica to the Genoese. Saint-Contest had to wait three months for a reply, and when the republic finally responded it did so under pressure. In April Versailles had prodded it into action by demanding a public apology from the Genoese commissioner in Corsica for an alleged insult to Cursay; if the apology were not forthcoming within eight days, French troops in Corsica would be withdrawn immediately. This form of harassment brought results. By mid-May Saint-Contest had the Genoese reply: The republic accepted the *règlements* on condition that French troops would leave Corsica and that Versailles would give a subsidy to support 1,500 Genoese soldiers on the island.[22]

Despite Richelieu's and many Corsicans' opposition to withdrawal,[23] the *règlements* on which Chauvelin had been working for two years were finally signed on September 6, 1752. The agreement, which became known as the "Convention of Saint-Florent," stipulated that the Genoese were to take total jurisdiction over the island; the French troops were scheduled to be evacuated in six months, or not later than March 1753.[24] A short time later, on September 26, France agreed to a subsidy for support of the Genoese troops scheduled to replace the French forces. The Genoese therefore had substantial reasons to rejoice, for they had won their principal demands. In December 1752, they received an additional piece of good news when they learned that Cursay had been arrested and taken to Antibes as a political prisoner. His replacement was the French officer who had secretly been corresponding with the ministry, Colonel de Courcy. He took the French troops from the island in the spring of 1753.[25] At that moment Versailles professed to believe that the island was pacified, although it had in fact withdrawn because, as Puysieulx had observed some months before the accommodation was concluded, the Corsican affair had developed into "such an excess of indecency and scandal." [26] The Corsicans soon gave the republic cause to repent its attitude of *méfiance* toward Versailles.

The lawyer Barbier, ever alert to the talk around Paris and the news in *gazettes,* frequently noted in his *Journal* the troubles in Corsica while Cursay was there. In April 1750, not hearing much news about the island, he speculated about its future. Everything suggests, he wrote, that if Cursay and French troops leave the island, troubles will begin again and Genoa will not be able to maintain its sovereignty. What will happen to Corsica then? Barbier thought that the *Infant* Don Philippe, who had been awarded the duchies of Parma, Plaisance, and Guastalla at Aix-la-Chapelle, would receive the island

94

so that he would have the title of king. This, Barbier believed, would be at the expense of France. Later, in January 1753, Barbier noted that at least part of his earlier prediction was coming to pass. He learned that the Corsican chiefs had met and shown strong opposition to Chauvelin's *règlements*: "They have loudly declared that they will not go back to obeying the republic under the conditions proposed, and that they would like to give themselves to some foreign power like England." [27]

The meeting of the Corsican leaders to which Barbier referred had taken place at Vallerusti on October 29 and 30, 1752. There the representatives of the people had discussed the *règlements* and had concluded that if they acquiesced they would be accepting total submission to Genoa. This was not altogether true, for the *règlements* were quite favorable to the islanders. But they had hoped that French mediation would give them only nominal dependence on Genoa; and for a year and a half they had been acting on this premise. By June 1751 they had organized their own government, headed by a Supreme Directory of twelve members forming a Council of State. Military power was lodged in a junta of twelve members and financial control in a junta of six members and a General Treasurer. The Council of State was scheduled to begin functioning on November 1, 1752. The other bodies were to begin after the French troops departed.[28]

The leader of this government was Gian Pietro Gaffori. Concerted, vigorous action placed him in control of the citadel of Corte and nearly all the island except the maritime places, that is, the *présides* or walled cities along the Corsican coasts, as soon as the French troops left. The Genoese were quite incapable of subduing the islanders alone, and their fears of France had kept them from realizing this painful fact. The same kind of shortsightedness led them to conclude that they would improve the situation by assassinating Gaffori. By October 3, 1753, the deed had been done with the aid of the Romei brothers of Corte: Gaffori was dead.[29] The assassination was a stupid blunder, an act that confirmed and intensified the

95

Corsicans' hatred for the republic and made Gaffori a martyr.

Until this time, the Corsicans had fought for their independence, but had lacked any real unity and national purpose. Gaffori's death gave them a national hero; but it also took from them the unifying influence of a national leader. Before the end of October, a new *Consulte* met at Corte to reform the Corsican Government, the initial plan for which had been built on Gaffori's leadership. The principal leader of the "Council of Regency" was Clemente Paoli, the eldest son of Giacinto Paoli who had been prominent since the 1729 revolt. Acting with him were three other council members: Tommaso Santucci, Simon-Pietro Frediani, and a Doctor Grimaldi.[30]

The new government immediately began efforts to consolidate its position. The first need was to justify the new revolution against Genoa in the eyes of Europe. On January 27, 1754, the *Consulte* published a manifesto to the courts of Europe, which stated, in part:

> Our first movements have had an echo in the paternal heart of kings. Pope Clement XII, Emperor Charles VI, and then the king of France became interested in our fate. In more recent times we have experienced the effects of the individual protection of the king of Sardinia and his allies. Since the peace of Aix-la-Chapelle, all the monarchs seem to have conspired against us. The republic has slandered the brave Marquis de Cursay and has had our General Gaffori assassinated. The Cain into whose hand it put the weapon has confessed everything in his prison, where he has been justly put to the wheel. Already it has stirred up spirits against some officers in the service of France. The hired assassins have received the blood prize, but this blood will cry out for vengeance, and Anthonys will rise in order to revenge our massacred Caesars. Perhaps we will even have an Augustus to establish the public peace on indestructible bases, which we have longed for such a long time. If the powers arm

against us, they know that we have sworn, by the Supreme God who has no equal, to die or to vanquish.[31]

The practical matter of internal organization was much more difficult than the wording of manifestoes. The national government had to get the island into condition to resist, and it spent the year 1754 attempting to achieve that end. It quickly learned, however, that Corsica needed a unifying presence, a leader. The people did not want juntas and committees; they wanted a general. A person had to be found who could command both the respect and the allegiance of the Corsican factions.

The mantle of leadership fell on Antonio-Filippo-Pasquale Paoli, second son of Giacinto Paoli and younger brother of Clemente. Born in the little village of Morosaglia on April 6, 1725, Pasquale Paoli had been reared in the tense atmosphere of continual rebellion against Genoa. In 1739 he had gone to Naples with his father when the latter and other Corsican chiefs left the island at the time of Boissieux's intervention. He studied under Antonio Genovesi, the celebrated Italian economist at the Royal Academy of Naples. When his studies ended in 1749, he became a sublieutenant in the Neopolitan Royal Regiment of Farnese and was assigned to serve at Longone on the island of Elba. Paoli was a soldier by choice and inclination, but he was bored by his service in Sicily and Elba. Resisting his father's advice to enter the church, he longed for some opportunity to exercise his *métier*. Finally, in 1755, he was rescued from his boredom by his nation's need for a leader.[32]

Having been suggested for leadership by his brother Clemente, Pasquale Paoli was recalled to the island early in 1755. He arrived on April 29 and landed secretly at the mouth of the Golo River on the eastern coast. For a short time he assisted the national government in its efforts to organize the island. Then, at a *Consulte* held at Saint-Antoine de la Casabianca from July 13 to 15, Pasquale Paoli was chosen General-in-Chief of the Corsican Nation. The edict announcing his

Pasquale di Paoli, 1769, by S. Caron
(Library of the Museum of Amsterdam).

election mentioned the discords and divisions that so disturbed the island's internal peace, and it decried the old and personal enmities that undermined the public good. Only the election of a General-in-Chief could mitigate against these evils. By unanimous consent, Pasquale Paoli had been chosen for this difficult task. To facilitate his work, Paoli had been given full powers except in "matters of State." These matters included revision of the constitution, law-making, and the "orientation général des affaires," for which Paoli would be bound to consult the representatives of the nation.[33]

Upon taking control of the government, Paoli immediately set about to restore order, to consolidate his power, and to prepare for the future of his nation. The first task involved rigorous administration of justice. The second entailed frequent visitations throughout the island to eliminate rival leaders, the most formidable of whom was Mario Emmanuele Matra. Paoli's running conflict with Matra did not end until March 1757, when the latter was finally killed in a battle with forces led by Pasquale and Clemente Paoli. The third task was the most difficult because it meant revising Corsica's laws and internal administration. At a *Consulte* held at Corte, November 16 to 18, 1755, Paoli's constitution was approved by the deputies of the General Assembly. It was based on the sovereignty of the people, delegated to deputies of the *Consulte*. Executive power was vested in the General-in-Chief presiding over and assisted by a Council of State consisting of three chambers: justice, finance, and war.[34]

To the extent that Paoli's power in Corsica and prestige in Europe increased, Genoa's fears were heightened. The republic had been in no position to enforce its sovereignty over the island in the spring of 1753, when French forces had been withdrawn. Thereafter it rapidly lost all control over the island's affairs except in the maritime places. When Paoli's determined leadership made a bad situation even worse, the republic was nearly powerless to do anything about it. All it could do was to ask King Charles of the Two Sicilies to recall his former officer. And all the Neapolitan king could do was

99

to order Paoli's dismissal from the Neopolitan army if he did not return to Naples.[35] As if the more vigorous independence movement on Corsica was not enough, the Austrian Hapsburgs selected this same moment to revive their claims to some of the republic's continental possessions.

In these circumstances, Versailles' policy toward Genoa and Corsica was again determined by its desire to maintain its Genoese foothold in Italy. Its position was clearly stated in the instructions sent to Jacques-Philippe Fyot de la Marche, comte de Neuilly, who went to Genoa as *envoyé extraordinaire* and *ministre plénipotentiaire* in 1754. These instructions reviewed Genoa's long neutrality, indicating that only the "injustice" of the Treaty of Worms caused it to join actively the Bourbon alliance. They pointed explicitly to article XIV of the Treaty of Aix-la-Chapelle, by which the republic was restored to full sovereignty over possessions it held before the war. Concerning Corsica, the instructions noted how close Genoa was to losing control over it and then briefly reviewed French military and financial assistance related to the island. This assistance was given because the king "was always disposed to give support to his allied powers who were oppressed."

The central objective of Neuilly's mission in 1754, however, did not concern the Corsican question. Versailles considered that issue in a state of rest after French troops had been withdrawn and the subsidies granted. The important problem at the time was Austrian pretensions to Genoese possessions on the continent. Vienna was fomenting trouble in the fief of Campo-Freddo and in the province of San Remo, which it contended was also a fief of the Empire. All this was done, thought Versailles, because "the Emperor would like to detach this republic from the French alliance, and to oblige it to take with the Court of Vienna some engagements that would put Genoa totally at its discretion." Neuilly was therefore ordered "to renew to the republic the assurances of protection that His Majesty has already given it several times [and] to make the Genoese realize that it is in their interest to keep at all times a rigid neutrality." If Genoa made any agreements with Vienna, "these agreements would make it absolutely dependent on the Court of Vienna, which would then become master to dispose of Genoese possessions . . . without leaving to the republic any hope of obtaining the support of His Majesty." [36]

Upon arriving at Genoa in September 1754, Neuilly quickly discovered that the problems being created by the Corsicans themselves were as serious as the republic's controversy with Vienna. Genoa's fears grew worse as Paoli consolidated his position in the island. Early in 1756, the republic again had recourse to Versailles and asked the French Government to provide an increased subsidy to meet the threat posed by Paoli and to send additional forces into the island. Louis XV was not unwilling to increase the subsidy, but before he did so he wanted to make certain that his money would be used effectively. In March the new secretary of state for foreign affairs (since July 1754), Antoine-Louis Rouillé, comte de Jouy, told Neuilly that the Genoese continued to press for a subsidy and that if the king consented he would take the necessary precautions to determine exactly the extent of the republic's need and how his money would be used. A few days later Rouillé specified the conditions under which Louis XV would increase the subsidy to Genoa. First, the king wanted to know in detail the state of Genoese troops and fortifications. Second, he would give the Genoese money only if they agreed to repair the strong places on the island and to reinforce the garrisons they kept there. To supervise the execution of these conditions, Versailles sent to Genoa a temporary ambassador, M. de Pujol. Pujol was to work with Neuilly and was told to examine "in the greatest detail the quality and number of troops that the republic actually has in readiness, both in *terre-ferma* and in Corsica, the strength of the garrisons in the fortresses and the state of the fortifications, especially in the island. . . ." His instructions also cautioned him to act in such a manner as "to give no subject of umbrage to the Genoese. While protecting them, the king wants to be careful of their delicacy and is quite far from any idea of occasioning in their minds any distrust of the purity and the generosity of his views." [37]

The reason for Versailles' renewed interest in Corsica is not difficult to discover. The Peace of Aix-la-Chapelle that ended the War of the Austrian Succession resolved nothing between France and England. Afterward there were constant clashes between these two colonial powers and by 1754 it was clear that the truce was broken and war should be renewed. One of the most important of the numerous incidents that pushed France and England toward open conflict was the English Vice-Admiral Boscawen's attack on the French fleet in June 1755. There was an immediate French reaction. The Maréchal de Noailles, in a memoir to Louis XV dated July 1755, suggested that England's offensive declaration of war left the king no uncertainty about what he must do. He must recall his minister from London and send the English minister home. He must attack English ships when advantageous, fortify Dunkirk and the colonies, and increase the size of the navy. It was also essential, Noailles argued, "to take early measures in order that the English do not seize Corsica." [38]

The Maréchal de Belle-Isle seconded these views on Corsica. His war plan, drawn up early in 1756, was adopted by Versailles in February of that year. It called for an invasion of England, Ireland, and Scotland and, at the same time, a blow at Minorca in the Mediterranean. If the latter tactic failed, French forces could retreat to Genoa, Corsica, or even the Spanish ports.[39] In these circumstances it was imperative that Corsica should not fall into English possession.[40] Belle-Isle was even more concerned about the island after Richelieu captured Port Mahon on Minorca in June 1756. He was informed that the English had some designs on Corsica, which they hoped would offset their loss of Port Mahon. He therefore pressed for some explicit agreement which would prevent Corsica's loss.[41]

The result of growing French anxiety over Mediterranean developments was a new treaty with the republic concerning Corsica. It was signed on August 14, 1756, and has become known as "The First Treaty of Compiègne." Its introduction assured Genoa of Louis XV's affection and his desire to end the troubles on the island. It also reiterated His Majesty's consistent objective: "to maintain the island of Corsica under the domination of the Serene Republic, which has possessed the legitimate sovereignty of it for several centuries." This principle was repeated in article V, where it was stated as the primary motive for the entire treaty.

The specific terms of the treaty support the conclusion that it was entirely defensive and was designed to keep the English out of the island and to maintain Genoa in its neutral position. France pledged an annual subsidy for the duration of the war and for six years after peace was signed. It promised artillery and munitions for the defense of the republic's continental possessions and contributions if Genoa would arm warships. Most important, France would send troops to Corsica, which would be recalled "at Genoa's first request after the re-establishment of the peace, without leaving them there for any cause or under any pretext whatever" (article V). These French troops were to replace Genoese forces in Saint-Florent, Calvi, and Ajaccio. French commanders were not to become involved in any judicial, administrative, or economic affairs, were not to harbor any Corsicans sought by Genoese authorities, and were pledged to support those officials whenever Genoa called upon them to do so, "both in order to support the exercise of its sovereign jurisdiction and for the perception of rights of entry into the aforesaid cities and their ports." Finally, if the republic were attacked, Versailles agreed to increase the subsidy and to come directly to its aid.[42]

Those who believe that after 1735 Versailles had secret plans to acquire possession of Corsica are hard pressed to explain the First Treaty of Compiègne. Villat and Cesari-Rocca repeated Driault's comment: "This First Treaty of Compiègne marks *un temps d'arrêt* in the evolution of the Corsican question towards its inevitable termination; it permits France to pass through the crisis of the Seven Years' War without accident from the direction of Corsica." [43] The treaty clearly does not fit into any plans to acquire possession of Corsica, which makes it seem an aberration from "the inevitable outcome" of the Corsican question. It does clearly correspond to the two-sided program that had been reaffirmed at Versailles in 1748 and 1749. Thus the Seven Years' War, like the War of the Austrian Succession, confirmed the French ministers in their approach to the Corsican question. They intended to keep another power out of the island and to maintain the friend-ship of Genoa by assisting it with subsidies and military aid. These goals were clearly stated by Rouillé both before and after the First Treaty of Compiègne was signed. In the spring of 1756 he informed the French minister in Genoa that the principal objective of French aid to Genoa was "to shelter the island of Corsica from all surprise." He also said that if France became the master of Fort St. Philippe in Minorca, the English would have to find some other stronghold in the Mediterranean, and their object would certainly be Corsica. Then, in September, Rouillé emphasized that French forces were sent to Corsica "to maintain the legitimate authority of the sovereign, and in order to shelter this island from the enterprises that the court of London intends to execute against this part of the Genoese possessions." [44]

How best to achieve these objectives was Versailles' dilemma, but by 1756 it had arrived at a solution. Its aims could best be achieved by garrisoning the island's maritime places (the *présides*) with French troops. The treaty of 1756 stated the terms of the French military intervention. The instrument for carrying them out was a force of 3,000 troops, which landed on Corsica in November 1756 under the command of Charles-Gabriel de la Croix, marquis de Castries.

Castries' arrival raised two questions, one of which was political: What would be the relationship of the French troops to Paoli's national government? Paoli, naturally, was disturbed by the presence of the French, for he had been on the verge of driving the Genoese from their last strongholds on the island. Moreover, he did not know precisely why the French had come. He therefore tried to discover from the

French commander the reasons behind the French intervention. Responding to his questions, Castries said that Louis XV had ordered him to maintain a strict neutrality so far as the Genoese and Corsicans were concerned. The French were there only to act against the English if they should attempt to seize the island.[45] This response set the tone of French relations with the Corsicans. The French troops did not interfere with Paoli's government or with his efforts to win the allegiance of his countrymen.

The second question posed by the arrival of the French troops was how the occupying forces would be deployed. Castries' instructions, as well as the treaty of 1756, specified that two battalions would be garrisoned at Ajaccio, two at Calvi, and two at Saint-Florent. As Castries' biographer remarked, this was "une vue des bureaux qui ne correspondait ni aux possibilités de cantonnement, ni à la sécurité du territoire." After he had become acquainted with the island, Castries proposed an alternative plan. He wanted one battalion at Ajaccio, one at Calvi, and four dispersed between Bastia and Saint-Florent to guard the two watersheds of the Nebbio region and to insure the French internal communications.[46]

Castries remained in Corsica long enough to put his plan into effect and then have it reversed by a ministerial change. The Comte d'Argenson, minister of war since January 1743, was disgraced and exiled on February 1, 1757. His successor, Antoine-René de Voyer, marquis de Paulmy, ordered Castries to return to the original plan for deployment of the French troops. Castries had already become embroiled with the Genoese in Corsica over jurisdictional and protocol disputes, and the reversal of his proposals irritated him further. He therefore appealed to his uncle, the Maréchal de Belle-Isle, to get him out of Corsica. Belle-Isle obliged, and in July 1757 Castries turned over command of the occupying forces to his replacement, Noël Jourda, comte de Vaux. Vaux withdrew the French forces from the interior of the island and concentrated them almost entirely at Calvi, which he deemed the only place capable of resisting the English if they decided to seize the island.[47]

Another ministerial change gave rise to a further re-evaluation of French intervention. In December 1758, Étienne-François, duc de Choiseul, became secretary of state for foreign affairs. Later, as we shall see, he turned his attention to the Corsican question and resolved it. At this moment, however, he had other, more serious problems on his hands. France, now actively engaged in a near global war against England and a continental war against Brandenburg-Prussia, needed funds and troops. Moreover, the French capture of Fort St. Philippe on Minorca had given them a measure of protection and security in the Mediterranean. For these reasons, it appeared French occupation of the Corsican *présides* was both wasteful and unnecessary. There were other considerations that suggested the need to reappraise French policy. The French troops in Corsica were insufficient to repel a really determined English attack. Most critical of all, there were constant and growing recriminations and conflicts between Genoese officials and French troops on the island. Choiseul considered these matters carefully and recommended that the French withdraw from Corsica.

Early in 1759 Choiseul communicated news of the change of plans to Neuilly and Belle-Isle. The king intended to withdraw at least four and perhaps all six of the battalions then located in Corsica, he wrote; this resolution being required by the present circumstances because the king wanted to do nothing "prejudicial to or even displeasing" to the republic.[48] Belle-Isle was totally unprepared, apparently, for this reversal of French policy. His reply to Choiseul said simply that he had not suggested withdrawal to the king and that he was ready to take the subject up in the Council in order to learn the king's decision. Belle-Isle advised leaving Vaux at Calvi with one battalion of troops. This move, he observed, is necessary for several reasons, which he proposed to discuss with Choiseul at the earliest opportunity.[49]

Belle-Isle's reasons must have been persuasive because Choiseul's next letters to Neuilly sounded a different note. French troops had been sent to Corsica, he observed, only to defend it against England. It was clear, however, that Calvi was the only place on the island capable of resisting a decisive attack. The king had therefore decided to leave one battalion at Calvi under Vaux's command and to withdraw the others. Genoa would undoubtedly be pleased, Choiseul added, ". . . because it has continually expressed its repugnance at seeing [French troops] in Corsica." A short time later Choiseul refused a Genoese request for increased subsidies. The king's financial burdens, he told Sorba, were already too great.[50]

The troubles between Genoese officials and French troops in Corsica continued for a few more months. There were few subjects that did not give rise to conflict, from petty matters like the lodgings for French troops to more serious matters like French relations with Paoli and other Corsicans. Finally, in exasperation, Choiseul concluded that the only way to end these problems was complete French withdrawal. French-Genoese relations had again developed into "an excess of indecency and scandal," and Corsica stood so low on the list of French priorities that Choiseul believed it was not worthwhile to prolong these conditions. In September 1759, Louis XV decided to withdraw the one French battalion left on Corsica.[51] French intervention had been successful, for it had discouraged the irresolute and vague thoughts that the English had about invading the island; this was its objective. But French intervention did not interfere with the growing strength of Paoli's national government. When French troops left the island in the fall of 1759, Paoli was entering the most glorious period of his popularity and influence.

Left to themselves, the Genoese did not know how to control Paoli. On the island, the Genoese commissioner, Don Filippo Grimaldi, tried military action, using some 2,000 to 3,000 German and Swiss mercenaries that the republic had hired. When his efforts resulted in defeat, the Senate recalled him in disgrace and then tried conciliation. In May 1761, six Genoese senators arrived in Bastia and published an edict of conciliation. Again their offers were refused. A *Consulte* held at Vescovato in the Casinca on May 24 proclaimed that no plan of conciliation would be considered as long as the republic occupied one piece of the island. The *Consulte* went further by deciding that only independence for the island would be accepted as a basis for negotiation. When its conciliatory approach failed, Genoa tried to exploit internal divisions among the Corsicans. In November it sent to the island Alerio Francesco Matra, to whom it gave both the title of *generalissimo* and funds for a war against Paoli.[52]

While Genoa adopted one expedient after another to detract from Paoli's prestige, Paoli was fortifying his position. In particular, he turned his attention to military, economic, and educational reforms. He toured the island extensively in 1761 for the purpose of rallying support for his government and discovering what reforms were needed. Everywhere he was acclaimed, especially by the peasants. He told his people that he intended to expel the Genoese forever and to make Corsica "a republic as famous as Holland." All he wanted was their support and time to accomplish his objectives.[53]

Considering these circumstances, any kind of recognition given to the Corsicans would only increase Paoli's prestige. Genoa was compelled to combat energetically any such menace; and this was precisely what was so disturbing about Paoli's ecclesiastical changes. As a son of the Enlightenment, Paoli believed fundamentally in ecclesiastical reform. It was a difficult task in a country so devoutly Catholic. Moreover, when Paoli emerged as the Corsican leader, the bishops appointed by the Genoese had sought safety in Bastia, which was still controlled by the republic's officials. Thus they left their flocks untended. Paoli recognized that ecclesiastical reform was badly needed, but at the same time he realized there were risks if he tried it himself. To facilitate this task, he therefore appealed directly to Pope Clement XIII for assistance. The Pope agreed to send an apostolic visitor to the island and chose for this appointment the Bishop of Segni, Monseigneur Cesare Crescenzio di Angelis.

The Genoese were enraged. Some Senators were convinced that the Papacy intended to revive former claims to the island, claims that went back to the eighth century. Others saw no dark designs in the Pope's action, but did realize that the act of sending an apostolic visitor was tacit recognition of Paoli's government. When its protests to Rome availed nothing, the Senate finally forbade Bishop Angelis to set foot on the island. Eventually the Genoese Senate offered a reward of 6,000 Roman *écus* for anyone who arrested the papal emissary. Despite all the republic's opposition, Mgr. di Angelis assumed a disguise and arrived in the island on April 23, 1760. He proceeded to work with Paoli toward a badly needed ecclesiastical reform.[54]

Paoli's growing support in the island was largely increased by Genoese blunders and the presence of the apostolic visitor. As a result, Genoese-Corsican relations had reached a new low by 1762. It was at this moment that Versailles sent to Genoa a new representative. Neuilly's replacement was Joseph Boyer de Fonscolombe, formerly *chargé d'affaires* at several European courts.

Boyer's mission involved particular attention to three special problems, the first of which was the controversy between the republic and Paoli over the apostolic visitor. Versailles' role in this controversy was curious. In May 1760, Agostino di Sorba, the Genoese representative to Versailles, tried to secure a French representation at Rome against the Corsican visitor. He was informed that the Bishop of Laon, who represented France at Rome, would be instructed to convey to the Papacy French concern that Genoese rights over Corsica should not be infringed.[55] Yet it seems clear that Versailles wanted no conflict with the Papacy over such an insignificant question. This judgment is supported by the instructions sent to Boyer, which were to take no part in the controversy over Rome's emissary to Corsica. He was to be a "passive observer." When approached, he was to say only that Louis XV was concerned and hoped for an accommodation through the mediation of the king of the Two Sicilies, who had voluntarily proposed his help in seeking a compromise.[56]

The second problem demanding Boyer's attention was the

question of Genoa's neutrality. The *pacte de famille,* which had been concluded on August 15, 1761, was followed in January 1762 by a declaration of war between Spain and England. The result was an increase in maritime activity in the Mediterranean, thus bringing into question the course that Genoa would take in the expanding conflict. In these circumstances, Versailles believed England would look for a pretext to draw Genoa out of its neutrality. Boyer was therefore to persuade the republic to persevere in "the principles of a wise and enlightened *politique* and in the most inviolable attachment to the Crown of the King." In addition, he was cautioned to press for the swift establishment of Genoese defenses in case the English should resort to some overt act.

The third problem with which Boyer was to deal was the Corsican question. Versailles informed him that he would most certainly be approached by Genoa for further assistance, and when such a request was made, Boyer was to say "in general terms that all powers owe it to themselves not to protect subjects in revolt against their legitimate sovereign, and that His Majesty always desires, with the same sincerity as the republic, that the peaceable possesssion of this part of its domains finally be secured." Other than this general statement, however, Boyer was to say that he had no instructions to deal with this question and that the republic's minister must take this matter up with the government at Versailles.[57]

Boyer was both a man of intelligence and a dedicated envoy anxious to please his superiors. After he came to Corsica in June 1762, he observed Genoese-Corsican relations for a few months and then summarized his conclusions in a "Mémoire politique sur la Corse," which he sent to Versailles on September 13. His memoir contains three important observations. First, the Corsicans would never submit to Genoa and the struggle would only bring ruin to the republic. Second, the island should be placed in the hands of another power; but it must be a power which would not alarm the other states and yet would be capable of taking advantage of Corsica's resources. These criteria, Boyer believed, eliminated the Emperor, the king of the Two Sicilies, the Pope, the Order of Malta, and the dukes of Parma and Modena. The only candidate left was the king of Sardinia, who had the capability to use the island's resources without threatening other states. To rebut those who might pose the danger of an alliance between Sardinia and England, Boyer argued that the *pacte de famille* and French ties with Austria effectively prevented Sardinia from making such a move.

The third point Boyer's memoir dealt with was how to compensate Genoa for its loss. He suggested that in return for Corsica, Sardinia should give up its claims to Plaisance, which since 1748 had been in the possession of Don Philippe. In return for Don Philippe's gain, Spain would pay a sum of money to the Emperor, who would cede to Genoa the right to the province of Pentremole or some imperial fiefs.[58]

Although Boyer's scheme can probably be dismissed as map-juggling by an ambitious and perceptive envoy, it does have some rather curious aspects. Certainly the most interesting was the absence of any mention of French possession of Corsica. This omission is the more interesting if one assumes that ever since 1735 the French plan had called for eventual sovereignty over the island. Driault did not explain Boyer's ideas. In his introduction to Boyer's instructions, he noted that the envoy "was naturally put *au courant* of the relations between Genoa and France." Yet when it came to Boyer's memoir, Driault was mystified; and he indicated that he printed the memoir only to show that Boyer "was not in on the secret of the intentions of his government, and that in good conscience a French agent, on the eve of the annexation of Corsica, was able to estimate it reasonable to fortify the power of the House of Savoy and to make of it a devoted client on the frontier of the Alps, between France and the Italian states subjected to the influence of Austria." [59]

Driault's professed surprise over Boyer's supposedly absurd proposal results from interpreting the facts to fit the thesis. Driault cannot have it both ways, for either Boyer was or was not informed about Versailles' intentions. If he had been informed, he presumably would not have written his memoir proposing to give Corsica to the king of Sardinia; since he did write it, he must not have been informed. But the inference is not justified, because it fails to take into consideration another alternative: the possibility that in 1762 Versailles had no definite intention of or plan to acquire sovereignty over the island.

One fact that supports this alternate explanation for Boyer's proposals is that its suggested solution to the Corsican question was not so patently absurd. Ever since the seventeenth century there had been at Versailles strong defenders of an alliance with the king of Sardinia. It had been the hopes for just such an alliance that contributed to the wretched record of French forces in the Italian campaigns during the War of the Austrian Succession. And when the war ended, one of the most persistent supporters of this policy was the Maréchal de Noailles, who proposed it again and again to Louis XV.[60] Thus Boyer was another proponent of the Sardinian alliance, who believed that Corsica might help to cement such a union of interests.

In addition, Boyer's background and experience make it difficult to accept Driault's argument that he was not informed about his government's intentions. Boyer came from a family of Aix-en-Provence and entered the diplomatic service as *chargé d'affaires* in Saxony (1752) and at Turin (1753). He was personal secretary to the Duc de Choiseul in Rome in 1754; after Choiseul's departure for the French embassy in Vienna, Boyer took over the French correspondence with Rome and from January to August 1757 was the *chargé d'affaires* there. Choiseul called him to Vienna where he resumed his duties as secretary and later, from November 1758 to June 1759, became *chargé d'affaires* at the Hapsburg court. His next assignment was *chargé d'affaires* at Liége (1760). Finally, in 1762 he was sent to Genoa.[61] Had Choiseul wanted a nonentity at Genoa, a person who would remain uninformed about the policies of his government, he surely would not have selected Boyer, a man who had twice been his personal secretary and had been an able diplomatic agent in several critical posts. Indeed, Boyer was selected as Versailles' *envoyé extraordinaire* to Genoa at a critical juncture in French-Genoese relations. From 1760 on, the Duc de Choiseul began to give increased attention to Corsica. During his ministry the long-lived and terribly frustrating Corsican question was finally resolved.

NOTES

1. Richelieu to Puysieulx, Oct. 3, 1748, AE–CP, *Gênes*, Vol. 125, fols. 269–271.
2. Puysieulx to Richelieu, Oct. 15, 1748, *ibid.*, Vol. 125, fols. 296–297.
3. The chronology of these events, documented by reference to Richelieu's letters, is given in a "Mémoire sur le passage des troupes du roy en Corse," [April 14, 1751], *ibid.*, Vol. 130, fols. 208–211.
4. Guymont to Puysieulx, Aug. 15, 1748, *ibid.*, Vol. 125, fols. 148–158.
5. Richelieu to Puysieulx, Oct. 3, 1748, *ibid.*, Vol. 125, fols. 269–271.
6. Christian Ambrosi, *La Corse insurgée*, p. 155. For Cursay's attempt to rehabilitate Corsica, see especially Chapter VII, "Un despote éclairé; L'oeuvre de Cursay en Corse."
7. Cursay to [Argenson], July 1, 1748, AG, *Arch. hist.*, A1 3305.42.
8. "Instructions envoyée à M. de Cursay," Sept. 6, 1748, *ibid.*, A1 3306.16.
9. Cursay to [Argenson], Oct. 29, 1748, *ibid.*, A1 3306.103.
10. Puysieulx to Cursay, Nov. 3, 1748, *ibid.*, A1 3307.3.
11. Belle-Isle to Cursay, Nov. 12, 1748, *ibid.*, A1 3307.15. A day later Belle-Isle wrote to Guymont (*ibid.*, A1 3307.17) informing him of the king's decision that Richelieu should continue the Corsican negotiations he had proposed "à fin d'établir d'une manière plus solide l'authorité de la république sur les peuples de cette isle en refondant de nouveau les formes du gouvernement de manière que la république ne les traiter plus en esclaves, et y exerce sa souraineté avec justice et moderation, et qu'en même tems [*sic*.] les peuples soumis a leur souverain jouissent paisiblement de leur liberté, observent leur loix, et n'abusent pas des privileges qui leur seront accordés."
12. See Guisard's instructions from Richelieu and Chauvelin dating from November 1748 and March 1749, AG, *Arch. hist.*, A1 3307.10, 3332.119–.120, and 3332.125 bis.
13. See Courcy's correspondence with Puysieulx and his successor, François-Dominique Barberie, marquis de Saint-Contest, in AE–CP, *Corse*, Vol. III, fols. 452, 464, 482, and Vol. IV, *passim*.
14. Puysieulx to Chauvelin, April 8, 1749, and to Chauvelin and Argenson, May 13, 1749, AE–CP, *Gênes*, Vol. 126, fol. 278, and Vol. 127, fols. 74–77.

15. Belle-Isle to Richelieu, Oct. 23, 1748, in A. de Boislisle, ed., *Mémoires de Richelieu*, p. 235. Richelieu's own brief account of his mission to Genoa is found in *ibid.*, pp. 117–121.

16. Driault, *Recueil*, pp. 217–219.

17. See the "Mémoire de griefs contre M. de Cursay remis par M. Sorba, ministre de Gênes," June 27, 1749, AE–CP, *Gênes*, Vol. 127, fols. 214–217; [Puysieulx] to Cursay, June 10, Oct. 18, Nov. 4, 1749, and Feb. 17, 1750, AE–CP *Corse*, Vol. III, fols. 7–9, 132–133, 184–185, 298–299.

18. Chauvelin to Puysieulx, Jan. 9, 1751, AE–CP, *Gênes*, Vol. 130, fols. 14–15.

19. Puysieulx to Cursay, March 10 and 24, 1750, and to Belle-Isle, May 22, 1750, AE–CP, *Corse*, Vol. III, fols. 315, 322–323, 355–357.

20. AN, T 1169 [1]. This letter, a copy, bears only the date "1752." Letter "T" of the classification in the *Archives Nationales* refers to the series *Séquestre*, i.e., documents confiscated during the Revolution.

21. "La College à Sorba," March 29, 1751, and Sorba to Saint-Contest, March 4, 1752, AE–CP, *Gênes*, Vol. 130, fols. 163–166, and Vol. 131, fols. 360–363.

22. AE–CP, *Gênes*, Vol. 130, fol. 264; Vol. 131, fols. 397–398, 442–448. Saint-Contest was secretary of state for foreign affairs from Sept. 11, 1751, to his death on July 24, 1754.

23. Richelieu to .... [Saint-Contest], April 8, 1752, *ibid.*, Vol. 131, fols. 402–407; AE–CP, *Corse*, Vol. IV, fols. 138–141.

24. *Ibid.*, Vol. V, fols. 61–157 contain three copies of the *règlements* in French and Italian.

25. The Abbé de Germanes, *Histoire des révolutions de Corse, depuis ses première habitants jusqu'à nos jours*, 3 Vols. (Paris, 1771–1776), II, 153; J.-M. Jacobi, *Histoire générale*, II, 215–216; AdBR, C 2920.

26. Puysieulx to Cursay, April 2, 1751, AE–CP, *Corse*, Vol. IV, fol. 123.

27. Edmond-Jean-François Barbier, *Chronique*, IV, 420; V, 334.

28. The form for the national government was drawn up at the Consulte d'Orezza in June 1751. The constitution has been published by Pierre Lamotte, ed., "La formation du premier gouvernement corse autonome," *Corse Historique*, No. 2 (1953), 12–23.

29. Harold Acton, *The Bourbons of Naples, 1734–1825* (London, 1956), p. 93, incorrectly places Gaffori's death in the year 1755. A good discussion of the assassination and its results, as well as of Gaffori's personal qualities as a leader, is in Rossi, Bk. X, par. 25–26, pp. 75–79.

30. Jacobi, *op. cit.*, II, 220–221.

31. Quoted by F. Girolami-Cortona, *Histoire de la Corse*, pp. 335–336.

32. An extensive, though uncritical, bibliography on Pasquale Paoli is found in Carmine Starace, *Bibliografia della Corsica* (Isola del Liri, 1943), pp. 363–393.

33. Tommaseo, *Lettere*, 1–2; Philippe Marini, "La Consulte de Caccia et l'élection de Pascal Paoli, 1752–1755," *BSHNC* (April–June 1913), 65–112. For Paoli's powers, see Rossi, Bk. X, par. 46–47, pp. 136–141, and Matthieu Fontana, *La Constitution du généralat de Pascal Paoli en Corse, 1755–1769* (Paris, 1907). Fontana, however, was much too uncritical and failed to deal with any of the major criticisms of Paoli's use of power.

34. For an extensive analysis of all phases of this constitution, see *ibid.*, *passim*. Fontana makes an interesting, but not altogether convincing, case against the oft-repeated notion that Paoli was the first to apply practically Montesquieu's theory of separation of powers. The events leading to Paoli's emergence as general-in-chief, including his controversy with Matra and his first acts, are the subjects of the anonymous memoir, "Historique des événements de Corse, de 1752 à 1755," AG, *Mém. hist.*, 206 [3].

35. Acton, *op. cit.*, p. 93.

36. Neuilly's instructions, dated August 28, 1754, are in AE–CP, *Gênes*, Vol. 134, fols. 287–291, 308–317.

37. Rouillé to Neuilly, March 2 and 16, 1756, *ibid.*, Vol. 136, fols. 84, 106; "Mémoire d'instruction à M. de Pujol," March 22, 1756, *ibid.*, Vol. 136, fols. 115–117.

38. Camille Rousset, *Correspondance de Louis XV et Noailles*, II, 398.

39. Julian S. Corbett, *England in the Seven Years' War; A Study in Combined Strategy*, 2 Vols. (London, 1907), I, 91, 98.

40. Baron de Treues, "Mémoire concernant l'ile de Corse," 1756, AN, K 1225.1; "De la Corse," August 1755, AE–CP, *Corse*, Vol. VI, fols. 71–72.

41. "Mémoire sur l'ile de Corse; événements principaux de 1731 à 1769, accompagné d'une projet militaire," AG, *Mém. hist.*, 248 [1]. This is a military memoir, written apparently in 1770. Belle-Isle's information on the English plans for Corsica was correct. See Corbett, *op. cit.*, I, 129–130, 135–137, 144, 153–154.

42. AE–CP, *Corse*, Vol. VI, fols. 91–101; AE–CP, *Gênes*, Vol. 137, fols. 231–241; Driault, *Recueil*, pp. 330–335; A. de Clercq, *Recueil de traites de la France*, XV, 34–39. Gaetan de Raxis de Flassan, *Histoire de la diplomatie française*, VI, 65–72, made the treaty appear a French threat to Genoa's sovereignty; he gave insufficient consideration to the forceful wording of article V.

43. Driault, *Recueil*, p. xcviii; Louis Villat, "La Question corse," p. 363; Colonna de Cesari-Rocca and Louis Villat, *Histoire de Corse*, p. 212.

44. Rouillé to Neuilly, April 13, May 18, and Sept. 23, 1756, AE–CP, *Gênes*, Vol. 136, fols. 145, 189–191; Vol. 137, fols. 412–413.

45. "Discorse del Generale Paoli nella Consulta del 1761," Tommaseo, *Lettere*, pp. 22–23; Jacobi, *op. cit.*, II, 235. Castries, who did not be-

lieve that ordinary means were suitable for dealing with a man as "cunning" as Paoli, was in favor of assassinating the Corsican chief. His suggestion was overruled by the Maréchal de Noailles, who counseled moderation. See the Duc de Castries, *Le Maréchal de Castries, 1727–1800* (Paris, 1956), pp. 32–33.

46. *Ibid.*, pp. 31–33.

47. The Abbé Expilly, "Description de la Corse: Journal itineraire du 23 novembre 1756," Dec. 6, 1756, AG, *Mém. hist.*, 1098.13; "Éclaircissement sur la localité des places occupées par les troupes du roy en Corse: Calvi, 1757," *ibid.*, 1098.18; Germanes, *op. cit.*, II, 175–177; Castries, *op. cit.*, pp. 33–34.

48. Choiseul to Neuilly, Jan. 2, 1759, and to Belle-Isle, Jan. 3, 1759, AE–CP, *Gênes*, Vol. 141, fols. 4–6.

49. Belle-Isle to Choiseul, Jan. 5, 1759, *ibid.*, Vol. 141, fols. 7–8.

50. Choiseul to Neuilly, Jan. 9 and 23, 1759, *ibid.*, Vol. 141, fols. 13, 25; Choiseul to Sorba, Feb. 11, 1759, *ibid.*, Vol. 141, fol. 44. See also Choiseul to Neuilly May 22, 1759, *ibid.*, Vol. 141, fol. 130, where Choiseul explicitly remarked that it was on Belle-Isle's advice that he decided to leave troops at Calvi.

51. Choiseul to Neuilly, Aug. 13 and Sept. 18, 1759, *ibid.*, Vol. 141, fols. 227, 256. The military correspondence for this period described vividly the issues upon which the French and Genoese officials clashed. See, for example, AG, *Arch. hist.*, A^1 3539.10 bis,-.11,-.44, and -.56.

52. Tommaseo, *Lettere*, pp. 20–22. Paoli's vigorous protest against Genoese action is found in a proclamation, "Il supremo Consiglio di Stato del Regno di Corsica," Sept. 7, [1762], in *ibid.*, pp. 29–32.

53. Germanes, *op. cit.*, II, 181.

54. The best treatment of the religious situation in Corsica is S.-B. Casanova, *Histoire de l'église corse*. There is much information on the apostolic visitor in Rossi, Bk. X, par. 98–129, pp. 257–344; and in Paoli's letters, Tommaseo, *Lettere*, pp. 5–18 and *passim*.

55. René Boudard, *Gênes et la France*, p. 124.

56. "Mémoire d'instruction au sieur Boyer de Fonscolombe," April 18, 1762, AE–CP, *Gênes*, Vol. 144, fols. 85–89.

57. *Ibid.*, Vol. 144, fols. 85–89.

58. *Ibid.*, Vol. 144, fols. 312–337.

59. Driault, *Recueil*, pp. 336, 342. Villat argued that Choiseul promised to read Boyer's memoir; but that the minister never got around to doing so ("La Question corse," p. 364).

60. See especially Noailles' letter to Chauvelin, Sept. 15, 1753, BN, *Fonds français*, 10661, fols. 61–70, and his letters and memoirs of Feb. 5 and March 7, 1751, and July 20 and 21, 1755, in Rousset, *op. cit.*, II, pp. 304–308, 311–324, 396, 400, 404, 407.

61. See Boyer's dossier in AE, Dossiers du Personnel, Vol. 11; Louis Farges, *Recueil des instructions données aux ambassadeurs et ministres de France*, Vols. IV and V, *Pologne*. 2 Vols. (Paris, 1884–1888), II, 114; and Gabriel Hanotaux and Jean Hanoteau, *Recueil des instructions données aux ambassadeurs et ministres de France*, Vols. VI, XVII, and XX, *Rome*. 3 Vols. (Paris, 1888–1913), III, 329–331.

CHAPTER V

The Duc de Choiseul: First Approaches
to the Corsican Question

The Duc de Choiseul was, with Fleury and Vergennes, one of the three most important ministers of eighteenth-century France. Originally from a family of Lorraine, he had been trained for a military career. His marriage to Louise-Honorine Crozat, granddaughter of Louis XIV's famous financier, had brought him wealth. His ministerial position at Rome, November 1753 to January 1757, and his ambassadorial appointment at Vienna, March 1757 to November 1758, had, given him diplomatic experience. His friendship with Voltaire and other *philosophes* had placed him in the mainstream of the Enlightenment. Finally, his friendship with Madame de Pompadour, among other court figures, had given him a position of enormous power. In December 1758, he was appointed successor to the Abbé (then Cardinal) Bernis as secretary of state for foreign affairs.[1]

We have already seen that Choiseul's first actions regarding Corsica were dictated by the necessities and pressures of the Seven Years' War. After his elevation to the ministry in 1758,

Étienne-François, duc de Choiseul, 1763
(from a print in the author's possession).

he at first advised withdrawal of French troops from the island,
then, upon Belle-Isle's persuasive advice, agreed to leave one
battalion at Calvi, and finally decided to evacuate the troops
entirely because they were needed elsewhere and because their
presence on Corsica threatened to worsen relations between
France and Genoa. Choiseul's attitudes toward Genoa and
Corsica at this time in no way suggest that he intended to
aggrandize France by securing possession of the island. But
his correspondence does indicate that he had already formed

120

some ideas on the Corsican question. It was obvious to him that all the Genoese efforts to compel submission had failed. Thus he concluded that a policy of compulsion was both erroneous in conception and ineffective in execution. Something more and something different was needed, for the gravity of the Corsican problem required grave reorientation of both Genoese thought and action. As early as September 1759, Choiseul observed that Genoa could no longer hope to subdue its island rebels unless it substituted "for the manner in which it has always governed this island, an administration absolutely different." Choiseul entertained little hope that the Genoese would or could do this;[2] he understood their form of government and its weaknesses too well.

At the same time, Choiseul complained bitterly about Genoese attitudes toward France.

The principal evil regarding the troubles in Corsica lies in the administration of the republic. The Genoese have not been able to resolve it, so they have appealed to France. But hardly have French troops arrived than the Genoese have made things disagreeable by their continual jealousy and requested that [the troops] leave. Thus the Genoese will be able to look only to themselves if the rebellion makes new progress, and finally drives them from the places that they still possess in Corsica.[3]

Choiseul made it quite clear that France was through giving its assistance to such ungrateful people as the Genoese, and in February 1760 he told Neuilly that "at present" the king was no longer interested in Genoa. Neuilly was to pay particular attention to three subjects: the internal situation on Corsica; the measures that Genoa took regarding its island possession; and English enterprises in the Mediterranean against Genoa, French commerce, or the French coasts in Provence and Languedoc.[4] This letter suggests that Versailles' interest in and concern for Genoa were declining, but that its concern for Corsica was growing because the English presence in the Mediterranean constituted a serious threat to French security. For the first time since the 1740s, the focus and perspective of the French ministry was brought to bear on Corsica first and Genoa second, rather than vice versa. This change was one aspect of a general reorientation in French policy under Choiseul; from 1759 on, Choiseul directed increasing attention to and force against Great Britain.[5]

Choiseul was thus vitally concerned about what happened in Corsica after French forces left the island in 1759. From 1760 on he actively solicited answers to the problem. As the number of proposed solutions increased, he started to do what he did so well: Applying the logical and rational mind that made him such an able secretary of state for foreign affairs, war, and the navy, he began to toy with alternatives. He did not restrict himself to the "secret plan of 1735," as Louis Villat suggested.[6] Although strict adherence to a single principle may be commendable as far as personal morality is concerned, in diplomacy it courts disaster. Arthur Wilson expressed this point well when he said, writing about Cardinal Fleury, that "the unending task of statesmen is to make a choice of the means at their disposal." [7] This statement applies equally well to Choiseul. His solution to the Corsican question resulted from an astute appraisal of alternatives and from making a choice among them. His end was to attain security for France in the Mediterranean, unattainable as long as the Corsican revolt against Genoa invited intervention in the island's affairs. Yet there was a choice of means, a choice which depended on the actions of both the Genoese and the Corsicans.

The flexibility of Choiseul's position was revealed as early as the summer of 1761. In June of that year Choiseul had been told that the republic was going to ask Spain for troops to assist them in their negotiations with the Corsicans. He doubted if the news were true; in any case, he observed, if the Genoese employed the protection and aid of some other power, "it will be quite essential that they do not conduct themselves vis-à-vis the troops that will be accorded to them as they have done with regard to those of the [French] king." By the fall of 1761

Choiseul had heard that the Genoese were seeking to make other, more far-reaching, arrangements involving Corsica. "It is not probable," he stated flatly, "that the Genoese have decided to sell Corsica." But he wanted the French consul at Genoa, François Régny, to pay particular attention to this rumor and to keep him informed about any developments related to it. "You will readily judge," he cautioned Régny, "that in case the Genoese believe themselves obliged finally to renounce this island, it will not be unimportant to the king to be warned in advance of [their decision], in order that His Majesty may take in consequence the measures that he will judge the most suitable to the good of his service." [8]

The question of French control over Corsica had thus been clearly posed as an alternative solution to the Corsican question even before the Seven Years' War ended. There were substantial reasons to consider it a viable alternative because events in Europe before the war had considerably changed the pattern of alliances. The Peace of Aix-la-Chapelle had established a more permanent settlement in Italy, and after 1748 the Austrians had turned away from Italy in order to concentrate their attention upon central European affairs and their force against Frederick II of Brandenburg-Prussia. Moreover, France and Austria were allies after 1756. As a result of these changes, France's Genoese "foothold" in Italy was not as strategically important as it had been formerly. Versailles could safely consider changing one aspect of the policy that had been established in the late 1730s, a policy whereby France aided Genoa in Corsica in order to maintain its "open door" to Italy.

Yet the expanding conflict with England required from Versailles continued vigilance in order the keep the island out of the hands of another power. Here the parallels between Minorca and Corsica were particularly striking. Minorca had been of strategic importance during the Seven Years' War, especially because the British were still lodged in Gibraltar and therefore posed a definite threat to France in the Mediterranean. As the Seven Years' War expanded and British gunboats blockaded Toulon, just as they had done in the previous war, the crucial position of Minorca and the crucial problem of Corsica became even clearer. So long as France held Minorca, control over Corsica's ports would reinforce and strengthen its Mediterranean position and security. If France lost Minorca, its control of Corsica would be the only factor preventing the Mediterranean from becoming a British lake. This last possibility was very real. From March to September 1761, Choiseul was involved in protracted but unsuccessful negotiations with Britain to end the war. One of the key points in these discussions was that France would exchange Minorca for the return of the West Indian islands of Guadeloupe and Marie-Galante. On this particular bargain France and England were agreed, though their lack of agreement on other issues caused the failure of these negotiations.[9]

It is therefore significant that Choiseul's increased concern about Corsica came at precisely the time when the English menace in the Mediterranean was growing and when Choiseul himself had proposed to sacrifice control of Minorca in return for restitution of important British West Indian conquests (which in fact happened in 1763 when the Peace of Paris returned Minorca to Great Britain). But Choiseul's observations on Corsica's importance were not merely speculations about future dangers. The immediacy of the problem was vividly demonstrated during December 1761 when word reached Versailles that Paoli had made contacts with the British. According to Régny's report from Genoa, Paoli was negotiating with London for its support against Genoa and in consolidating his position with the island. In return, Paoli would provide 1,500 soldiers for the English army and cede to Great Britain control over two Corsican ports. Régny said that he received this information via Leghorn and also from the Genoese secretary of state. Versailles was visibly disturbed by this news. César-Gabriel, duc de Praslin, who had been handling the Corsican correspondence since October 1761, told Régny that this matter merited his greatest attention and that he should seek to arouse both the Genoese "vigilance and fear" over it. Three

weeks later Praslin stated the issue bluntly: "Genoa can consider Corsica lost if the English establish themselves in St.
Florent, and the Genoese Government ought to neglect nothing
in order to prevent this calamity." [10]

Yet in 1761 did resolution of the Corsican question neces-
sarily mean or require French sovereignty over the island?
René Boudard discovered a document that raises this question in the reports that the Genoese minister to Versailles,
Agostino di Sorba, sent back to Genoa in July 1760. At that
time Choiseul told Sorba that in his personal opinion the only
solution to the Corsican question was to sell the island to
France. Thereafter, Boudard reported, Choiseul drew up a
plan to appease Spain and Piedmont in case the republic did
cede Corsica to France. Sorba reported on this plan in April
1761. His report included the following phrase: "Plaisance
would then be given to the king of Sardinia and the *Infant*
[Don Philippe] would have been consoled by the grant of a
kingdom." Apparently the words "a kingdom" refer to Sardinia; thus the following changes were in Choiseul's mind:
Corsica would go to France, Plaisance to the former Sardinian
king, and Sardinia to Don Philippe. Genoa would be compensated for its loss by the restitution of five Imperial fiefs.
Boudard added, however, that Choiseul "had to modify his
views, while taking account of the Genoese fluctuations and
reserves." Moreover, Boudard insisted that Choiseul was not
so "Machiavellian" in his pursuit of the island as is often
charged; it is unjust to say that he made every effort "to lead
the republic to share his views, with the tacit assistance of
Sorba." [11]

Boudard's findings reveal several points about Choiseul's
approach to the Corsican question. They show, first, that Choiseul personally considered increasing the power of the king
of Sardinia in northern Italy. He therefore could have been
sympathetic to the general views of Boyer, though not perhaps sympathetic with Boyer's specific proposal: namely, to
give Corsica to the king of Sardinia.[12] Yet Choiseul's map-
juggling has a doubtful aspect. Surely he could not suppose

that the king of Sardinia would give up Sardinia for Plaisance, especially because it was from Sardinia that the "king" received his title. Boudard's findings suggest, secondly, that Choiseul's personal views were quite flexible. If he entertained the idea that the only solution to the Corsican question was to sell the island to France, he also realized that France had commitments to Genoa which could not easily be discarded. Those commitments had to be considered in any solution to the Corsican question. At the same time, French security in the Mediterranean had to be considered also.

A complicating factor regarding Choiseul's motives toward the Corsican question is the story told by the documents. If Choiseul had definite plans to acquire Corsica after 1761, he kept them to himself. The documents dealing with his approach to the Corsican question do not indicate that he initially planned to acquire possession of the island. Instead, they suggest that his principal objective was French possession of some strategic maritime places on Corsica. By securing control over these strategic places he would strengthen French power in the Mediterranean without totally renouncing the commitments that Versailles had made to the republic. The documents further suggest that not until subsequent developments convinced Choiseul that his limited objective could not be obtained did he broaden that objective. Not until he became certain that there would be no maritime places for France without sovereignty over the entire island did he choose sovereignty as the basis of his *politique*. Only an examination and interpretation of those documents will reveal if the story they tell is credible.

Choiseul's search for a solution to the Corsican question got off to a shaky start in 1760, the year after French forces had left the island. In reply to his active solicitation, the number of proposals increased. One of the most elaborately reasoned proposals was presented to the minister in a "Mémoire au sujet de la Corse," written in June 1760.[13] The memoir suggested that Corsica definitely merits "the ministry's" attention. The basic question was "how much these advantages [of Corsica] would be increased if the property of this state was to be joined to the kingdom of France. This idea, *thoroughly remote as it is* [italics added], can take place by a consistent piece of work: secrecy is the standard of it." Because Corsica was suitable only to certain nearby powers, the writer continued, France should not lose sight of the possibility that a convention among those powers could decide the ownership of it. In any case, Genoa risked being annihilated if the other powers remained neutral. Up to this point its policy had been to seek French assistance in regaining its maritime places. Once this had been accomplished, the republic had asked for withdrawal of the assisting forces, thus leaving the Genoese in possession of the maritime places and free to wreak their vengeance on the islanders. Meanwhile, the Corsicans were raising one generation after another in bitter hatred against the Genoese.

The memoir suggested that, because the mediation attempted in 1756 had failed, it was time to formulate a new plan. This plan should consider that Corsican affairs may develop along five possible lines: (1) Corsica will remain divided between Corsicans and Genoese: (2) The island will revert to Genoese domination, "with or without restitutions;" (3) The Corsicans may acquire complete liberty; (4) A foreign power, or a prince of the house of France, will acquire the domination of it; (5) France will acquire the sovereignty "either entirely or under the title of protection, either from the republic, which is no longer able to keep possession of it, or from the free Corsicans who have driven out the Genoese." After a detailed discussion of these five possibilities, the memoir's author endorsed the last. "The most essential object of the minister," he wrote, "is to work with some Corsicans to make [their] submission voluntary and to have them do it in such a way that it does not appear to any power, and especially to the republic, which is the most interested, that [France] has suggested it to them."

Another memoir to Choiseul, written by François-Claude, marquis de Chauvelin, in February 1760, posed different alternatives. He suggested only two means for resolving the troubles in Corsica. One of these was force, which had never been used because of its dangerous consequences. The second was by negotiation, which might succeed if the "true source of the dissensions" were attacked. In other words, "lasting calm can only be achieved by a common *rapport* between the two nations." Chauvelin then referred to his plan of pacification that was approved by the ministry in 1748. Shortly after his plan was accepted, he added, "it was decided that the object was purely military and not political. From then on I ceased to be charged with it and other arrangements, which have not had the success that was hoped for, were taken." Chauvelin concluded that there was no use going into detail on the matter until he knew Choiseul's intentions.[14]

The Chauvelin plan of 1748 involved a convention, some written *rapport,* between Corsica and Genoa. French troops would remain in the island until they were certain the agreement would be kept. Although he looked forward to future evacuation by the French forces, Chauvelin believed that France should hold certain guarantees as protection for its maritime interests. These guarantees included the maritime places, that is, the *présides* or walled cities of Calvi and Saint-Florent.[15]

The two memoirs of 1760, plus the earlier plan Chauvelin had presented in 1748, contain the central ideas that Choiseul subsequently blended into a policy of his own, one that was developed only gradually and that paid particular attention to alternative solutions. It was, in effect diplomatic *savoir faire.* Thus Choiseul's developmental diplomacy and his astute perception of differing alternative solutions lie at the root of the final political resolution of the Corsican question. Choiseul followed the implicit recommendations of the anonymous memoir of June 1760 by bargaining with both Genoa and Paoli. He followed Chauvelin's recommendations in working toward an accommodation between the two quarreling parties. This, at least, is the story told by the documents, which do not answer all the relevant questions. The documents do not say what motives lay behind this bargaining, nor do they reveal how sincere Choiseul was in working for an accommodation between the republic and its island possession.

Although Choiseul began to solicit ideas as early as 1760, he was in no position to take action until 1763 when the Seven Years' War ended and Europe was again at peace. When he finally did act, he did so in the best tradition of cloak-and-dagger diplomacy by making informal approaches to Paoli through a special agent, Joseph Meissonnier de Valcroissant, then a captain in the *Chausseurs de Fischer*. In the fall of 1763 Valcroissant was sent to Corsica to sound out Paoli about a treaty with France. He carried out his task well, and by December he and Paoli had arrived at an agreement concerning French-Corsican relations.[16]

The agreement, signed by Paoli and Valcroissant on December 9, 1763, contains eleven separate articles. The first four stipulated Corsica's obligations. The "Corsican Nation" agreed to expel the Genoese and their allies from the island and to consider all France's enemies as enemies of Corsica when the Corsican Government became consolidated. Paoli promised to turn over to France one of the maritime places *(présides)* as a guarantee of the treaty, although he gave up no economic or civil rights over that strategic place. France reserved the right to approve any treaty, offensive or defensive, peace or war made by Corsica and to establish the maximum number of warships and troops that the nation could possess. Finally, France had the right to recruit soldiers and sailors throughout the island.

Articles six through nine dealt with French obligations to the Corsicans. Article six promised French men and munitions to any of the places in Corsica that needed them during time of war, "as [Louis XV] judges it most advantageous to his interest and to those of the Corsican Nation, which will never be separated from each other." His Majesty also promised (article seven) that he would furnish 400,000 *livres* per year during four years for the establishment of two regiments of 1,100 men each, plus a 1,600,000 *livres* subsidy. Once the regiments were armed, the subsidy was to be reduced to

200,000 *livres* per year, which would be used for the maintenance of one regiment. Articles eight and nine promised the loan of eight cannons and the supply of as much powder as the king "jugera à propos proportionnée à sa générosite et à sa grandeur." Article nine ended with the proposal that His Majesty would give his royal word "to assist and support the Corsican Nation in all occasions and with all his forces [and] that His Majesty will consider it with a paternal eye just the same as he considers and treats his own subjects."

Of the two concluding articles, article ten stated that Corsica agreed to supply hostages as security for its promises. Article eleven stipulated that Louis XV would decide whether the treaty was to be kept secret or to be made public.[17]

Choiseul's first reaction to his agent's work was on the whole quite favorable. Valcroissant even received a promotion to the rank of Lieutenant-Colonel. Yet the minister did have some important comments and questions. He said that he was not able to reply directly to a letter concerning the agreement from Paoli "because a vague response signifies nothing [and] a positive response would be compromising." Obviously Choiseul did not trust Paoli with any evidence linking him personally with the negotiations. Yet he did note that the king adopted the first six articles of the proposed treaty as "the basis of a treaty *plus en forme* when circumstances permit it." Article seven required some explanation, both because of its vagueness and because "the rebels have sufficient forces at present to take Bastia [and] Saint-Florent and they do not need to raise troops for this." The request for a subsidy was not absolutely refused, although Choiseul wanted to modify its provisions. France would agree to grant 400,000 *livres* per year for four years so that Corsica could firmly establish its government. The commander of the French troops on the island would have the power to supply these sums in installments whenever they were needed. Choiseul also asked one more concession for France: In return for guns and powder furnished by the French, the king was to be allowed to extract wood products for his navy.[18] The end of the ninth article was adopted, although the question of hostages (article ten) was to be considered only when more detailed treatment was undertaken.

The attention Choiseul gave to article eleven, concerning the king's power to decide whether the treaty should be secret or public, indicates the subterfuge involved in his bargaining with Paoli. Above all, Choiseul wrote, everything in this memoir must be kept secret "because all it contains, and even M. de Valcroissant, will be disavowed if the republic of Genoa has the least knowledge of it. The General ought to realize the consequences of this."

> L'on envoye en poste M. de Valcroissant après du lui pour lui faire connaitre *tout* [*tout* is crossed out in the minute of the letter] ce qui est contenue dans ce mémoire et *les vraies intentions* du Roy et l'on compte qu'il pourra être de retour ici avec des observations et l'aquiescement du général. . . . [Italics in manuscript.] [19]

Despite the promotion Valcroissant received in consideration for his work, Choiseul's attitude toward his agent soon changed. For one thing, Valcroissant was not an astute secret agent. Word soon reached the republic that he was heaping invectives upon it and that he was advising Louis XV not to get mixed up in the Corsican affair because the islanders would soon free themselves.[20] Even more important, while Choiseul was negotiating with Paoli, he was also dealing with Genoa, and the Genoese negotiations promised quicker results with fewer risks. They seemed to promise, in effect, what became one of the key points in Choiseul's policy toward the Corsican question: greater security and greater strength for France in the Mediterranean through occupation of the *présides* on the island. It is significant that this had also been a key provision of the treaty Valcroissant negotiated with Paoli.

By the beginning of 1762 the republic was on the verge of losing what little territory was left to it in Corsica. It had tried conciliation, external force, and internal subversion;

all had failed to suppress or even to retard the growing independence movement led by Paoli. Moreover, the Corsicans had declared that they would enter into no negotiations that failed to recognize the island's independence and had sought British support for their movement. A crisis in Genoese-Corsican relations was rapidly approaching. The republic had no alternative but to solicit aid once more from the court of Versailles. In February 1762 Sorba made a formal request for French subsidies.[21]

For a moment Praslin became philosophical. "The principles and maxims of Machiavelli," he observed, "are usually peculiar opinions which he claimed to apply only to the weak powers of Italy which choose them only too often for rules of their conduct in the exercise of their authority." But Praslin did little other than listen and wait for Genoa to specify more clearly what it wanted from France. Meanwhile, during the months that followed the republic's request, Boyer and his secretary, Michel de Pinet, kept the ministry informed about Genoa's actions and apprehensions. Boyer reported that Genoa feared Sardinian designs on Finale and other fiefs belonging to the republic, to which Praslin replied that "we will not undertake to deliver them from their disquietudes in this respect, although I have reason to believe that they are by no means founded." Praslin himself read news in the *gazettes* suggesting that England wanted Corsica for one of the English king's brothers. He thought it an unlikely story but told Boyer to watch the impression that it made on the Genoese.[22]

The reason why the republic was slow in pursuing its initial request for subsidies was its internal divisions. Within the Petit Council there was a three-way division. One faction wanted simply to conserve the places held in Corsica without sending additional troops. A second faction, composed largely of young men, wanted to make a determined effort to suppress the Corsican rebels but could not agree on the means. Some of these wanted assistance from French troops; others preferred the aid of an Imperial prince. A third faction did not want to talk about Corsica at all, which Boyer interpreted to mean that they were either ready to abandon the island or to come to an agreement with another power concerning its fate. After receiving this report on Genoa's internal divisions and indecisiveness, Praslin urged Boyer to redouble his efforts to learn the republic's decision and to insinuate that it would not be prudent for it to dispose of Corsica without Louis XV's approval. "I will speak in the same sense to M. de Sorba," he added.[23]

Not until June 1763 did the Genoese finally reach a decision on what action to take. After a great deal of debate in the Petit Council, it was decided to go on the defensive and to conserve the places that were still held on the island. Even to do this, however, required outside assistance. The Petit Council debated whether it should meet Louis XV's demand that France be given St. Florent "in perpetuity" in return for his aid. But it decided on a different course of action. Early in August 1763, the Genoese Government finally "begged" France to send troops to Corsica "to conserve, reduce, and pacify this island under the republic's domination"; it asked Louis XV to fix a definite limit on the time that his forces would remain on the island.[24]

This request caused a flurry of activity in the French Government. Praslin sent Choiseul a copy of Sorba's new requests, saying that he would wait for Choiseul's reply before he made a response to Genoa. Although Choiseul was clearly determining French policy, he wrote to Sorba saying that he did not know what Louis XV had decided to do, but that when the minister of foreign affairs informed him of the king's decision he would conform to it. At about the same time Praslin wrote to Genoa to inform Michel, Boyer's secretary, from whom he had been receiving reports while Boyer was on leave in France, that he was either badly informed or had been deliberately misled into believing that the king had made any propositions regarding Corsica. All this was camouflage, for the breakthrough had finally occurred. On August 15, Praslin wrote to Boyer in

Provence telling him to return to Genoa immediately because "the state of affairs of Corsica . . . has become so perplexing and so critical" that he was needed in Genoa at once.[25]

There is no need to follow here the projects and counter-projects of the long and laborious negotiations between France and Genoa that eventually, in January 1764, led to an agreement whereby Louis XV consented to renew his subsidy to the republic and to send French troops to Corsica yet another time. However, two aspects of these negotiations deserve emphasis. First, it boded ill for French-Genoese relations that the atmosphere in which they were conducted was one of mutual suspicion. At one point Versailles submitted its proposals as an "ultimatium," and on another occasion Praslin lectured Sorba about the "indecency of the silence" with which the Genoese treated Boyer. Versailles was visibly insulted when Genoa replied in kind by asking it to "guarantee" the agreement about to be signed. The fact that the two parties agreed at all is evidence of how earnestly France was seeking to reinforce its Mediterranean security by frustrating any possible agreement between Paoli and the British. It was also evidence of Genoa's desperate condition vis-à-vis the Corsicans; at precisely this time there was every reason to believe that Paoli's Corsicans would soon drive the Genoese from St. Florent, one of the republic's remaining strongholds on the island.

Second, Versailles demanded as "an absolute condition" for renewing its aid to the Genoese that they turn over to France one of the Corsican présides. France would keep this strategic port "not by title of ownership, but as a deposit as long as His Majesty will consider it necessary or expedient for the good of his service and for the self-interest of the Genoese." This demand confirms the nature of Choiseul's intentions regarding Corsica in 1763 and 1764. He did not seek sovereignty over the island, although he did seek a measure of French control over and security in the Mediterranean through long-term possession of one of Corsica's ports. Choiseul failed in this objective because Genoa rejected it even more absolutely than Versailles had demanded it. He therefore accepted an alternative, that of temporary control over several Corsican ports, and the formal agreement between Versailles and the republic was finally signed at Compiègne on August 6, 1764.[26]

According to the so-called "Second Treaty of Compiègne," France agreed to send troops to guard Bastia, Ajaccio, Calvi, Algajola, and Saint-Florent for a period of four years. The commander of these troops had jurisdiction over crimes committed against the occupying forces and by French soldiers. Otherwise the French troops were not there to make war against the Corsicans and were not to exercise any sovereignty over civilian matters. Article twelve pledged the French commanders to work with Genoese officials "to facilitate the re-establishment of order and tranquillity in this island," and to this end they were authorized "to maintain such business as they will judge suitable with all the inhabitants of the island indistinctively, and to make known to them the interest that His Majesty takes in the pacification, on which depends the reciprocal happiness of the Sovereign and his subjects." Article fifteen affirmed Genoese neutrality, indicating that the presence of French forces in no way compromised it.[27]

Although the essential differences between this Second Treaty of Compiègne in 1764 and the First Treaty of Compiègne in 1756 were few, they were nevertheless important. Two more maritime places, Bastia and Algajola, were added to the list of places French forces would guard. Most important, the sections giving French commanders the right to conduct business with the Corsicans and to inform them of the peaceful intent of the French troops was a new stipulation. It expressed Versailles' certainty, learned from long experience and expressed frequently in letters and memoirs, that the republic and Corsica would never reach an accommodation without outside mediation. It also left a loophole for continued discussions with Paoli.

One of the immediate consequences of the Second Treaty of Compiègne was the disavowal of Valcroissant and the cancellation of his promised pension. Valcroissant protested from

Leghorn. He pleaded the damage to his honor. He recalled to Choiseul his faithful service and the many wounds he had suffered for his king. In despair he suggested that there was no recourse for him but to join the service of the king of Portugal, or Prussia, or Denmark. His efforts were in vain. Finally, in the spring of 1765, Choiseul gave him permission to enter the service of another power, so long as that power was not France's enemy. Valcroissant was mystified by this curious permission, because he knew of no actually declared enemies of France.[28] For the moment his disgrace was complete.

A second consequence of the 1764 treaty was still another expedition of French troops into the island. In December 1764, seven battalions of infantrymen and 100 artillerymen under the command of Louis-Charles-René, comte de Marbeuf, landed at Bastia. This development did not surprise Paoli, who had begun to speculate about the "imminent arrival" of French troops as early as 1762. Since that time, the rumor that the French were coming had circulated freely throughout the island. Paoli was not intimidated by the French. He was angry, because he believed that French forces in Corsica constituted an infraction of his nation's just rights. But he also believed that they had not come to wage war on the islanders and that their purpose was only to occupy and defend the *présides* still remaining to Genoa. Paoli therefore counseled moderation to his fellow countrymen. He took defensive measures to protect his government's position; otherwise he decided to wait and see what developed.[29]

When Marbeuf landed in the island, he immediately received some remonstrances from Paoli and some queries about the intentions of his government. He assured Paoli that he had come to Corsica only to act as a mediator between the republic and the Corsicans and to defend the maritime places. Paoli, who in no way desired to augment trouble between his government and Versailles, thereupon ordered his troops to raise their siege of the *présides* occupied by French forces. He allowed the French to secure provisions from the interior and agreed with Marbeuf on some rules regarding the relationships between the islanders and the French troops. The result was *una buona corrispondenza* between Paoli and the French.[30]

Because Paoli wanted to be certain of Marbeuf's intentions, he sought reassurances from higher authority. On January 5, 1765, he addressed a memoir to Choiseul requesting the reasons for the French expedition to the island.[31] The ensuing correspondence was to last for three years. Choiseul replied to Paoli's memoir on February 12. For more than a year, he informed the Corsican general, Genoa had been pressing Louis XV to act in Corsica. The king had at first refused, owing to past failures of his efforts to pacify the island. He had finally agreed, however, and had sent his agent Valcroissant to inform Paoli of his intentions. Choiseul had rejected the project that resulted from Valcroissant's interviews with Paoli, because it was a proposal that could only be acted upon when stability had been restored in the island with Genoa's consent. Stability and pacification of the island were the sole reasons why French troops had been sent, said Choiseul. Paoli should understand this clearly and should act accordingly. Above all, he should respect the presence of the French troops.[32]

Although Paoli was willing to work with Choiseul for stability within the island, he placed some requisite conditions upon any project of pacification. Such a project, he wrote, must accord with the declaration made by the *Consulte* of Casinca in 1761, which declared that Corsicans would never listen "to any proposition of accommodation with the Genoese, which, as a preliminary step, does not recognize our liberty and the independence of our government and [which] cedes to [Genoa] the smallest piece of land that it still holds" in Corsica. If the republic agrees to this condition, Paoli continued, the Corsicans "will take all proper and convenient measures that will be recommended to them by their equity and their natural moderation in order to accord to the Genoese all that they believe necessary to the glory and interests of their republic."[33]

It is quite clear that Choiseul did not like the tone of Paoli's vague letter and memoir. Not only had Paoli said very little, but he had said it in a tone of unconcealed pride. As a result, Choiseul's next communication to Paoli sounded a harsher note. On May 21, he wrote two different letters to Paoli. In one he repeated the assurance that the only reason French troops were sent to the island was to seek to procure for Corsica "the tranquillity and liberty" to which the proclamation of the *Consulte* of 1761 referred. However, Louis XV also wanted "to procure for the republic of Genoa [his] former ally, all that can be accorded to the glory and the interests of the said republic." The Corsicans, Choiseul continued, may "either wish to end the troubles while assuring a recognized and guaranteed stability to their form of government, or wish to perpetuate the troubles for some particular interests, or, finally, they have no fixed project." If the last, "humanity, the happiness of the island, and their personal tranquillity require that they form a project." If the first, there was no better time to achieve it with Louis XV's help. But if they continued the troubles, then "the king has nothing to negotiate with the Corsicans; and according to their response, in which His Majesty will distinguish perfectly the intentions of the said General and of the Nation, the king will take the measures that he will judge convenient under the circumstances." Although Louis XV did not like to threaten "so positively" the Corsican nation, he wanted it to be known that he "would take effective and prompt measures by sea and land to establish in Corsica the respect that is due his armies."

Another letter, written the same date, was of a different tone. It held out the hope of subsidies for Paoli's government after his intentions were known. It asked Paoli to send to Versailles someone he trusted to negotiate the many things that could not be treated in writing. Finally, it offered to Paoli or his brother Clemente the command of the French regiment *Royal-Corse*.[34]

These two letters gave Paoli a choice. If he cooperated with the French pacification, Corsica could hope for tranquillity and, supposedly, for liberty and independence also. Moreover, there would be some reward for Paoli himself. If he did not cooperate, the threat of force was clearly stated. Although Paoli profusely thanked Choiseul for the latter's offer of command over the *Royal-Corse,* he was compelled to refuse this position. The principle of the liberty and independence for his nation, he explained, guided all his actions and was at the time his chief concern.[35]

For the moment the negotiations floundered while Versailles was deciding what to do next. On the island there were minor troubles between the French forces and the Corsicans. Yet Versailles did not use force. Paoli was in frequent contact with Marbeuf, through whom he learned that Louis XV and Choiseul were not pleased with his actions.[36] And on March 18, 1766, Choiseul wrote directly to the Corsican chief. He reminded him that Louis XV intended to hold the maritime places for Genoa for several years, but that he did not intend to go beyond his treaty with the republic. He did not intend to wage war on Corsica; if he had to, however, he would increase his troops on the island in order to insure them the respect they deserved. In conclusion, Choiseul noted that he had been in touch with Sorba, the Genoese minister to Paris, who had indicated that the republic wanted to come in to an accommodation with the islanders. Choiseul therefore asked Paoli to submit a project for settlement indicating the Corsicans' viewpoints. He was to submit his proposals separately and to identify those to be communicated to Genoa and those for Louis XV alone.[37]

Within a month Paoli had formulated his plan for an accommodation. Pacification of the island, he wrote, must have as its basis the declaration of the *Consulte* of Casinca of 1761, which stated that the liberty and independence of Corsica must be secured and that Genoa was not to have any territory in the island. Once these stipulations were recognized, Corsica would agree to pay a tribute of 40,000 *livres* per year as compensation for the republic's financial loss and to sign with the republic both a perpetual treaty of alliance and a treaty of commerce. When the treaty was concluded, Louis XV was to agree to turn over the maritime places to the Corsican Government.[38]

Choiseul was miffed by the Corsican general's reply and by the nature of his proposals. He informed Paoli that he was instructed to communicate the latter's memoir to Genoa, but not the letter, which rather bluntly stated that the republic must give up all its rights to the island.[39] He felt compelled, however, to tell Paoli that "you always take a tone of equality between your nation and the French nation, which is indefensible." Do not do anything that will require the king to enforce obedience, Choiseul warned:

> Believe that it is as a friend and for your interest that I give you this advice, and do not force us to make a proof disagreeable to the heart of the king . . . and from which the republic will draw all the advantage, because if your conduct obliges the French troops to stay in Corsica, after the four years have ended, the king will necessarily end by espousing the *droit* of the Republic [;] and far from having achieved the good of the Corsican Nation, it will only become more unhappy for it. This letter merits all your consideration.[40]

If Choiseul was miffed by Paoli's egalitarian tone, Genoa was both angry and frightened. Having received from Choiseul some papers regarding the general's proposals, the Petit Council examined them carefully. It found the subject "displeasing." It complained of the delay in presenting Genoa with the information. It argued that, in substance, Paoli's proposals would mean complete abandonment of Genoese sovereignty, abandonment of the maritime places to the Corsicans, and "the establishment of a new sovereignty in the middle of the Mediterranean." The proposals, Sorba informed Choiseul, were unacceptable. They were formulated by an illegitimate assembly; it was astounding, he said, that such an assembly could present them in such an irrevocable tone to a court

140

whose affection for the republic was so well known. Moreover, if these proposals were accepted, they would mean the republic's ruin; and Louis XV had given his assurances that he would never agree to anything that would mean the ruination of his ally.

Genoa's complaint ended with a diatribe against the Corsicans' character, the dangers they presented to the republic, and the possible danger they might pose to France if they decided to ally with another power. The republic was resolved never to agree to a treaty with the Corsicans that gave the islanders sovereignty over the island or allowed them to hold the maritime places. Apart from that, Sorba informed Choiseul, "we are ready . . . to enter directly with the Court in any other negotiation regarding this island that is able to be more in conformity with the glory of the king, with the penetration of the ministers of His Majesty, and with the security of our republic." [41]

Once Genoa had so emphatically rejected the Corsican proposals for an accommodation, there was not much more that Paoli could do as far as negotiating with the republic was concerned. He faced a difficult dilemma. At least publicly, he professed to believe that a peaceful settlement of the island's problems under French mediation was the best solution.[42] On the other hand, he was the leader of a proud people whose hatred for their foreign governors had been developed through centuries of real and imagined wrongs, a hatred that had been strengthened by the successes and reforms of Paoli's national government. All Paoli's bargaining powers were limited by the strong national position posed in the declaration of the *Consulte* of Casinca of 1761. Thus when negotiations on that basis failed, Paoli was left with one alternative. He must prepare his country and opinion in Europe for the eventual withdrawal of French troops from the island. His preparations began in earnest early in 1767.[43]

The first thing Paoli did was to inform the Corsicans about the failure of the recent negotiations. In a declaration published for his people, he traced Corsican-French-Genoese relations from 1764. He referred to the extremities to which the Genoese had been reduced in that year, which had led to the appeal to France for help that had brought French troops to the island. The troops had come, he reported, not to wage war on Corsica, but to use the occupation as a time for reaching a solid accommodation. Then he reminded them that in May 1765, the Grand Council of the Corsican Government had proposed its terms. In rejecting them the republic had once "again rendered useless and unfruitful the mediation of His Very Christian Majesty." Noting the Corsicans' fervent desire to end the war and to maintain their liberty, he warned his followers that Genoa hoped to profit from their divisions, but that the Grand Council would issue instructions to avoid this eventuality. Concerning the French troops, Paoli issued instructions to maintain harmony with them; but at the same time he pointed to the necessity of making preparations for the eventual evacuation of the French forces, which would be the object of the *Consulte* to be convoked in May. Therefore the Corsicans must choose their representatives with care "to the end that, with unanimous consent and with the greatest effectiveness, they are able to choose while ordering the most certain means of continuing the war with fire in the assurance of ending it happily and of chasing our enemies from the kingdom entirely." [44]

Several days after this decree was published (January 1767), Paoli tried to prepare the courts of Europe, and especially France, for renewed Corsican action. In one memoir he placed the island's position before the sovereigns of Europe, explaining Genoa's rejection of Louis XV's mediation and arguing that Genoa's only title to the island came from "a barbarous and violent" invasion. In another memoir he flattered Louis XV for his peace overtures and the "impartiality" of French justice. Arguing that Genoa would have been less reluctant to negotiate if French troops had not occupied Saint-Florent, he asked Louis XV to make up for the wrong done to Corsica in this case by repaying them with "any of the means that the grandeur of [his] soul and his royal generosity will suggest to him." Finally, Paoli asked Louis XV to secure liberty for Corsica under his protection, thereby tying the interests of the Corsicans to those of his crown. In a special letter to Choiseul, Paoli besought the French minister to help in presenting this memoir to Louis XV. The Corsican general said he was certain Louis XV and his minister would not regard lightly Corsica's attachment to France. These three memoirs, written in the first month of 1767,[45] make it clear that Paoli realized that a critical and decisive stage in French-Corsican relations had been reached.

While Paoli was presenting his cause to Europe, he was at the same time taking more vigorous action against the Genoese. On the sea, his small navy saw renewed activity against Genoese shipping. In January 1767, he sent a special expeditionary force to capture the small island of Caprajá, located just off Corsica's northeastern tip.[46] If he succeeded in capturing Capraja, he would be in an even better position to attack the commerce of the Genoese. Moreover, the cannon on Capraja would allow him to breach the walls of the citadel at Bonifacio, which overlooked the narrow strip of sea between Corsica and Sardinia and which was still held by Genoese forces. In preparation for this eventuality, Paoli sent 1,000 of his troops to surround Bonifacio in March.[47]

With the collapse of the negotiations over Paoli's propositions, Choiseul had begun to put pressure on both the Genoese and the Corsicans. Through his envoy to Genoa, Boyer, he assured the Senate that French troops would be withdrawn from the island when the treaty of 1764 expired. Although the Genoese secretary of state for foreign affairs, Gerolamo Gherardi, expressed astonishment, Boyer gave him no hope for prolonged occupation after 1768. Gherardi then replied that the republic was disposed "to enter directly into a treaty with France concerning Corsica, which will . . . most conform to the glory of the king, the penetration of his minister, and the security of the republic." The republic therefore wanted to be instructed concerning French thoughts on such a treaty.[48]

Gherardi's statement did not go beyond Sorba's proposal of

September 1766. Indeed, he used almost exactly the same words Sorba had used. His reply indicated that the republic was simply willing to let France lead and that it had no policy of its own to present. Not until Paoli's maritime activity and his attack on Capraja badly frightened the republic did its representatives make a further declaration of Genoa's intentions. In March 1767, the Senate sent to Sorba a "plan" for the proposed treaty with France, which the Genoese minister was ordered to communicate to Choiseul. The plan called for the cession of all Genoese rights of sovereignty and ownership to France. Under its provisions, Corsica was never to be independent, was never to have a naval establishment or possess the maritime places, or in any other way be able to threaten the commerce and peace of the republic. Louis XV was to recover the island of Capraja for Genoa and was never to admit the shipping of the "Barbary States" to Corsican ports. Other articles stipulated the return of goods confiscated from Genoese or individual Corsicans and the freeing of prisoners; the cancellation of all Corsican concessions and privileges within the republic; the prevention of smuggling by Corsican ships flying the French flag; the confiscation by the French of all artillery in Corsica; and a guarantee by Louis XV of all Genoese possessions. Finally, there was to be some monetary compensation given to the republic by France, and Genoa was to continue to furnish salt to the island.[49]

On the same day that the Senate sent its plan to Sorba, Gherardi told Boyer much the same thing in Genoa. The republic, Gherardi explained, would let Corsica enjoy its independence as long as Genoa did not have to recognize it formally, and as long as the island never made treaties of peace or war, paid a tribute to Genoa, and sent a deputation to Genoa every ten years to pay homage to the republic. Boyer, in recounting these propositions to Choiseul, said that the threat to the island of Capraja had done more to bring the republic to negotiations than all his representations. The Genoese, he believed, really wanted to end the Corsican affair with French help.[50] Boyer did not elaborate nor indicate *how* the Corsican affair was to be ended with French help. Probably his representations had been directed toward discovering just what Sorba and Gherardi meant when, in September 1766 and January 1767, they indicated Genoa's willingness to enter into a treaty with France concerning Corsica. Through Boyer, Choiseul was applying pressure on the republic to clarify its proposition.

As soon as Choiseul received the Senate's propositions he began to put pressure on Paoli. In a long letter dated March 23, 1767, Choiseul adopted a lecturing tone. He said that the Corsican general accentuated excessively both his own efforts to establish peace and the obstinancy of the republic in refusing Corsica's proposals. States were held "by *droit* and by occupation," he told Paoli. When the latter was lost, the former remained. But if ". . . the Sovereign who has lost the occupation of his dominions by force abandons his *droit* by a treaty, nothing remains to him for ever." Thus, Choiseul concluded, Genoa was right in refusing Paoli's proposals, for it received no indemnity for its *droit*.

> If the Corsican nation desires to obtain by a treaty the abandonment of the republic's right of sovereignty without offering some compensations for the cession of this right, it is not possible to hope for any success from the negotiation, because the republic will never consent to lose voluntarily a right that cannot be taken from it and the king is not in the position of being able to force it to such a sacrifice in pure loss for itself.

Then Choiseul posed some alternative actions. If Corsica really desires peace, he continued, it must be willing to give up something. A suitable compensation would include leaving Genoa the title of King, letting it keep some places in Corsica, and giving homage to it each year. These conditions alone would lead to the abandonment of Genoese sovereignty. If they were to be accepted, France would again approach the republic for some accommodation. If not, the other alternative was a suspension of arms for ten or fifteen years. In such a situation, it would be wise to partition the maritime places, giving some to Genoa and some to Corsica. But let it be clearly understood, Choiseul remarked, that "in both measures proposed, the king, as a guarantor of the arrangement that will be made, will keep one place in the kingdom of Corsica during several years, if the first means was adopted, and during the suspension of arms, if it was the second."

Choiseul's letter to Paoli ended with a clear warning. The minister noted that he had not yet presented these terms to Genoa, although he had been instructed to present them. But if he were a Corsican, he would choose the first alternative, "because in fact it is to triumph only by obtaining without contestation and with a voluntary consent, under the mediation of a great power, a sovereignty in exchange for a few places and for a formality of homage." You and the nation must decide which to choose, Choiseul urged.

> [If neither succeeds] circumstances and time will deter-
> mine the events in Corsica, and in the same manner that
> the Corsican Nation addresses itself to all the sovereigns of
> Europe to have them judge its situation, and without doubt
> to interest them in it, it is strongly to be feared that the
> republic of Genoa will come to terms with some powers
> concerning its right of sovereignty, which is contested by
> no one, and that then the Corsican Nation, after many
> years of struggle, will find itself obliged to submit to a
> foreign authority, from which it will not cast off the yoke
> as easily as it seeks to cast off that of the republic.[51]

Choiseul's letter of March 23 to Paoli again contains his demand for French possession of one maritime place on the island. It is significant to note that this demand appeared from the beginning, when Choiseul sent Valcroissant to Corsica, and that it continued to reappear in all Choiseul's negotiations with both Genoa and Paoli. The "maritime places" referred to can best be defined as the *présides,* or the walled cities along the Corsican coast. These cities included Calvi, Bastia, Saint-Florent, Ajaccio, Algajola, and Bonifacio. Just as the power that controlled Port Mahon controlled Minorca, so too the power that controlled these walled cities controlled Corsica and the area of the Mediterranean around the island. It was even possible that control over just one of those cities, Calvi, could lead to domination over the area around Corsica.[52] Thus French possession of one maritime place in Corsica would provide security against foreign attack for the French Mediterranean coasts.

Yet the proposals Choiseul suggested to Paoli were clearly not acceptable, as the Corsican general soon made clear. Although Paoli was willing to pay homage to Genoa and to let it retain the title of king in Corsica, he could not in conscience accept the provision leaving the republic some places within the island. This, he said, would not give Genoa any compensation for its lost sovereignty. Moreover, the republic would use its possessions to disturb the peace in the island to create divisions among the people. The result would be "perpetual uneasiness." A suspension of arms would be even less satisfactory, because Genoa would have all the advantages. But Paoli did offer monetary compensation for the republic's loss of the martime places. He suggested the enfeoffment of Bonifacio for two or three years, during which time the Corsicans would pay a sum of money to Genoa as its feudal lord. During the same period, he added, he wanted French troops to occupy Bonifacio as a guarantee of the republic's good faith.[53]

Thus in June 1767, Choiseul's negotiations with Paoli were deadlocked. The fact that Choiseul was partly responsible for these conditions is suggested by both the tone and the proposals of his March 23 letter, written immediately after he had received Genoa's first definite suggestion of a treaty ceding the republic's rights over Corsica to France. Up to this point Choiseul's correspondence with Paoli had been fairly amicable and his words of caution fairly temperate. Suddenly he adopted both a lecturing and threatening tone, and presented proposals that in no way recognized the principles of the *Consulte* of Casinca of 1761, which called for recognizing Corsican liberty and, in effect, expelling Genoa from the island. Both the alternatives Choiseul proposed left Genoese forces in the island. Even worse, Paoli would have to give up an additional maritime place to the French. With "a few" of the *présides* going to Genoa and one to France, Paoli would be restricted almost entirely to the interior of the island. These restrictions so thoroughly mutilated the declaration of the *Consulte* of Casinca that Choiseul could hardly have believed them acceptable to the Corsican leader.

The change in Choiseul's attitude toward Paoli can be traced to the Genoese proposal of March 1767 which suggested that under the right circumstances they were willing to talk about ceding Corsica to France. It is, of course, possible that Choiseul never took seriously his negotiations with Paoli. Yet these negotiations constituted one way for him to achieve his objective of French security in the Mediterranean, even if making a bargain with Paoli was low on his list of priorities. What is significant is that the Genoese offered him a more interesting and less dangerous alternative for resolving the Corsican question, an alternative which had been suggested to Choiseul and which he had considered as early as 1760. Thereafter, each time a rumor or official report stated that the republic sought to make a bargain with another power regarding Corsica, the alternative of French possession of the island must have appeared more desirable. Certainly the French ministers frequently said that if Genoa considered giving up Corsica the king wanted to know of their decision immediately. Again and again they cautioned the Genoese that Louis XV had so much invested in aid to Genoa and so many interests at stake that he must be consulted first if the republic decided to end its Corsican troubles by giving up its control over the island.

The timing of Genoa's offer to discuss cession of Corsica is also significant. The offer, however vague it was and however ambiguous its wording, was made a year and a half before the treaty of 1764 was to expire and French troops were to be withdrawn from Corsica. Moreover, it was made at precisely the time when Paoli's strong nationalist stance seemed to doom both the chances for a Genoese-Corsican accommodation and the key point of all Choiseul's discussions with Paoli: namely, French possession of one or two strategic places on the Corsican coasts.

Finally, it is significant that the Genoese offer was made at a time when a rapidly growing controversy between Great Britain and Spain threatened to involve France in another Anglo-French conflict. This controversy involved possession of some one hundred islands off the southern coast of South America, known to the French as the "Malouines" islands and to English speaking peoples as the Falkland islands. The issue was whether they would be controlled by Spain or England. France was involved because Louis Antoine de Bougainville had established a French settlement on East Falkland (one of the two important islands) in 1764. Two years later Choiseul agreed to recognize Spanish claims to the islands. But by then a full scale controversy had developed between France's ally under the *pacte de famille* and the British, with Spain urging that a British settlement on West Falkland should be destroyed and with the Earl of Egmont, Great Britain's First Lord of the Admiralty, claiming that the Falkland islands were "the key to the whole Pacific Ocean." Choiseul's role in this conflict was to recommend a moderate and temperate policy for the Spanish Government.[54] Yet he was aware that his advice might not be followed, and thus France might be drawn into another war with Great Britain. If this happened, the conflict would obviously spread to the Mediterranean and jeopardize French security there if the Corsican question remained unresolved.

Considering these circumstances, it is not surprising that, after March 1767, Choiseul worked to secure a favorable solution to the Corsican question by making a bargain with the republic. But the terms of the bargain were not clear, and Genoa's resolve to rid itself of its island possession was not firm. Therefore, the other alternatives had to be kept open until Choiseul was certain that Genoa was sincere and would deliver on its offer. He had a great deal of work ahead of him when all negotiations with both Paoli and Genoa were temporarily interrupted by the expulsion of the Jesuits from Spain. He was able to use this event to clarify Genoa's terms and to strengthen its resolve.

NOTES

1. Although a definitive study of Choiseul remains to be written, there is an extensive monographic bibliography. Some of the most important studies are: Roger H. Soltau, *The Duke de Choiseul: The Lothian Essay, 1908* (London, 1909); John F. Ramsey, *Anglo-French Relations, 1763–1770: A Study of Choiseul's Foreign Policy* (Berkeley, 1939); G. P. R. James, *Eminent Foreign Statesmen,* 5 Vols. (London, 1832–1838), V, 217–239; Alfred Bourguet, *Le duc de Choiseul et l'alliance espagnole* (Paris, 1906), and *Études sur la politique étrangère du duc de Choiseul* (Paris, 1909); Pierre Calmettes, *Choiseul et Voltaire, d'après les lettres inédites de Choiseul à Voltaire* (Paris, 1902); Maurice Boutry, *Choiseul à Rome; Lettres et mémoires inédites (1754–1757)* (Paris, 1895); Louis Blart, *Les rapports de la France et de l'Espagne après le pacte de famille, jusqu'à la fin du ministère du duc de Choiseul* (Paris, 1915). Pierre Muret's study of "Choiseul, duc de Stainville, madame de Pompadour et le cardinal de Bernis (1719–1758)" remains unpublished. See BN, *Nouvelles acquisitions françaises,* 13505.
2. Choiseul to Neuilly, Sept. 18, 1759, AE–CP, *Gênes,* Vol. 141, fol. 256.
3. Choiseul to Neuilly, Feb. 19 and Dec. 29, 1760, and Jan. 20, 1761, *ibid.,* Vol. 142, fols. 63, 413; Vol. 143, fol. 8.
4. Feb. 12, 1760, *ibid.,* Vol. 142, fol. 58.
5. For the general change in Choiseul's policy, see the comments in Eric Robson's chapter on "The Seven Years' War" in *The New Cambridge Modern History,* Vol. VII, *The Old Regime, 1713–1763,* J. O. Lindsay, ed. (Cambridge, Eng., 1957), p. 475.
6. Louis Villat, "La Corse napoléonienne," p. 439; Colonna de Cesari-Rocca and Louis Villat, *Histoire de Corse,* p. 214.
7. Arthur M. Wilson, *French Foreign Policy,* p. 19.
8. Choiseul to Régny, June 30, July 28, Aug. 18, and Sept. 21, 1761, AE–CP, *Gênes,* Vol. 143, fols. 154, 182, 197, 230.
9. *Mémoire historique sur la négociation de la France et de l'Angleterre, depuis le 26 mars 1761 jusqu'au 20 septembre de la même année, avec les pièces justificatives* (Paris, 1761), pp. 79, 85–86, 113, 162, 176. This important source was reprinted by Johnson Reprint Corporation in 1966.
10. Régny to Praslin, Dec. 14, 1761, and Praslin to Régny, Dec. 29, 1761, and Jan. 19, 1762, AE–CP, *Gênes,* Vol. 143, fols. 274–275, 283; Vol.

144, fol. 17. César-Gabriel de Choiseul, duc de Praslin, was Choiseul's cousin and assumed most of the duties as secretary of state for foreign affairs when Choiseul became secretary of state for war in October 1761. Although Praslin continued to hold this office until April 1766, it was Choiseul who made foreign policy decisions during this time.

11. René Boudard, *Gênes et la France*, pp. 128–129.

12. For further evidence of Choiseul's pro-Sardinian position, see his "Mémoire justificatif presenté au roi par Choiseul in 1765," in Pierre Calmettes, ed., *Mémoires du duc de Choiseul* (Paris, 1904), p. 392. On the authenticity of Choiseul's memoirs, see Émile Bourgeois, "Une nouvelle édition des mémoires de Choiseul," *Revue Historique*, LXXXVIII (May–Aug. 1905), 83–91. Bourgeois sharply criticized Calmettes for using the word *mémoires* and for giving the appearance of unity to the pieces he collected when there was in fact no unity at all.

13. AE–CP, *Corse*, Vol. VIII, fols. 231–234. The manuscript is in the formal secretary's hand and does not bear the author's name. Nor does internal evidence reveal the author, although he was clearly well informed about Genoese-Corsican relations. It is reasonable to conclude that this memoir was written by a *commis des affaires étrangères*. Chief clerks in the various departments frequently wrote such memoirs. For an example dating from March 1755, see Richard Waddington, *Louis XV et le renversement des alliances: Préliminaires de la guerre de sept ans, 1754–1756* (Paris, 1896), p. 157.

14. AE–CP, *Corse*, Vol. VI, fol. 109. The author indicates that to his quality as *envoyé extraordinaire du roy* was added that of *plénipotentiaire*, a description that fits Chauvelin. Chauvelin was ambassador to Turin from 1753 to 1765.

15. For Chauvelin's memoir of 1748, see V. de Caraffa, ed., "Mémoires historiques sur la Corse par un officier du régiment de Picardie (1774–1777)," *BSHNC* (April–June 1889), pp. 21–22.

16. The dossier on Valcroissant in the Archives du Ministère de la Guerre does not indicate when or where he was born. It merely gives his military ranks: July 16, 1757, Second-Lieutenant; Oct. 1, 1758, Captain; 1760, *acquitté*; Feb. 1, 1764, Lieutenant-Colonel of the Dragoons with 800 livres. The series *Pensions de la Trésorerie Royale* in this same repository does not indicate that Valcroissant ever received a pension. In 1770 he was sent to Turkey as a French agent. See Didier Ozanam and Michel Antoine, eds., *Correspondance secrète du comte de Broglie*, II, 240–241.

17. AN, Q¹ 291, "Copie des articles convenus entre le général de Paoli et le sieur le colonel Meissonnier de Valcroissant, 9 décembre 1763."

18. Ever since the 1730s, the French Department of the Marine had shown great interest in exploiting the forests of Corsica for the French navy. For evidence of this interest, including some reports on

Corsican forests, see especially, AM, B [1] 60, 61; B [2] 340, 342, 389; B [3] 387, 571, 579. See also Paul W. Bamford, *Forests and French Sea Power, 1660–1789* (Toronto, 1956), p. 107.

19. AN, Q [1] 291, "Réponse aux articles ci-dessus, dictée par M. le duc de Choiseul dans son cabinet, present M. le duc de Praslin, à Meissonnier de Valcroissant, qui a dû en laisser une copie signée de sa main, restée entre celles de M. le duc de Choiseul, à Versailles, le 27 février 1764."

20. Chauvelin to Praslin, June 9, 1764, in Driault, *Recueil*, p. 363.

21. Sorba to Praslin, Feb. 7, 1762, AE–CP, *Gênes*, Vol. 144, fols. 28–31.

22. See Praslin's and Boyer's letters of Dec. 26, 1762, Jan. 4 and Feb. 8, 1763, *ibid.*, Vol. 144, fol. 417; Vol. 145, fols. 12, 37–38.

23. Boyer to Praslin (in code), Feb. 21, 1763, and Praslin to Boyer, March 22, 1763, *ibid.*, Vol. 145, fols. 43–50, 88.

24. Michel de Pinet (Boyer's secretary) to Praslin, June 27 and Aug. 1, 1763, *ibid.*, Vol. 145, fol. 210; Vol. 146, fols. 49–54.

25. See the correspondence in *ibid.*, Vol. 146, fols. 48, 92–93, 109.

26. For these negotiations, see *ibid.*, Vol. 146, fols. 102ff. Versailles' demand is stated clearly in a letter from Praslin to Boyer, Sept. 27, 1763 (fol. 187). Genoa's adamant refusal to cede France a Corsican port is in Sorba's memoir of Sept. 10, 1763 (fols. 148–153).

27. AE–CP, *Corse*, Vol. VIII, fols. 255–258; A. de Clercq, *Recueil*, XV, 87–90.

28. Valcroissant to Choiseul, Sept. 23, 1764, Dec. 27, 1764, and March 22, 1765, AN, Q [1] 291. Sometime later Valcroissant was restored to the rank of major and in 1776 he unsuccessfully petitioned for a 4,150 *arpents* concession of land in Corsica. See the "Ministerial Minute" in AN, Q [1] 298 [1].

29. See Paoli's letters to the comte Rivarola and the nun Maria Domenica Rivarola, Dec. 9, 1763, Aug. 22, 1764, Sept. 3, 1764, Sept. 15, 1764, Tommaseo, *Lettere*, pp. 34, 43, 57, 59–60. See also the "Resolutions prise par tous les principaux chefs . . . Oct. 1764," AN, Q [1] 291.

30. Paoli to the nun Rivarola, March 18, 1765, and "Consulte della 20 maggio, 1765," Tommaseo, *Lettere*, pp. 67–70. Marbeuf's reply accorded with his instructions of Sept. 27, 1764. See AG, *Arch. hist.*, A[1] 3635.17.

31. The Abbé L. Letteron, ed., "Carteggio fra Sua Eccellenza Pasquale de Paoli . . . e il Signor duca di Choiseul . . . ," *BSHNC* (Sept. 1886), 447–451. Hereafter cited as *Carteggio*.

32. *Ibid.*, pp. 451–453; Tommaseo, *Lettere*, pp. 99–100.

33. Paoli to Choiseul, March 12, 1765, *Carteggio*, pp. 459–464, and Tommaseo, *Lettere*, pp. 100–102.

34. *Carteggio*, pp. 464–467. The regiment Royal-Corse was created by an ordinance dated August 10, 1739. For a brief description of its origin

and history, see Paul-Louis Albertini and Georges Rivollet, *La Corse militaire*, pp. 61–80.

35. Paoli to Choiseul, June 17, 1765, *Carteggio*, pp. 468–471.
36. Paoli to Choiseul, Feb. 11, 1766, *ibid.*, pp. 478–481.
37. *Ibid.*, pp. 481–484.
38. Paoli to Choiseul, letter and memoir of May 18, 1766, AE–CP, *Corse*, Vol. VI, fols. 123–145; Tommaseo, *Lettere*, pp. 107–110; *Carteggio*, pp. 493–494.
39. Choiseul to Paoli, June 10, 1766, *ibid.*, pp. 506–507; Tommaseo, *Lettere*, pp. 110–111; AE–CP, *Corse*, Vol. VI, fol. 149.
40. Choiseul to Paoli, June 9, 1766, *Carteggio*, pp. 504–506.
41. Sorba to Choiseul, Sept. 6, 1766 (copy), AN, Q[1] 291.
42. Declaration, "Consulte dell'ottobre del 1764," Tommaseo, *Lettere*, pp. 60–62.
43. Buttafuoco to Choiseul, Jan. 3, 1767, AG, *Arch. hist.*, A[1] 3644.1. Matteo di Buttafuoco was at the time a colonel in the regiment Royal-Corse. He was strongly pro-French and, as will be indicated, became the liaison between Paoli and Choiseul in their last efforts to reach an understanding.
44. "Generale, e Supremo Consiglio di Stato del Regno di Corsica di Nostri Diletti Popoli, Corte di 27 (gennaio) 1767," AN, Q[1] 291.
45. The memoirs to the sovereigns of Europe and to Louis XV are dated January 31, 1767, as is Paoli's letter to Choiseul. All three are found in AN, Q[1] 291.
46. Alexandre Grassi, "La prise de Capraia (1767)," *RC*, IV (1923), 130–133; anonymous, "Relation du siège et de la prise de Capraja par les Corses . . . du 16 mars au 29 mai, 1767," AG, *Mém. hist.*, 248[1].
47. Boyer to Choiseul, Jan. 26, Feb. 23, and March 16, 1767, AE–CP, *Gênes*, Vol. 151, fols. 28–29, 45, 60–62.
48. Boyer to Choiseul, Jan. 12, 1767, *ibid.*, Vol. 151, fols. 18–19.
49. "Plan: Traduction littérale," sent to Sorba with his instructions of March 16, 1767. AN, Q[1] 291.
50. Boyer to Choiseul, March 16, 1767, AE–CP, *Gênes*, Vol. 151, fol. 63.
51. Choiseul to Paoli, March 23, 1767, *Carteggio*, pp. 523–526, and Tommaseo, *Lettere*, pp. 111–114. The reference to Paoli's interesting other powers in the island is a reference to England. In October 1765, James Boswell, the English globetrotter, came to Corsica for a five-week visit. When he left he had an interview with William Pitt about English interest in the island, all of which Choiseul knew. See Buttafuoco to Choiseul, Feb. 1, 1767, AN, Q[1] 291.
52. During the Seven Years' War French military personnel considered Calvi the only important maritime place because it alone was capable of resisting the English if they tried to seize the island. AG, *Mém. hist.*, 1098.18.

53. Paoli to Choiseul, June 3, 1767, *Carteggio,* pp. 526–532, and Tommaseo, *Lettere,* pp. 114–116.

54. On the Falkland Island crisis, see the able study by Julius Goebel, Jr., *The Struggle for the Falkland Islands: A Study in Legal and Diplomatic History* (New Haven, 1927). The quote from the Earl of Egmont is taken from Lawrence Henry Gipson, *The British Empire before the American Revolution.* Vol. XII, *The Triumphant Empire: Britain Sails into the Storm 1770–1776* (New York, 1965), p. 6. This volume contains a concise summary of the issues involved in the controversy. See also Paul Vaucher, *Recueil des instructions données aux ambassadeurs et ministres de France . . . ,* Vol. XXV–2, *Angleterre, Tome 3, 1689–1791* (Paris, 1965), pp. 431–432, 463ff.; and D. A. Winstanley, *Lord Chatham and the Whig Opposition* (Cambridge, Eng., 1912), pp. 370ff. Winstanley makes a good case for the sincerity of Choiseul's recommendations for peace and moderation.

CHAPTER VI

The Final Phase: The Duc de Choiseul
and French Acquisition of Corsica

The expulsion of the Jesuits from Spain was an event pleasing to the *philosophes* but shattering to many sincerely devout churchmen. It was not the novelty of the attack against the Jesuits that was so disturbing. For many years they had been buffeted by writers of the age. In 1757 Sebastian Joseph Cavalho, marquis de Pombal, launched his attack on them in Portugal, and the Society was expelled from that state in 1759. Then, in November 1764, the Society was suppressed in France. Whatever novelty there was in action against the Society in 1767 resulted from the fact that this time their foe was Charles III of Spain. Spain had been the real home of the Jesuits and Charles III, as its king, was supposedly the defender of the Church. Therefore, his arrest and deportation of the Spanish Jesuits had a profound impact.

Once the Jesuits had been expelled from Spain, the problem was where to send them, and it was an attempted solution to this problem that involved Corsica. Although both Pope Clement XIII (1758–1769) and the republic refused to accept any of the Jesuits in their lands on the continent,[1] Genoa did allow Spain to send some of them to Corsica. Genoa's willingness to burden the island with still another problem placed Choiseul in a dilemma. On the one hand, there was a very difficult problem of supply for the French forces guarding the *présides*. Should the Jesuits be sent there, the problem of provisions would be compounded, for, at the time, there was a quite general fear of famine in the entire island. The harvests of the preceding two years had been very small, and by 1767 both grain and meat, which were never plentiful, were in great demand. Both Marbeuf and Paoli had informed Choiseul about the growing misery of the islanders.[2]

On the other hand, France was tied to Spain by the *pacte de famille,* and it could not very easily block the entry of the Jesuits if Charles III wished it and the republic agreed. In these circumstances, Choiseul decided to let the Jesuits come to Corsica *par interim,* or until something else could be done with them. On May 11, 1767, he ordered Marbeuf to let them land without difficulties and "to follow in their regard the rules of humanity." At the same time, he informed Madrid that France would not provision the Jesuits.[3]

As he had predicted, Choiseul's problems were immediately compounded, for he soon learned that Genoa would not help in any way with the Jesuits' subsistence. On July 7, 1767, Marbeuf reported that nearly 2,600 Jesuits had arrived, and that the commanders of the Spanish ships wanted to distribute them at Calvi, Algajola, and Ajaccio. He also complained about the inaction of the Genoese officials, who refused to take charge of the Jesuits' distribution, and expressed his concern over the difficulties in caring for them and the possible impact of their arrival on the Corsican people. "It may indeed happen," he said, "that the inhabitants, in the fear of dying of hunger, will not want to receive them." [4] Shocked by this new demonstration of the republic's irresponsibility, Choiseul had a trump card left. He and Louis XV decided that the only solution was to withdraw the French forces from the places where the Jesuits had been received. Accordingly, in July the French troops were withdrawn from Calvi, Algajola, and Ajaccio. Only ten men were left at each place to act as pickets.[5]

French withdrawal from the three strategic places caused considerable alarm in Genoa, which may have been precisely what the withdrawal was designed to accomplish. The Genoese feared Paoli would seize the chance to occupy the *présides* from which the French had departed. They therefore urged Marbeuf to stop the withdrawal and informed him that they had sent a special representative to Versailles concerning this matter. Marbeuf replied only that he had his orders and must carry them out.[6]

The Genoese fears and their subsequent actions kept Boyer alarmed throughout the months of July and August. He was warned on August 3 that Genoa might try to secure Spanish troops as replacements for the French forces, for the treaty of 1764 would expire within a year. By August 17 he thought the Genoese had already attempted this, but that they had done it to get financial aid from Versailles, and they had by then renounced the project. On August 24 he had second thoughts. The Genoese, he wrote, ". . . want either subsidies, or Spanish troops to replace French troops in Corsica, or they intend (which seems more likely), to engage the king of Spain to mediate between Genoa and France." Finally, on August 31, Boyer reported with relief that Genoa had learned there would be no subsidies from the Spanish and that Charles III did not want to become involved in the Corsican question.[7] The republic's concern over Corsica was certainly very real in the summer of 1767; otherwise the Genoese might have realized at once how little success they would have in petitioning Spain for troops, subsidies, or mediation. As long as the *pacte de famille* existed, there was little chance that Spain would interfere in a venture in which its French ally was so deeply involved.

The Jesuit problem not only disturbed Genoa, but it also delayed Choiseul's response to Paoli's propositions of June 3, to which he finally replied on July 25. He cautioned Paoli that the fate of the French pickets lay in the Corsicans' hands, and that they should not interpret the limited number of French troops on the island as a sign of French weakness or irresolution. If some definitive accommodation were not arranged by the time the treaty of 1764 expired, then the Corsicans "serez les maîtres d'user de vos droits respectifs." Meanwhile, Choiseul added, "it is essential that the republic not be allowed to believe, as it has already claimed, that the king evacuated the places because he was secretly in accord with you on this possession." Concerning Paoli's proposals for an accommodation, Choiseul professed to believe that they had sound chances of success. He told Paoli that they contained a "conclusion satisfactory for all parties," and that Paoli was in a "very advantageous" situation if he would only be patient. At the same time, however, he vetoed Paoli's request that France occupy Bonifacio. Then, in a more haughty tone, he added that if France "for the general good," decided to keep some places in Corsica, it would do so without answering either to the republic or the Corsican nation. In such an eventuality, Louis XV would decide which places were the most convenient to occupy.[8]

Paoli had heard Choiseul's lectures before, and this one did not break the relationship between them; indeed, for the moment they seemed to be getting along splendidly. Paoli agreed to continue his cooperation with the French, despite their reduced numbers and the disadvantages to his nation. It would be different, he said, if Genoese troops had replaced the French, because the Genoese were incapable of neutrality. For his part, Choiseul thanked Paoli for the latter's cooperation, indicating that at a time when he had "countless difficulties to overcome, unjust reproaches to fight, and foreign [diplomatic] negotiations to destroy," Paoli's cooperation was most welcome.[9]

Yet Choiseul injected a new note in his letter of thanks, and his comment abruptly shattered the apparent harmony between Paoli and himself.

I think that for the security of an arrangement that may be made, it will be necessary that France keep two places *en propriété* in Corsica; and if the island of Capraja is the only obstacle that remains to you vis-à-vis the Genoese, I believe that *we will be able* [italics added] to sacrifice it to the republic in order to obtain its free and categorical consent to the arrangements that will assure the liberty of the Corsican Nation.[10]

Paoli did not need much intelligence to see through these phrases. They reveal that Choiseul was primarily concerned with French security and strength in the Mediterranean, and that any Genoese-Corsican accommodation would be tailored to accomplish this principal French objective. To obtain that security, Choiseul now openly said that he wanted the owner-ship of two definite places on the island. And if Capraja blocked his plans, he was perfectly willing to let the republic have it despite the loss to Corsica.

If Choiseul were now seriously considering sovereignty over the entire island, he undoubtedly would have been even more willing to let the republic have Capraja. Genoese possession of Capraja had, in fact, been one of the terms that the republic had suggested if it should cede its sovereignty over the island to France, and there is evidence that Choiseul was now quite serious about the alternative of full sovereignty. Up to the summer of 1767, his correspondence concerning the Corsican question had contained only references to French control over a strategic place on the island. His correspondence suggests that he did not want sovereignty over the entire island and that his designs were directed only toward Calvi. This was the position that Marbeuf signified in a letter to Choiseul dated June 12, 1767. "The plan established until the present time," Marbeuf wrote, "has been to consider Calvi as the only place interesting for France by the ease of the passage [from it] to Italy." [11] This statement indicates clearly that Marbeuf had been aware of only a limited interest that Choiseul had in Corsica. If Choiseul had for some time planned to acquire sovereignty over the entire island, Marbeuf was not in on the secret.

Yet Marbeuf's letter to Choiseul also indicates that in the

summer of 1767 Choiseul was changing his objectives and was taking Marbeuf into his confidence. After noting that Calvi had been Versailles' only interest, Marbeuf continued: "When the object changes, and when the affairs have a direct interest with the Nation, this place loses its advantage. It is located on a rock totally separated from the continent, . . . and for this reason it is not in the position of imposing on the Nation." Marbeuf concluded his assessment of the situation by pointing out the advantage of Bastia and the absolute necessity of possessing Saint-Florent.[12]

Additional evidence that Choiseul was either taking his officials into his confidence or was developing a broader *politique* is found in a long letter to him from Boyer. It is dated June 8, 1767, within four days of the time Marbeuf signaled the change in Versailles' object. Boyer began by thanking Choiseul for revealing to him the minister's "plan secret relativement à la Corse." [13]

Although both Marbeuf and Boyer noted a change in Choiseul's policy toward Corsica early in June 1767, neither correspondence threw much light upon Choiseul's approach to the Corsican question. First, what was the "secret plan" concerning Corsica that Choiseul revealed to his subordinates in that month? Did it involve French sovereignty over certain maritime places on the island or over the entire island? If the latter, was sovereignty over Corsica a broadening of Choiseul's original intention to acquire sovereignty over merely a few maritime places? Or was it merely taking the wraps off Choiseul's long-term project, a project he may have had from the beginning of his ministry? Finally, to what extent were Choiseul's negotiations with Paoli sincerely undertaken? These questions are especially difficult to answer because, even after Choiseul revealed his "secret plan" to his subordinates, he continued to negotiate with both the republic and Paoli. His negotiations involved certain pressures on both parties.

Ever since Genoa had first posed the possibility of ceding Corsica to France in September 1766, Choiseul had waited for more explicit information concerning its intentions. Time and again the Genoese Government vacillated and temporized. The Corsican invasion of Capraja had promised for a time to give it a firmer resolve, but by March 1767, a former Senator named Pinelli had won a majority of the Petit Council to his side against giving up the island. Choiseul was still waiting for details on the cession in August.[14] From then on Boyer began to insist on a "clear and categorical" explanation of the cession of Corsica. When French forces withdrew from Calvi and Ajaccio because of the arrival of the Jesuits, he let it be known that Genoese fears for these two places were irrelevant if their proposition for cession of the island had been made in good faith. It availed him nothing, for toward the end of August he still awaited the clear and categorical explanation.[15]

Suddenly in mid-September Boyer changed his approach. Instead of seeking a definitive answer, he informed Gerolamo Gherardi, the Genoese secretary of state, that Versailles waited *sans impatience,* for Genoa's propositions concerning the cession. Gherardi was astonished by these words, which he interpreted as indifference on the part of Versailles. But Boyer explained "the true sense of this word by making [Gherardi] realize . . . the interest that the king does not cease to take in the advantages and the tranquillity of the republic." These words, Boyer further explained, were the most natural to use in describing the French Government's request for additional information from the Genoese on the cession of Corsica to France. A short time later Boyer indicated that the Genoese wanted additional information from Sorba, who was in Paris, before they explained their plan further. This information included: whether France would agree to the "quite extraordinary condition" never to cede Corsica to another power; and whether France wanted all of the places on the island, leaving none to them, or whether France would be content with some of the places, "as if the offer that we have been made for the entire cession of Corsica did not anticipate this request." Boyer was quite confused about Genoa's actions. He believed that they either wanted to gain time, had decided not to cede the island, or wanted to discern French designs.[16]

Choiseul was not pleased by Boyer's interpretation of the words *sans impatience*. On September 28, he informed Boyer that his explanation was incorrect.

You could have indeed spared yourself the pain of seeking such an unnatural interpretation to give to the word *impatience* that you found in my dispatch . . . , and you will do well, if you find the occasion, to tell M. Gherardi that, having reflected further on the subject, you erred by modifying the meaning that is in question, and that you are strongly convinced that it ought to be taken very literally, and that in this case for us *sans impatience* is to say *avec indifference*.

For his part, Choiseul continued to urge indifference, patience and resignation throughout the first three months of 1768.[17]

While Choiseul was making the Genoese extremely nervous by his apparent indifference, he continued to negotiate with Paoli on the basis of French sovereignty over two maritime places. Choiseul's letter to Paoli of September 12, 1767, which was cited earlier, had for the first time bluntly stated his aims. Whatever course the negotiations take from now on, he had said, Versailles wanted "two places *en propriété* in Corsica." Paoli did not like the sound of that. His reply indicated only that he was not authorized to give an absolute answer, although he did suggest that Choiseul could surely find a way to secure definite advantages for France and dignity for the French crown without "ownership" of two maritime places in the island.[18]

The Corsican general's vague reply caused Choiseul to return to this subject in a letter written to Paoli in October. Affairs had reached a point, he wrote, where they could no longer be treated through letters. Therefore,

it is essential that you send M. [Matteo] de Buttafuoco here [to Fontainebleau] as soon as possible with instructions which authorize me to develop completely to him my plan concerning Corsica, and with enough knowledge of your intentions that he is able to inform me of them, and that we [can] form together a reasonable project. Without that, I repeat to you, all that we do will lead to distrust between us; and [when] the French leave Corsica, I predict to you that another nation will arrive, . . . whose dispositions will surely not be as favorable to the Corsican Nation as the dispositions of the king.

In the same letter Choiseul scolded Paoli for not explaining himself clearly regarding French interests in the island:

It is not natural for you to think that His Majesty will get involved in Corsican affairs without drawing from them some advantage. Now this advantage can be no other than that of conserving there some places useful to the navigation of his subjects: and the king thinks he renders to the Corsican Nation a great enough service by assuring to it forever its liberty and its independence, in order that it not make difficulties in approving advantages for France which are not injurious to the Nation. . . . We have arrived at a relationship in which it is no longer a question of phrases or of words; a plan must be drawn up.[19]

There are two ways to interpret this, the first of which is to take it at its face value. Interpreted thus, the letter indicates that Choiseul's bargaining with Paoli was sincere—that is, Choiseul would leave the interior of Corsica to Paoli's government so long as French security measures were definitely provided for by a plan conserving to France "some places useful to the navigation" of His Majesty's subjects. The second interpretation is that Choiseul hid from Paoli his real plan to acquire sovereignty over the entire island. He merely used diplomatic finesse to calm Paoli until he made the necessary arrangements with Genoa.

Although the latter interpretation may seem more credible, it is not supported by Choiseul's correspondence with Marbeuf which suggests that the "secret plan" Choiseul revealed in June was not a plan to secure sovereignty over Corsica. Choiseul wrote a long letter to Marbeuf on October 20, the same day he wrote to Paoli the letter just cited. The first part is concerned with the military and commercial value of Cap Corse, the finger-like projection of land jutting out from the island and pointed toward Provence. "I see [from your letter and memoir of October 10th] that it is possible and easy to occupy with success and militarily Cap Corse, the object of my views in all the Corsican affairs," Choiseul wrote. He realized there might be trouble from the Genoese, the Corsicans, and perhaps also from foreign powers, but here was where his plan entered into the discussion. "I have led the Genoese, or I believe to have led them," he continued, "to the point of offering to the king their right on the totality of Corsica, in a fashion that His Majesty finds himself free to negotiate with Paoli instead of and in place of the republic." Thus far Sorba had suggested to Choiseul the propositions he sought, but the minister believed that Sorba had done so only to discover what the French intentions were. There were possible complications in the fact that the republic was negotiating with Spain to have Spanish troops replace the French forces in the island, but Choiseul saw little hope of success in such negotiations. Other complications resulted from the fact that Paoli did not really want to accommodate himself with the Genoese and "has had the daring to refuse to France the two places in Corsica." Turin and London, moreover, were becoming alarmed about developments in the island.

In analyzing these circumstances, Choiseul decided there were three possible courses of action. The first, which he preferred, was to continue negotiations "either with the republic or with Paoli, [and] in this negotiation to endeavor to make sure of both parties or of at least one. If I succeed in having the right of the republic ceded to the king, I will be in a strong position *vis-à-vis* Paoli on the conditions that the king will prefer to accord him." Choiseul did not fear that Paoli would receive help from London or Turin, "because one will not wage war for Cap Corse." If, however, Genoa did not cede its right to the island in France's favor, and yet Paoli fell into line on the French demands, then Choiseul would remind Paoli of his proposals, would prevent Spain from aiding Genoa, and would let Paoli act as he saw fit. "At the end of four years I will effectively abandon everything, except for Cap Corse, which the king will keep in his own name without any pretext, while favoring the conquests that Paoli will be able to make on the Genoese." Although not specifically stated, the letter implies that it was in view of this plan that Choiseul had asked Paoli to send Buttafuoco to Fontainebleau for consultation on Corsican affairs.

Choiseul naturally faced the possibility that his preferred plan would fail. As an astute diplomat, he had two alternative plans formulated. The first was to occupy Bastia and Saint-Florent, thus giving France control of Cap Corse, without further negotiation. The second alternative was to leave the island when the 1764 treaty expired, with the understanding that if war broke out "we would again seize these two places for our utility." If the negotiations did not bring results in six months, then the king would decide between these two alternatives, Choiseul concluded. As an afterthought, he notified Marbeuf that Spain had asked for asylum for two hundred Jesuits coming from America. Sooner or later, he added, the Jesuits "will leave or perish from misery. But we are not able to quarrel with Spain for this object, especially while having the project of preventing it from sending troops to Corsica." Choiseul much preferred, he said, to have Jesuits in Corsica rather than Spanish battalions.[20]

This lengthy letter to Marbeuf may be another maneuver in Choiseul's diplomatic finesse. On the other hand, it may reveal that as late as October 1767 Choiseul did not definitely intend sovereignty over Corsica, but that he was still toying with alternatives. There are arguments for both interpretations. As to the first, it is possible to argue that some references within the letter cast suspicion upon it. Such is the case with Choiseul's plan to prevent Spain from aiding Genoa and his preference for Spanish Jesuits rather than Spanish battalions in Corsica. The danger that Spain would oppose French acquisition of the island was hardly very great, especially after France had given Louisiana to Spain in 1763. The letter is also suspect for the absence of any reference to French acquisition of the island which had certainly been a distinct possibility ever since the republic first suggested cession. Thus Choiseul's alternatives may have been merely a cover for his strong acquisitive intentions, which were all the stronger because he had so recently been forced to renounce France's empire in America. He may merely have given the impression that he was considering the alternatives to acquisition. Instead of actually toying with alternatives, he may have been toying with both Paoli and the Genoese.

Choiseul was certainly capable of such diplomatic cunning; yet capability does not prove actuality. Thus it is possible that as late as October 1767 he was actually considering alternatives to complete sovereignty; a number of arguments support this interpretation. First, as has been indicated, there was the "secret plan" regarding Corsica that was revealed to Marbeuf and Boyer in June 1767. The minister's long letter of October 20 to Marbeuf does not indicate, however, that his plan called for acquisition of the island. It suggests, instead, that all Choiseul's interests in the island dealt with the *présides* of Bastia and Saint-Florent. Choiseul's correspondence with Paoli supports this supposition, for the two places on the island that Choiseul demanded from Paoli were undoubtedly these two cities.

Secondly, there were advantages for France in sovereignty over these two maritime places, which would give France control of Cap Corse, whereas there were some real disadvantages in sovereignty over the entire island. If French security in the Mediterranean could perhaps be achieved by the limited sovereignty over Bastia and Saint-Florent, it would be advantageous for France not to have to bear the entire costs of governing and administering Corsica. Another advantage from limited sovereignty, as Choiseul clearly indicated, was that no one would go to war over Cap Corse, the clear implication being that war might break out if France secured sovereignty over the entire island. This point is given additional force by the fact that in 1767 Choiseul was not ready for war. "Political affairs," he had written in 1765, "must be managed in a fashion that the war does not take place earlier than 1769." At that time he did not know whether war could be prevented until 1769, but he believed it necessary to use all available efforts in avoiding conflicts that might lead to war.[21]

A third argument suggesting that Choiseul sincerely considered limited sovereignty a viable alternative is found in his admission that if he failed to secure control of Cap Corse by treaty, he proposed either to occupy it without further negotiations or to leave Corsica in 1768 and seize Cap Corse when war broke out. If he intended full sovereignty over Corsica, it is certainly possible that he did not take either Marbeuf or Boyer into his confidence, as the practice of hiding real intentions from diplomatic representatives was a common feature of eighteenth-century French diplomacy. But would he have revealed to his subordinates his plans for such unmitigated territorial rapacity as the seizure to which he referred and yet not reveal to them his plans for securing possession of the whole island through the more normal diplomatic means of a treaty? If his apparent quest for sovereignty over a limited number of places in Corsica were only a pose for posterity, would he have revealed to posterity such a damaging alternative as outright seizure of certain strategic places?

If the foregoing arguments are correct, they indicate that in the fall of 1767 Choiseul sought temporary sovereignty over Corsica, which was to be accorded by Genoa and which was intended only as a means to circumvent Versailles' numerous guarantees of its Genoese ally's possessions. After that had been accomplished and the king's "honor" had been preserved, Choiseul intended to negotiate with Paoli concerning the *présides*. These strategic places were, in any case, a must for French security in the Mediterranean. If Choiseul could gain them by negotiation, he could achieve his objective and, at the same time, avoid the danger of a conflict with Paoli's Corsicans and with other European states which were interested in Corsica's fate.

The limited nature of Choiseul's intentions regarding Corsica and the sincerity of his negotiations with Paoli cannot definitely be proved. The kind of security Choiseul demanded involved Paoli's willingness to partition his island nation, and that Paoli was unwilling to do. Thus Choiseul never reached an agreement with Paoli. Following the minister's earlier request, Buttafuoco was sent to France in December 1767. He brought with him a plan for a treaty between France and Corsica, which he presented to Choiseul on January 4, 1768. The plan suggested that only with French consent could the republic acquire another power's troops to hold its island kingdom. Deprived of this, Genoa could only cede the island to France. Once this was accomplished, France would give the places it then held to Paoli's government, would grant freedom and independence to the island, and would persuade other powers to recognize this independence. Corsica would give France "protection," would allow military occupation of Bastia and Saint-Florent and would ally with the Bourbon family if Louis XV so desired.[22]

Choiseul replied to the plan within two days. Still giving the impression that he was weighing alternatives, he suggested that three things might happen: Genoa might cede Corsica to France; it might treat with the islanders under French mediation; or it might try to establish its rights and give up all thoughts about an accommodation. If the third possibility developed, Genoa would need another power's assistance, in which case France would have nothing to say about the matter. (This statement was plainly untrue if, as Choiseul told Marbeuf, he would prevent Spain from giving aid to the republic.) If the republic chose the second alternative, France would keep two places *en propriété* as a condition for executing the mediation. If the first possibility occurred, France would treat directly with Corsica and would assure the island its liberty and independence. In return for this protecion, and as compensation for conditions the republic would ask, France would "irrevocably" keep Bastia and Saint-Florent, with full sovereignty over Cap Corse. A line drawn between Bastia and Saint-Florent would mark the limits of the French possession. This article, Choiseul warned, is a *sine qua non,* for Louis XV "is tired of guarding these places for other powers. Thus either the king's troops remain in the two places of Corsica which I have indicated to you, as in places belonging to the king, or all His Majesty's troops will evacuate Corsica, and will hand it over to its future destiny as soon as the time for the evacuation specified in the treaty made with the Genoese [in 1764] has arrived." It would be possible, Choiseul threatened, for the king to buy these places from Genoa, which would agree provided France helped restore its power in the rest of the island. The Corsican nation should therefore not cause trouble over the ownership of these places, but should "put itself entirely at the king's disposition." [23]

In all Choiseul's correspondence with Genoa, there had been no mention of a sale of Cap Corse to France if Versailles would help the republic to bring the rest of the island to submission. He was clearly putting pressure on Paoli and in the process was escalating his demands. In March 1767 he had told Paoli that France wanted one of the *présides.* In September he had demanded two places *en propriété.* But if Paoli did not act quickly, he said in January 1768, Genoa might cede Corsica to France. If this happened Versailles might still negotiate with Paoli, but its price for protection of the general's Corsican government would be Bastia, Saint-Florent, and all of Cap Corse. On the other hand, the French might bargain with Genoa instead and help it to suppress the Corsican rebels in return for the two places that Paoli was so reluctant to give up. The point was shockingly clear: Paoli would lose something no matter how the negotiations ended; but he would lose less if he came to terms now.

The choice before Paoli early in 1768 was extremely difficult. If he followed Choiseul's plan, the rewards were enticing for they included Corsican independence under French protection. Yet the price was high; it was in fact too high for Paoli because it most certainly would mean his dismissal as the Corsican chief. Already some of the features of the national-democratic state were in evidence. Paoli's office was an elective office which depended on his ability to please the majority of his people. Therefore, should he accede to the loss of a portion of his nation, he would stand convicted of betraying all that nation had stood for and all that had been represented by its most solemn declaration at Casinca in 1761. Moreover, the price was too high for the Corsican nation itself. A country as poor as Corsica could not afford to lose its most important cities and its northern extremity. Versailles was still acting on the principle of allegiance to a king as the symbol of nationalism, a nationalism that could change as the allegiance changed. But as early as the 1760s the Corsicans were posing new nationalistic symbols.

For these reasons, Paoli naturally refused Choiseul's terms. Stating his arguments cogently, the general asserted that it was natural for France to want some advantages, but must it obtain those advantages by the ruin of Corsica? He again referred to the principles of *Consulte* of Casinca of 1761. He none too subtly suggested that other powers, especially London and Turin, were interested in the fate of the island, and he pointed to his good faith in all the negotiations. Finally, he offered to France a treaty of perpetual alliance in peace and war, a treaty binding Corsica to all French objectives, and an association with the *pacte de famille*. More he would not and could not offer, for to do so would be to betray his people.[24]

In presenting Paoli's response to Choiseul, Buttafuoco pointed to France's image of neutrality and impartiality. This image, he argued, would be destroyed if Versailles demanded Bastia and Saint-Florent. He suggested that France needed the Corsicans' loyalty, for together they could control the Mediterranean. But if Versailles demanded sovereignty over the maritime places, it would have to use force to obtain it. He noted that French sovereignty in the island would drastically upset the balance of power and would bring into play the interests

170

of other powers. Finally, he argued that the people of Cap Corse were especially noted for their patriotism and their love of liberty. There would be serious trouble if Versailles tried to enforce its sovereignty over such people. To avoid this trouble, Buttafuoco again proposed the plan of a military guard over the maritime places. France would be paid for its help by Corsican allegiance to its interests and by its predominant influence in the island.[25]

Paoli's and Buttafuoco's objections, appeals, and threats availed them nothing, and by the end of February 1768 the negotiation with Paoli was finished. Both sides expressed disappointment that no agreement had been reached, but all was over except the formal notes of regret. On March 8, Choiseul reported to the *Comité* that "he did not consider it convenient to continue the negotiations with Paoli." [26] Even had he been sincere in his negotiations with the Corsican general, he was clearly not a person who would content himself with vague promises of influence within the island. This is the reason suggested by the documents for the failure of Choiseul's negotiations with Paoli. There was an even more basic reason why those negotiations failed: They ran afoul of two later developments of the western world, nationalism and democracy. Choiseul naturally did not recognize these two concepts that were formulated later during the American and French revolutions. Of course, a third explanation is possible: that he never intended his negotiations to succeed because from the moment he became secretary of state for foreign affairs he worked to add Corsica to the crown of France. In any case, at the time Choiseul had little chance to mourn the breakdown of these negotiations. As his dealings with the Corsican general collapsed, he was succeeding in his negotiations with the republic.

From the beginning of 1768 there was in Genoa "la plus grand fermentation" over the Corsican question. Loss of the island of Capraja, fear for Bonifacio, and Buttafuoco's trip to Paris for consultation with Choiseul were the factors that most disturbed the Genoese and finally convinced them that the question needed their concerted attention. In January several meetings of the Petit Council were held to discuss the problem. It was particularly difficult to resolve because the Genoese were divided into four parties. Some wanted to use French forces to help Genoa conquer the Corsicans. Others preferred to wait for a more favorable time and try to reach an agreement with the islanders without foreign mediation. Still others thought that for the moment they should weakly oppose Paoli and wait until the republic was in a position to take stronger action. Finally, the fourth party wanted to continue the mediation with French help.[27]

The doge at the time was Marcello di Durazzo, who had been elected early in 1767. He was an ardent patriot and republican who believed that the republic needed outside help and that only France could provide the kind it required. At the same time, he was particularly concerned over the possibility that Corsica would fall into French hands without stipulations guarding Genoese interests. Therefore, late in February 1768 he proposed to the Petit Council a resolution ceding the island to France. The resolution passed by a two-thirds majority, over the protests of a minority who contended that the required majority was four-fifths, not two-thirds. The constitutional problem was circumvented by the explanation that the proposal had been discussed in 1767, was therefore not a new subject, and thus needed only a two-thirds majority to pass.[28] The plan for cession of the island to France was almost exactly like the one proposed in March 1767.[29]

In reporting these proposals to the *Comité* on March 8, Choiseul said that only three alternatives were possible: accept, refuse, or modify. He preferred not to advise on which alternative to choose, but he did comment on what action not to take. The Genoese policy, he reported, was one of revenge against Corsica, a policy that would be fulfilled if Louis XV agreed to subjugate the islanders by force. Therefore, the more the Genoese pressed Versailles about the urgent nature of these proposals, the more Choiseul believed they should not be accepted entirely. France's chief interest was making certain that Corsica did not fall into the hands of the English. Therefore, France must occupy the ports of the island either by an agreement with the nationals or by force.[30]

Choiseul's comments to the *Comité* were reflected in Louis XV's "Réponse . . . au plan proposé par la républic de Gênes le 3 mars 1768," which was sent to Boyer on March 16.[31] The king's reply began with a general statement of the professed French policy:

> The king has never thought of uniting the island of Corsica to the domain of his kingdom, and His Majesty does not believe that this union can be useful to his crown. The king's views have always been directed toward an accommodation between the republic and the Corsican Nation.

This accommodation, Louis XV's reply continued, no longer seemed possible because such great differences separated the republic and the Corsicans. To subjugate the islanders as Genoa would like them subjugated would mean the use of force; but it was obvious that the use of force and the continued control of the islanders "would be very onerous to the finances of His Majesty, who will not be compensated for it by the sovereignty of such a poor island." In these circumstances, the *Réponse* continued, it is not possible to accept the cession of the island with its attendant conditions. The king was willing to procure for Genoa the benefits it desired through the island's cession, but he did not wish sovereignty over the island, "the domain of which is useless to him and could be very onerous to him."

Therefore, Louis XV proposed: (1) He would occupy Bastia, Saint-Florent, Calvi, Ajaccio, and Algajola, *en toute souveraineté* as recompense for the expenses he had incurred by conserving them to the republic. (2) These places were to be returned to Genoa when it paid France the sums spent in their conservation. (3) Any agreement made with the Corsicans relative to these places would be done with Genoa's consent. (4) If in the future the interior of the island submitted to Louis

XV, it would be held under the same conditions as those cover-
ing the maritime places. (5) The island of Capraja would be
returned to Genoa, but not before 1771. (6) The king would
not positively deny Barbary ships entrance to Corsican ports
because of his treaties with the Barbary powers. He would,
however, make certain that they did not trouble the republic,
"autant qu'il sera possible." (7) The king alone would decide
if confiscated goods were to be returned to Genoese and to
individual Corsicans. (8) Louis XV agreed that Corsicans would
lose all their privileges in Genoa. The concluding five articles
dealt with a perpetual guarantee of Genoa's possessions, the
exercise of police powers and justice in the king's name, prevention of smuggling under the French flag, and disposition of
the artillery on the island. One article stipulated that the
French, and not Genoa, would furnish salt to the island.
Finally, the king wanted to know Genoa's intentions by May,
so that he could make "the preparations necessary for the ship-
ment of troops and [for] avoiding the commotion that such
a negotiation may produce in the cabinets of Europe." There
was no mention of a sum of money to be paid to the republic.

Boyer presented this *Réponse,* or, as he called it, "Choiseul's
contre-projet," to Gherardi in Genoa on March 28. The Genoese minister could not reply to it because he lacked the authority, but Boyer thought that Gherardi was favorably impressed. The agreement was nearly finished, with only the
question of the sum of money to be paid to Genoa left to
determine. This last provision was worked out by mid-May,
and the definitive treaty was signed in Paris on May 15. Boyer
signed the ratification in Genoa on May 31.[32]

In its final form the treaty was almost exactly the same as
Choiseul and Sorba had worked it out; it constituted a fusion
of Sorba's plan of March 1768 with Choiseul's *contre-projet*.
Louis XV did agree, other treaty terms to the contrary not-
withstanding, to keep Barbary ships out of French-controlled
Corsican ports except when they were in trouble. He also
agreed to restore to their owners goods confiscated by the Corsicans. In one separate and secret article, he consented never to

abandon the places scheduled to be occupied by French forces to the Corsicans or to a third power. A second secret article stipulated that France would pay the republic 200,000 livres per year for ten years, as compensation for arrears of subsidies granted before 1764 and as a mark of the king's "sincere friendship."

The most controversial article of the treaty has been article IV. In this article Louis XV agreed "to conserve under his authority and his domination all the parts of Corsica that will be occupied by his troops until the time Genoa asks from France the restitution of them and the request for which is made in the form of repaying the expenses that the actual expedition of the troops and the cost of their maintenance may occasion." In view of this stipulation, it is possible to argue that Genoa "pawned" the island rather than sold it to France. Yet it is generally agreed that this article made the cession of the island appear provisional and was inserted in the treaty to camouflage from foreign powers and from the sensitive Genoese the permanent nature of French sovereignty. The decisive factor, of course, was the republic's inability to repay the expenses of French occupation. In any case, whether the republic sold or simply pawned its island possession is merely a fruitless academic argument for the effect was the same. Genoa had given up its troubled and troubling Mediterranean possession. Relieved of their burden, the Genoese very quickly began to think about the economic rejuvenation of their republic.[33]

Thus the political-diplomatic phase of the Corsican question was closed. Choiseul had won for France a new possession, the last addition acquired under the Old Regime. Moreover, the "solution" to the Corsican question found by Choiseul consisted in annexation of the island without the necessity of allowing other, neighboring powers, who were also more or less interested in Corsica, the benefit of claiming or obtaining "compensations." The treaty that ceded Corsica to France was of such a nature that it avoided the thorny question of compensations. It should be added, however, that in this case compensations were not so necessary to balance the acquisition of a power that had borne losses of the magnitude of those sustained by France at the Peace of Paris of 1763. Choiseul's successful "solution" to the Corsican question was prepared by French losses in the Seven Years' War and by the peace that followed the disasters of that war.

As to why Choiseul had won Corsica for France, there are two possible answers. The answer given by documents in the French ministerial archives and the National Archives suggests that Choiseul was constantly preoccupied with the Corsican *présides,* which would gain for France additional security in the Mediterranean. Those documents suggest that Choiseul negotiated with Paoli to leave the Corsican government control over the island's interior. They suggest, finally, that when Choiseul's negotiations with Paoli failed, he adopted a policy of sovereignty over the entire island. It was a policy that meant added expense in payment to Genoa and in administering the island. It was also a policy that posed the danger of war with England over Corsica's acquisition. Choiseul accepted the expense and the danger of war because France otherwise would have received no security in Corsica. In fact, France ran the risk of being edged out of the island entirely. Another war between France and England was bound to occur anyway, in preparation for which Choiseul had been making naval and military reforms. To have been squeezed out of Corsica on the eve of such a war would have invited a Mediterranean disaster for France possibly greater than that of the Seven Years' War. The danger of such a disaster was particularly great precisely because, after 1763, France no longer controlled Minorca.

The second answer to why Choiseul acquired Corsica is considerably different. It is perhaps more speculative than the former, because it has less documentary evidence to support it. It is, rather, based on a different interpretation of the documents that tell the story of Choiseul's quest for the *présides.* This second answer suggests that from the beginning of his ministry Choiseul worked to acquire the island. His subordinates were not informed of the nature of his ambitions.

He cautiously dealt with Paoli to keep Corsica pacified, but he never really intended to pursue his bargaining with the Corsican general. At the same time, Choiseul led Genoa to the position where it voluntarily gave up its sovereignty over the island. He used a variety of means to bring the republic around to his viewpoint. He bargained with Paoli, actually withdrew most of the French troops from the *présides*, and invited one of Paoli's representatives to Versailles. All these actions were designed to frighten the Genoese into giving up their possession of Corsica. It is, in short, a story of penetrating diplomatic *savoir faire* and of secret diplomacy in the best tradition of the eighteenth or any other century.[34]

Whichever interpretation is the most credible depends largely on a general assessment of Choiseul and of the policies he pursued. John Fraser Ramsey suggested that Choiseul's general policy after 1763 was based on the idea that William Pitt would start a war with France as soon as possible. For this eventuality Choiseul prepared by trying to prevent England from building a northern coalition with Sweden and Russia, and by making every effort to maintain "the System of the South," which included Spain, the Two Sicilies, the Austrian Hapsburgs, and France.[35]

Corsica clearly fit nicely into Choiseul's "System of the South." In fact, a Corsica in English hands would weaken the entire system. Yet did French security in Corsica require sovereignty over the entire island? Possibly it did not, especially if French forces were securely established in Cap Corse, Bastia, and Saint-Florent. Herein lies the critical question: Would Choiseul have been contented with sovereignty over the northern extremity of the island? The French archives offer no clear line for Choiseul's thinking on this question. Just as the key to Minorca was Port Mahon, so the key to Corsica was Cap Corse, with Bastia and Saint-Florent. This suggests that Choiseul could have gained security for France in the area around Corsica through possession of the dominant and dominating part of the island.

Yet the parallel between Minorca and Corsica is not entirely apt. The former island did not have a rebellious population and a nationalist movement similar to that on Corsica. Thus Choiseul could never have been certain of a secure establishment in the northern extremity of Corsica while Paoli continued to dominate the interior. Surely forty years of rebellion pointed to a clear moral of the Corsican question. So long as rebellion in the island continued, it invited outside intervention. Outside intervention meant insecurity for France in the Mediterranean. Thus the key to the Corsican question was not merely French occupation of the *présides*. It was, instead, filling the political vacuum within the island. That objective required French control over all Corsica at one time or another. Even if Choiseul would have been contented with French possession of the *présides* in 1767, sooner or later France would have had to acquire full sovereignty over the entire island. Only full sovereignty would have brought France the Mediterranean security that Versailles so obviously wanted and, as past experience had shown, so desperately needed.

It is therefore probable that Choiseul believed from the beginning of his ministry that the only real solution to the Corsican question was for the republic to sell it to France. Yet events as much as design accounted for the fact that this sale took place in 1768 rather than later, and the critical event was Paoli's inability to make the kind of bargain that Choiseul demanded. The irony of the Corsican question was that forty years of revolt for liberty and independence from Genoa eventually created the kind of atmosphere that meant the loss of those objectives when they might have been secured through negotiations with Versailles. The prospect of limited liberty and limited independence, which Paoli could not accept, came face to face with the prospect of limited security and limited power for France in the Mediterranean, which Choiseul could not accept. The result was another chapter in "The Tragic History of Corsica."

Choiseul's own assessment of his acquisition of Corsica provides the key to his reasoning, although it simplifies the agility of his approach to the problem. Before his fall from power in December 1770, Choiseul presented to Louis XV a memoir defending his ministry. Included in this memoir was an assessment of Corsica's value to France and a defense of Choiseul's acquisition of the island. The English, Choiseul argued, had been more fully aware of Corsica's potential than had France. The English realized that it provided important support for French commerce in the Levant and that it would procure for Louis XV "an easy way to dominate all the shores of Italy." Fortunately, Choiseul had been equally interested, for he believed that not only would possession of Corsica accomplish these objectives, but that possession would make France and Spain the dominant powers in the Mediterranean. For these reasons Choiseul acted to secure the island. The English never really knew what happened, he claimed. "Corsica was under the domination of Your Majesty before the English had the time to think of the means to oppose it." [36] Choiseul might have added, as a later scholar did, that the minister's ability to act so swiftly in securing the island before England could take preventive action was related to his restoration of the French navy.[37] He can perhaps be pardoned, writing as he was in a *mémoire justificative,* for not emphasizing the fact that France had to conquer Corsica from Pasquale Paoli and that this conquest, which took two years, cost France both in monetary terms and in *gloire.*

NOTES

1. François Rousseau, *Règne de Charles III d'Espagne, 1759–1788,* 2 Vols. (Paris, 1907), I, 236–237.
2. Marbeuf to Choiseul, July 29, 1766, AG, *Arch. hist.,* A¹ 3638.82; Paoli to Choiseul, June 7, 1767, *ibid.,* A¹ 3644.48.
3. Choiseul to Marbeuf, AE–CP, *Gênes,* Vol. 151, fols. 95–96.
4. Marbeuf to Choiseul, AG, *Arch. hist.,* A¹ 3644.58. In July 1768, 800 more Jesuits arrived in Corsica. Marbeuf to Choiseul, July 14, 1768, *ibid.,* A¹ 3647.17.
5. Marbeuf to Choiseul, July 2, 7, and 21, 1767, *ibid.,* A¹ 3644.55, -.58, -.60.
6. Marbeuf to Choiseul, July 21, 1767, *ibid.,* A¹ 3644.60.

7. See the correspondence between Boyer and Choiseul on Aug. 3, 17, 24, and 31, 1767, AE–CP, *Gênes*, Vol. 151, fols. 208, 221, 237, 244–245.

8. Choiseul to Paoli, July 25, 1767, *Carteggio*, pp. 534–536; Tommaseo, *Lettere*, pp. 116–118.

9. Paoli to Choiseul, August 5, 1767, *Carteggio*, pp. 536–538; Choiseul to Paoli, Sept. 12, 1767, *ibid.*, pp. 539–540, and Tommaseo, *Lettere*, pp. 118–119.

10. Choiseul to Paoli, Sept. 12, 1767, *Carteggio*, pp. 539–540, and Tommaseo, *Lettere*, pp. 118–119.

11. AG, *Arch. hist.*, A¹ 3644.50.

12. *Ibid.*, A¹ 3644.50.

13. AN, Q ¹ 291. Although the letter is not signed, internal evidence reveals the author to be Boyer. It is written from Genoa and refers to the author's dispatches concerning information communicated to him by Gherardi, the Genoese secretary of state for foreign affairs.

14. Boyer to Choiseul, March 23 and Aug. 3, 1767, AE–CP, *Gênes*, Vol. 151, fols. 67–69, 208.

15. Boyer to Choiseul, Aug. 3, 17, 24, 31, and Sept. 7, 1767, *ibid.*, Vol. 151, fols. 208, 221, 237, 243–244, 249.

16. Boyer to Choiseul, Sept. 14 and 21, 1767, *ibid.*, Vol. 151, fols. 254–256, 258–259.

17. Choiseul to Boyer, Sept. 28, 1767, Jan. 1, Feb. 9, and March 1, 1768, *ibid.*, Vol. 151, fol. 263; Vol. 152, fols. 17, 31, 46.

18. Paoli to Choiseul, Sept. 24, 1767, *Carteggio*, pp. 541–544.

19. Choiseul to Paoli, Oct. 20, 1767, *ibid.*, pp. 544–546; AE–CP, *Gênes*. Vol. 151, fol. 284.

20. Choiseul to Marbeuf, Oct. 20, 1767, *ibid.*, Vol. 151, fols. 281–283.

21. "Mémoire justificatif . . . 1765," in Choiseul, *Mémoires*, p. 394.

22. Buttafuoco to Choiseul, Jan. 4, 1768, *Carteggio*, p. 566. See also the "Projet d'un traité entre la France et les Corses," AE–CP, *Corse*, Vol. VIII, fol. 276. Someone has written the date "vers 1767" on this document; but it is clearly the treaty proposed by Buttafuoco in January 1768.

23. Choiseul to Buttafuoco, Jan. 6, 1768 (copy), *Carteggio*, pp. 567–569, and Tommaseo, *Lettere*, pp. 121–123. Tommaseo incorrectly dated this letter October 6, 1768.

24. Paoli to Buttafuoco, memoir and letter, Feb. 5, 1768, *Carteggio*, pp. 569–579, and Tommaseo, *Lettere*, pp. 128–129.

25. Buttafuoco to Choiseul, letter and memoir, Feb. 28, 1768, *Carteggio*, pp. 582–589.

26. "Corse, du 8 mars 1768," AE–CP, *Corse*, Vol. VI, fol. 313. This document contains notes on Choiseul's report to the *Comité*. The *Comité* was a council established by Cardinal Fleury to study state questions. The Marquis d'Argenson considered it a *petaudière*, i.e., a bear-

garden or a noisy and disorderly assembly. [Cited by H. Carré, *Le Règne de Louis XV (1715–1774)* (Paris, 1909), p. 134 (Vol. VIII, Pt. 2, of Ernest Lavisse, ed., *Histoire de France depuis les origines jusqu'à la Révolution*).] Choiseul obviously used the *Comité,* but how often and for what purposes he used it is not clear.

27. Boyer to Choiseul, Jan. 11 and 25, 1768, AE–CP, *Gênes,* Vol. 152, fols. 12, 19–20.
28. Boyer to Choiseul, Feb. 9, 1767, Feb. 1 and 23, 1768, *ibid.,* Vol. 151, fol. 37; Vol. 152, fols. 25–26, 44.
29. For the plan submitted in 1767, see *supra,* chapter V. For the plan submitted in 1768, see "Plan, traduction littérale, presenté par M. de Sorba par order de ses maîtres," March 3, 1768, AE–CP, *Corse,* Vol. VI, fols. 307–314.
30. "Corse, du 8 mars 1768," *ibid.,* Vol. VI, fols. 313–314.
31. *Ibid.,* Vol. VI, fols. 320–325.
32. Boyer to Choiseul, March 28 and May 31, 1768, AE–CP, *Gênes,* Vol. 152, fols. 69, 138. The treaty is found in this same volume, fols. 109–125. See also Driault, *Recueil,* pp. 370–375. For the Genoese side of these negotiations, see Piera Combi, "La cessione di Corsica alla Francia da parte della Repubblica di Genova," *Archivio Storico di Corsica,* II (1926), 22–106.
33. Boyer to Choiseul, March 21, 1768, AE–CP, *Gênes,* Vol. 152, fols. 65–66.
34. J. W. Thompson and S. K. Padover, *Secret Diplomacy: A Record of Espionage and Double-Dealing: 1500–1815* (London, 1937), pp. 120–179.
35. John Fraser Ramsey, *Anglo-French Relations,* p. 146. Ramsey's evidence for Choiseul's general policy after 1763 is convincing. The evidence for his statement that "Choiseul's influence was always exerted to avert war" between France and England (pp. 147–151) is less convincing. To make Choiseul out to be a peaceful minister of France is to miss the point: namely, Choiseul wanted peace until he was ready to fight a war with some chance of success, which in his thinking meant after 1769.
36. Choiseul, *Mémoires,* pp. 245–246.
37. Paul Maurel, *Histoire de Toulon* (Toulon, 1943), pp. 111–112.

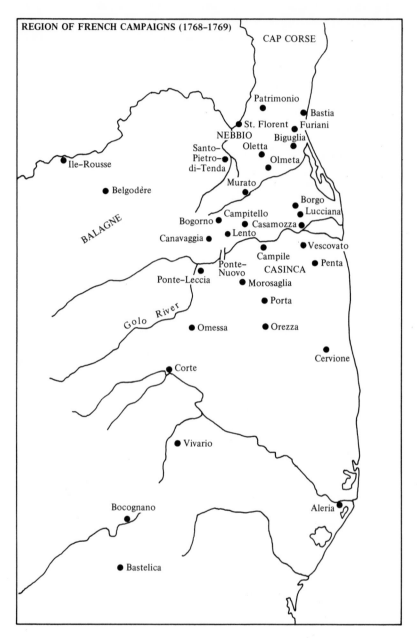

REGION OF FRENCH CAMPAIGNS (1768–1769)

CAP CORSE

Patrimonio

Bastia
St. Florent • Furiani
NEBBIO
Biguglia
Santo–
Pietro–
di–Tenda
Oletta
Olmeta
Ile–Rousse

Belgodère

Murato

Borgo
Lucciana
Campitello
Bogorno •
Casamozza •
Canavaggia •
Lento

BALAGNE

Vescovato

Campile
CASINCA
Penta
Ponte–
Nuovo
Ponte–Leccia
Morosaglia

Porta

Golo River
Omessa
Orezza

Cervione

Corte

Vivario

Bocognano
Aleria

Bastelica

Region of French Campaigns in Corsica, 1768-1769

CHAPTER VII

The Conquest of Corsica, 1768-1769

Although one student of Corsican history attributes French acquisition of the island to Providence,[1] there can be little doubt that the deed was accomplished by a man, in the person of Choiseul, and he therefore deserves any credit or blame to be meted out for that French territorial acquisition in the Old Regime. Of late, the praise has outweighed the blame, except among modern Corsican nationalists. But they gloat in having had revenge by giving France Napoleon. Whether censured or applauded, one fact is certain: the acquisition was ably accomplished, and represents an important factor that helped to rank Choiseul's ministry as one of the most successful of eighteenth-century France.

Yet Choiseul's Corsican policy was not an unqualified success. Assured by Marbeuf of the extensive sympathy for France among the Corsicans, Choiseul believed there would be no open hostilities as France took possession of the island.[2] Only by hindsight can he be judged harshly on this account. Who would have thought that Paoli's Corsicans would single-handedly challenge the might of France? Yet as Choiseul began to make plans for fulfilling the treaty of 1768 and combatting the dangers of foreign hostility toward it, a startling fact became apparent. Paoli and many of his "brave Corsicans" were not content to be sold like sheep. France would have to conquer the island to attain sovereignty over it.

It is quite certain that when Choiseul agreed to the treaty ceding Corsica to France, he did not intend to fight a war of suppression against the islanders. Marbeuf had been advising against such a war since the beginning of 1766. He had informed Choiseul that war in Corsica presupposed two ends, the first of which was to reduce and subjugate the island totally. This would be extremely difficult, Marbeuf contended. It would mean an enormous number of troops, much attention to road-building, and gigantic expense. The second presupposed end, which involved "punishing" the islanders by depriving them of agricultural and commercial advantages, was to Marbeuf's thinking more reasonable. In order to accomplish this goal, he advised preventing all communication between Bastia and Saint-Florent and cutting Cap Corse off from the rest of the island.[3]

Added to Marbeuf's explicit recommendation against a war of suppression is the fact that in all his extensive correspondence his comments about war in Corsica were brief and infrequent. Like Choiseul, he was aware of alternatives, and the possibility of war in the island always existed. Yet Marbeuf had little faith in the success of any such venture, an opinion seconded by the Sieur Paulain, *commissaire ordonateur* for the troops sent to the island in 1764. As early as March 1767 Paulain had posed the possibility that Genoa would redouble its efforts to secure French help in suppressing the Corsicans. He advised against granting such assistance by pointing out that there were no resources at all in the island for a war.[4]

The fact that Versailles did not intend a war of suppression is further supported by its unpreparedness. Not until March 30, 1768, did Choiseul begin to plan reinforcements for French forces in Corsica, nearly a month after Sorba presented his proposal for a treaty of cession. Even then all planning was vague and indecisive. In a memoir of that date, annotated

184

in Choiseul's hand, the minister evaluated some precautions to take for sending six to ten thousand troops to the island.[5]

The fundamental reason for Versailles' military unpreparedness was that it hoped to avoid waging war to suppress rebellion; but a second reason was its belief that there would be no real trouble in implementing the treaty. In this respect, much of the blame for the tragedy that developed lies with Marbeuf. This French commander never understood either Paoli or the hold the latter had on the Corsican people. He thought that Paoli terrorized the islanders with fear and that the only reason he did not make more progress with them was because Paoli kept the important people from seeing him. Before the treaty was signed in May, he advised that France had only to assure the Corsicans liberty and independence and they would support French interests in the maritime places. Indeed, he continued in this opinion even after the treaty had been concluded. On June 7 he informed Choiseul about the growing disunion among the islanders and then added: "We will perhaps have more difficulty preventing them from fighting each other than avoiding war on our own account." Three days later Marbeuf told Choiseul that the Corsicans were weak and inexperienced. A large part of the inhabitants wanted to be French, he said; and except for those with personal interests (that is, Paoli), all they wanted was perpetual possession of the island. Yet if Marbeuf was overconfident, he was also becoming more cautious. He advised Choiseul to move carefully because the Corsican nation believed that France had signed the treaty with Genoa ". . . only to deceive it and to enslave it." [6] As subsequent events showed, his concern was justified.

Marbeuf's reports tended to give Choiseul a false sense of security. On May 29 he informed Paoli that French troops were not coming to Corsica to cause trouble for the Corsican nation, "which His Majesty honors with a special protection." Then he added that the commander of the French troops in Corsica "will be ordered to join with you to avoid all steps that might harm the Nation." Choiseul even suggested that the state of Corsica was not changed for the moment and that the French commander could easily renew negotiations for an accommodation between Paoli and the republic, "the success of which is so essential for the good of both." In conclusion, Choiseul warned the Corsican general that "while waiting this success, the Corsican Nation will no longer answer to anyone but the king, whose bounty and protection it ought never doubt." [7]

Although Choiseul seemed confident about Paoli's cooperation when writing to the general himself, he was less optimistic in his other correspondence. To Buttafuoco he wrote that Paoli was setting a trap, which he would use Choiseul's letters to spring. "Il est bien fin," he continued, "mais cependant il faut qu'il acquière encore quelque finesse pour que nous tombions aussi grossièrement dans les panneau." Choiseul's advice to Paoli was to be calm and follow French leadership. But, Choiseul added, "I doubt that [Paoli] will take this course; and in this case I am sorry. What is certain is that he has missed the chance that I offered him so many times." [8] Choiseul could not forego the "I told you so" comment in concluding his correspondence with Buttafuoco. His final letters made it clear that the next move was up to Paoli.

These assurances to Paoli that France did not intend a war against him constituted the first step in Versailles' policy toward Corsica after the treaty of cession was signed. The second step involved drawing up plans for reinforcing French forces in the island and for sending the necessary officials. François-Claude, marquis de Chauvelin was chosen as commander of the French troops. It was a logical choice, because Chauvelin had for many years been associated with the Corsican question and presumably understood the islanders will. Yet, as Dumouriez later noted, Chauvelin's military experience was limited. After having served in the War of the Austrian Succession, he had become a diplomat. By 1768, "he had lost the habit of war, and understood nothing about it." [9] For *intendant de justice, police, et finances,* Choiseul on May 10 appointed Daniel-Marc-Antoine Chardon, *maître des re-*

quêtes, former administrator of Sainte-Lucie, and recognized (at least by the *philosophes*) for his role as *rapporteur* in the celebrated review of the case of Sirven.

There was considerable discussion concerning the number of troops that should be sent to Corsica. Noël Jourda, comte de Vaux, suggested that a force of twelve battalions, one legion, *canons à la Rostaing,* and *mortiers* could conquer the island in two months. But Choiseul apparently did not believe a force that size was sufficient, and on April 22, 1768, he ordered that the troops for Corsica would consist of sixteen battalions and two legions. Ten battalions were to leave for Corsica in June. The four battalions already on the island were to stay there until relieved by the last four of the sixteen battalions that were scheduled to land. The entire contingent was ordered to be ready to be sent to the island before August. Choiseul's order included provisions for artillery, *génie, régie,* transportation and necessary equipment.[10] The embarkation of this force took place from June to October, with the last battalions arriving early in October, after the major battles of the 1768 campaign had been fought. All the preparations were marked by extreme confusion, which also indicated Versailles' unpreparedness for military intervention in the island. If we are to believe Dumouriez, he alone, with some help from a certain Truguet, captain of Toulon, was responsible for the fact that ten battalions and one legion departed from Toulon in June.[11] It cannot be said, however, that modesty was one of Dumouriez's virtues.

The plan of occupation followed closely a proposal Marbeuf made in February 1766, when France was being pressured by the Genoese for more active military support in the island. The first step in his plan involved establishing the communications between Bastia and Saint-Florent, hence cutting Cap Corse off from the rest of the country. The second step was to cut off the Balagne, which provided grain and wine for the interior of the island. Marbeuf repeated these proposals in another memoir, dated simply "1768," with some additional provisions including a large road from Cap Corse to Corte and roads from Corte to all the maritime places.[12] When the first reinforcements, consisting of ten battalions and one legion, arrived in June, Marbeuf immediately set out to secure the communications between Bastia and Saint-Florent. This action caused much consternation among the Corsicans.

A more difficult decision was what to do if outside help were sent to the Corsicans. In response to a request from Choiseul, Jean de Lenchères, aide-de-camp and brigadier de cavalerie, turned to this problem early in May. "It is very difficult," he argued, "to succeed in entirely cutting off the communications between the island and the continent." [13] Lenchères really had nothing constructive to offer, and the ministry itself made the critical decision. If the Corsicans opposed the landing of French troops, the French navy was to protect them with artillery. If English ships were in the area, the French naval commanders were to pay no attention to them. If the French ships were attacked, they could defend themselves; but France intended to accomplish the landing without beginning hostilities.[14]

Paoli was understandably confused by what was happening. Although he was aware of the rumors that the French and Genoese had come to some agreement,[15] he had no way of knowing exactly what that agreement was. Yet he was not totally unprepared for the cession of Genoese rights over Corsica to France as Lenchères contended.[16] As early as April he had news of "la cessione" and expected the imminent arrival of many French battalions in the maritime places.[17]

For all his confusion and uncertainty, however, Paoli was clearly determined not to be deceived. At a *Consulte* held on May 22, even before the arrival of French reinforcements, he rather philosophically called his nation's attention to the dangers surrounding it. Desire alone, he stated, was not enough to make a people free, for all nations who aspired to liberty were subject to great vicissitudes. Then he added:

The state and the prerogative of a free people are an object too important, too worthy of the general administration, not to excite the envy of the greatest peoples of the world; and if this was not so, how is it that the French, who are one of the greatest powers of the Universe, would fall upon us to annihilate a Nation which has more courage than fortune and which, in its rustic simplicity, maintains a conduct that is a reproach for the greatest part of Europe. . . .

Corsica, Paoli continued, made Europe realize the great weight of the chains that crushed it. Then he ended his speech by an appeal to the courage of Corsican youth and by invoking the spirits of the dead.

Brave youth [,] now is the decisive moment. If you will not resist the storm which threatens you, both your name and glory are destroyed. . . . Honored spirits of your ancestors who, by having given us liberty at the price of your lives, found yourselves transported into heaven, do not be afraid that you will be tormented by your descendants. They are firmly resolved to live free and to follow your glorious example.[18]

In addition to his appeal to Corsican patriotism, Paoli began to make more definite and more practical preparations. He sought to convince his people that France intended to conquer the island and then, after a few years, return it to the Genoese. It now became increasingly clear that the vagueness of the treaty of May 15 was a mistake. It may have been intended to convince other powers that the cession was only provisional; but the Corsicans did not know that, in reality, the cession to France was definite. Therefore, Paoli was able to cite the danger of being returned to the republic in order to get support from his people. In addition, Paoli called for a body of volunteers consisting of one hundred young men, which would be used as a fast moving shock force wherever it was needed in the island. Paoli was actively preparing for "a defensive war," giving the impression that the only fighting would be against the Genoese.[19]

Meanwhile, Marbeuf had problems of his own with which to contend. Until Chauvelin arrived in the island in August, Marbeuf was the ranking officer. His letters to Choiseul reveal him as a man of feeling, actively engaged in a task for which he had little sympathy. He was pleased by the obvious joy the population of Bastia expressed at being under the French King, a joy voiced through cries of *Vive le Roy,* through celebration of a *Te Deum,* and through the lighted, festive air the city took on in the evenings. Yet he saw great pathos in the Corsican situation. Few Corsicans wanted to be in the first troop of one hundred volunteers, he reported. When some Corsicans offered the king their services, Marbeuf indignantly replied that the king did not intend for them to fight each other. If he was forced to make war, he said, only the king's troops would be involved. Over and over he reiterated one central theme: We must move carefully and cautiously, for the Corsicans are persuaded we intend to deceive them and to make them slaves again.[20]

Marbeuf's military and logistical problems were equally serious. He had to supervise work on the roads, which French troops undertook to develop as soon as they landed. By mid-June some four thousand French troops were working on the roads every day, with the help of a French architect sent to Saint-Florent about the same time. Marbeuf also found all the casernes and buildings that had belonged to Genoa in a state of advanced deterioration.[21] Equally serious was the confusion over what the French forces should be doing. They were soldiers, and as yet there was no war for them to fight. On June 25, Marbeuf complained of the many errors being made because there were no rules to guide the conduct of the officers, who exercised an authority foreign to their military character. All people with duties here, he said, must be "patient, just, and easily accessible." Finally, Marbeuf urged Versailles to send admiralty officers to combat danger from the Turks, who had not been informed that the Corsicans were subjects of Louis XV. He also recommended pardon to former French deserters in Corsica if they should stay on the island.[22]

Marbeuf's advice to move slowly was not followed at Versailles, where there was growing impatience over the slow progress being made on Corsica. During July the French Government ordered Marbeuf to finish the first step of the occupation plan by seizing Cap Corse.[23] On July 30 and 31 hostilities technically began when Marbeuf's troops began to occupy that part of the island. By August 5 French forces had secured the communications between Saint-Florent and Bastia, and before the end of August the entire province of Cap Corse was reduced. Paoli's troops resisted fiercely for a time, but eventually they withdrew from Cap Corse. Paoli did not attempt to drive the French from Cap Corse because he feared an immediately attack into the interior of the island. Thus he established his quarters at Murato and sent his brother Clemente to Oletta with some four thousand men. These positions were held until the beginning of September, when the campaign of 1768 officially began.[24]

On August 5, shortly after fighting began in Cap Corse, Louis XV finally published *Lettres Patentes* dealing with the subjugation of Corsica. The official document mentioned the treaty whereby Genoa voluntarily ceded its rights of sovereignty over the island to France. From then on, France became "charged with the government and the independent sovereignty of the Kingdom of Corsica," a sovereignty Louis XV intended to exercise only "for the good of the people of this island, our new subjects." The king ended by proclaiming "the sentiments of his paternal heart" for "the prosperity, the glory, and the happiness of our dear people of Corsica in general, and of each individual in particular." [25]

Chauvelin and Chardon arrived on the island in August, and Chauvelin immediately began to draw up plans for military operations. He also called to Choiseul's attention the inconvenience of turning the island of Capraja over to the Genoese, which had been stipulated by the treaty of cession, because the Corsicans in the interior would believe that the same fate awaited them.[26] One of Chardon's first acts was to expel the Jesuits, for the Order had been suppressed on the continent and now Corsica was part of France. There were over three thousand on the island at the time. Their revenues were put *en séquestre* and sent into a special *caisse* controlled by the Sieur Gauthier, who had been appointed *trésorier de la caisse civile*. Before they left, each father received a pension of 400 *livres* and each brother a pension of 250 *livres,* plus *un petit trousseau.* Some of the Jesuits left on Spanish ships and some on the French ships that carried the main body of French troops to the island; all were sent to Genoa.[27]

Although Paoli clearly realized that the French were closing in on him, in public he kept up a brave front. In an address to his people on August 28 he made good use of the rather advanced ideas he had gathered from reading Locke and Montesquieu. He expounded on the principle of the sovereignty of the people and appealed to the contract theory of government. The Corsicans may have been obliged to recognize Genoa in virtue of a contract with them, he argued, but the same motives did not exist relative to submission to France. Once Genoa had abandoned its sovereignty over the island, the Corsicans had every right to remain free and independent.[28]

In private, however, Paoli showed less confidence. In a letter to Octave Colonna d'Istria, who was president of the *junte d'observation* for Celavo, Ornano, and Cauro, Paoli expressed his grave concern over a number of subjects. In this letter, dated August 28, Paoli explained that he had left Cap Corse only with the greatest reluctance. Although he still hoped the English would come to his aid, he regarded Cap Corse as lost. Only superiority at sea could have kept it, which was impossible without English ships. He was disturbed by the lack of experience in some of his men and the lack of courage in others. He abhorred the relative ease with which the French troops moved within the island. Most earnestly of all, he denounced French perfidy. Observe, he told his correspondent, their ambiguity over the treaty of cession, especially whether the cession was temporary or perpetual. Note how they have translated the French word *confié* by the Italian *trasmetto*. The word *confié* meant that France was to exercise sovereign power. But the exercise of such power required an act of *parlement* declaring Corsica incorporated into France. It also meant that Louis XV should take the title King of Corsica. This France could not do, Paoli exclaimed, for "it knows very well that the other powers will never let it take possession of Corsica." [29]

To the feeling of discouragement Paoli felt at seeing his island ceded to France was added a sense of futility when he considered opposing French occupation of the island—but this did not mean that he was prepared to submit to French domination. Although he knew that Chauvelin had been commanded to pursue the war with vigor, he believed many Corsicans would not be content to be sold by Genoa. He realized that misfortunes would follow if the islanders resisted, but he believed that they would not bear the shame of letting themselves be treated like slaves by the republic. Even if they secured no help from England, Paoli insisted, they would resist, for they would not voluntarily relinquish "the liberty which has cost [them] so much." Finally, Paoli concluded, he did not want history to reproach him with having sacrificed the benefits gained after forty years of war and bloodshed.[30] Thus Paoli fully expected the approaching disaster; but to secure a favorable judgment from the muse Clio, he was prepared to pay the price. He did not have long to wait.

On the verge of opening his campaign against Paoli, Chauvelin jotted down his estimation of the Corsican general. "He is an ambitious person," Chauvelin wrote, "who wants to dominate [his people] and to make a great name for himself." Chauvelin, born and bred in the environment of the Old Regime's ruling classes, did not understand the forces at work within Paoli's Corsica. Thus he saw in Paoli nothing more than an opportunist. He believed that if the French made progress in the island while, at the same time, they destroyed

Paoli's prestige abroad, the Corsican would abandon his native land and would flee. As an opportunist, Paoli naturally had money put away in Swiss, Dutch, and Italian banks; it was a conclusion that Chauvelin did not doubt for a moment. Paoli, thought Chauvelin, "will have the appearance of sinking under the ruins of his country; he will play the role of an illustrious [but] unfortunate person, which is one of the objects of his ambition." Chauvelin also believed that two-thirds of the Corsicans wanted to free themselves from Paoli's tyranny. This tyranny, Chauvelin thought, rested on Paoli's ability to exploit the fear of being returned to Genoa and on his threats to ruin all areas of the island and all individuals who favored France. It was a tyranny sustained by Paoli's control over the powerful families of the island, a control exercised through hostages Paoli had taken and who were presently enrolled as students at his University of Corte. It was a tyranny supported by the Corsicans' hopes for assistance from England. Paoli used these hopes to stall for time until the winter, when he believed he would receive English aid.[31]

Chauvelin's appraisal of Paoli and the weakness of the Corsican general's *crédit* within the island made him dangerously optimistic about his campaign, which began in the first days of September. In reality the campaign lasted less than two months and took place in the Nebbio, the area immediately south of a line between Bastia and Saint-Florent. Before it ended, Chauvelin's overconfidence and bad tactics had given Paoli a sound victory. Contrary to Chauvelin's optimistic appraisal of the situation, there was no immediate French progress, only French defeat.

French troops marched into the Nebbio on September 5. At once Charles-François Dumouriez took the formidable positions of Croce, Maillebois, and Saint-Antonio. Antonie-Joseph-François des Lacs du Bousquet, marquis d'Arcambal and Colonel of the regiment of Roverque, took Furiani. Thereafter, the French army divided. Marbeuf with six battalions and one legion occupied the heights of Saint-Antonio and the villages of Furiani and Biguglia. Grandmaison, with four battalions and one legion, occupied the heights of Saint-Nicolas, stretching out before Olmeta and Oletta at the head of the Nebbio. When the campaign opened Paoli's troops had been at Oletta and Murato; but when faced with the initial French attacks he withdrew his forces toward the Golo River in a line extending from Bevinco to the *Étang* of Ciurlino. He was particularly intent upon placing a natural defense barrier between the French forces and his capital city of Corte. Thus the vigor of the French troops' initial movements, aided by Paoli's strategic withdrawal, carried French forces through the Nebbio region and beyond. On September 8 they occupied the villages of Borgo, Vignale, and Lucciana. On the same day, French troops commanded by Arcambal moved into the *pieve* of Casinca, south of the Golo River, and occupied the villages of Vescovato and Penta.

French penetration of Casinca alarmed Paoli and prompted a Corsican counterattack on September 9. Paoli's troops quickly drove the French from Vescovato and the next day they defeated Arcambal's forces at Penta. The rout was hardly complete, but it led Chauvelin to make a critical decision. Fearing that penetration of the Casinca would overextend his forces and threaten his communications, Chauvelin on September 18 ordered all French troops to withdraw from the Casinca. At the same time, he decided that Borgo must be held, despite warnings from Dumouriez and the ranking officer at Borgo, Colonel François-Louis-Hyacinthe, comte de Ludre, concerning the weakness of the French forces at that village. The fears for Borgo seemed unjustified for a time, because French withdrawal from the Casinca ended major action on the island until early in October. Yet when Paoli began to move again it soon became clear that the fears for Borgo had been valid; it was there that the real French disaster of the 1768 campaign occurred.

Paoli's forces began to move again on October 4. They quickly seized the weakly defended village of Lucciana and then moved on to Borgo. Chauvelin, committed to a decision to hold Borgo, formed a 1,000-man force in an attempt to relieve it. His efforts were in vain. French forces seized four or five of the houses on the edge of the village, but could go no further. Ludre's troops within Borgo tried several times to break through the Corsicans surrounding them, but their efforts also failed. The French disaster was complete. When Chauvelin ordered retreat at the end of the day (October 9), French casualties numbered almost 200 killed or wounded. On October 10 Ludre surrendered his 530-man contingent, plus 20 cannons. Chauvelin's tactics had not only lost him several major battles; they had also gravely compromised the prestige of the French army. The inexperience of the French troops and their commander played a large part in their defeat. Overconfidence, bad planning, and bad communications were also significant factors.[32]

Chauvelin's defeats were so disastrous that anyone without his long service on behalf of Louis XV and without the king's personal friendship most certainly would have suffered immediate disgrace. As it was, Chauvelin was allowed to continue in his capacity as commander until the end of December 1768. In October and November he tried to hold onto the Nebbio region, with the aid of reinforcements sent to supplement his quite obviously insufficient forces. Even this tactic failed. Chauvelin won back Oletta, but suffered further defeats and constant harassment from Paoli's forces around Ometa and Murato. By early November Paoli's troops occupied most of the villages in the Nebbio region.[33]

Even before his last military efforts failed, Chauvelin adopted a policy of divide and conquer. He confiscated the possessions of persons loyal to Paoli and made "un example terrible" of some of the more important. He told the representatives of the provincial assemblies that he regarded them as the real representatives of the people, thus trying to create divisions between them and Paoli. Finally, he worked to attach to France the province of Balagne and especially the *pièves* of Moriani, Tavagna, Orezza, and Alesani, in all of which there was some opposition to Paoli.[34]

Paoli's prestige was increased considerably by the French de-

Battle of Borgo, Oct. 5-9, 1768
(Jean Ange Galletti, *Histoire illustrée de la Corse*. Paris, 1863).

feats. Under normal conditions he would have been in a good bargaining position—and this is precisely what he thought. On September 14, he proposed negotiations for peace. He suggested a two-month armistice so that he could call a *Consulte* and seek its advice. He also proposed an exchange of prisoners. The most important point in all negotiations, he urged, was to give Corsica the assurance that it would never be returned to Genoa. Once the nation had been put at ease concerning this point, then all other issues could easily be resolved.[35]

But Paoli did not limit his activities to negotiations with the French. Internal affairs demanded his attention, for his leadership was being challenged by diverse factions within the island. This was especially true of the province of the Balagne. In December Paoli called together a provincial *Consulte* of the Balagne and through this assembly established *une junte de guerre ou inquisition*. The six members of the junte were to meet every ten days, or more often if necessary. Each had the authority to arrest suspects. Three members could punish sedition by prison, exile, or fines. Harsher punishments could only be dealt with by Paoli and his Supreme Council. The junte's powers were extensive, for it could punish people for "imprudent and unlawful words, even though [spoken] without any seditious intent, about the affairs of state and against the persons charged with the actual government." [36]

Although Paoli did receive the benefits of an armistice in November, there seems to have been no real question at Versailles of negotiations for peace. Chauvelin, sick and discouraged, asked for and received his recall, leaving Marbeuf in charge to re-establish the communications between Bastia and Saint-Florent. The winter of 1768–1769 was extremely difficult for the troops on the island, but otherwise there were few events of significance.

While Marbeuf braved the winter in Corsica, Choiseul, Louis XV, and the king's Council were busy planning how best to overcome the damage of the previous campaign. Choiseul feared that Corsica might become "la theâtre d'une guerre qui pouvait être importante." Only two alternatives seemed possible; to come to an agreement with Paoli or to drive him out by force. The latter course would be hindered by transportation problems and by lack of materials and, if it were chosen, extensive planning would have to be undertaken first. Some projects for an accommodation with Paoli were proposed, one of which was to leave Paoli in control of an internal Corsican Government located at Corte while France occupied the maritime places and Cap Corse; this was precisely the basis for Choiseul's earlier negotiations with Paoli. In the end, however, French "honor" decided the issue. French prestige, which had suffered badly in the 1768 campaign, had to be recovered, which was possible only by defeating Paoli. In January 1769, despite the expenses of the 1768 campaign, Louis XV decided in Council "to use all the means necessary for the submission of Corsica." [37] The French Government would pay the price to avoid another Borgo.

Once the decision had been made, Choiseul immediately turned to the planning necessary for success. He chose as Chauvelin's replacement Noël Jourda, comte de Vaux, who sometime earlier had written offering his services in Corsica.[38] At the time Vaux was second in command in the *Trois-Évêches* and governor of Thionville under the Maréchal d'Armentières. He had served in Corsica in the year 1738–1739 and in 1757. He had also distinguished himself in the Seven Years' War. All evidence pointed to his ability as an officer, and he had the additional advantage of knowing something about the island of Corsica. On January 19, Choiseul asked Vaux to come to Versailles for consultation on the coming Corsican campaign.[39]

Choiseul also wrote to prepare Chardon for the coming campaign. Last year, he told Chardon, there was no question of great troop movements. Hence the king had not provided campaign equipment for the officers. But things were different now, and Choiseul went on to describe the plans to provide bread and forage, to which the officers were entitled. In another letter to Chardon, Choiseul warned his intendant of the task that lay ahead. The number of troops for the 1769 campaign would be twenty-four thousand, Choiseul noted. He added that he knew Chardon well enough to believe that the latter had already taken measures to provide subsistence for them.[40] The spring of 1769 found Vaux actively preparing for the approaching campaign. During the last part of March he was at Toulon. For a time contrary winds delayed his sailing, but finally he left for Corsica on April 5. On the ninth he was reporting progress of work done on the roads. His troops, which arrived in the island from March to early May, caused considerable alarm among the Corsicans.

But the Corsicans' resolve to defend their place in history had not yet weakened. At a *Consulte* held in March in the Casinca, Paoli's Corsicans voted unanimously to defend their nation until death. They also voted a *levée en masse,* which required all able men between sixteen and sixty to prepare for the nation's defense.[41] The *levée en masse* constitutes a striking illustration and a natural culmination of tendencies within Corsican society during the eighteenth century. Throughout the long forty years that the Corsicans had been rebels they had referred to their country as a Nation and to their leaders as patriots. Now, under the pressure of foreign danger and the threat to their particular revolution, the Corsicans developed institutions and principles that appear decidedly modern in form and spirit. We have seen that in December 1768 Paoli's government established a special tribunal with extensive powers to hunt out and punish suspects. The *levée en masse* that was formulated three months later established the principle of the nation in arms and committed Paoli's Corsican followers to total war. A quarter of a century later the French formulated similar institutions and expounded a similar spirit and principles in order to meet similar dangers from within and without.

However modern the Corsicans' spirit, it was not sufficient to overcome their French opponents, whose plans for the 1769 campaign were systematic and thorough. Moreover, there were now at least forty-five battalions of infantry and three regiments of cavalry with which to carry them out. Some of the troops were distributed in the maritime places, so that the active force available for the campaign was only about half its apparent size; but this still left Vaux with twenty battalions, which on May 2 were drawn up before Murato. On that date the artillery Vaux expected arrived, and he decided to open the campaign the next day.[42]

Vaux's plan of attack was relatively simple. It involved, first, occupation of the mountains called Tenda; second, occupation of the Nebbio; third, the seizure of Corte. Marbeuf, commanding the left wing, was to seize Borgo, enter the Casinca and occupy Campile, and then cut Paoli's retreat. The right wing, commanded by Arcambal, was to secure the Col de San-Giacomo and then enter the Balagne. Vaux, commanding the center, was to drive Paoli out of Murato and then free the mountain passes north of Lento and Canavaggio.

As planned, French troops opened the campaign on May 3, with immediate success. Marbeuf, with five battalions, easily seized Borgo and Arcambal moved toward the Col de San-Giacomo with little resistance. Heavy fighting occurred at Murato, where Vaux finally forced Paoli's retreat. By May 6

Marbeuf, swinging in an arch pointed southwest, was moving toward the strategic point of Ponte-Nuovo, after having sent expeditionary forces into the Casinca. Vaux, after prolonged fighting, finally seized the passages near Lento and Canavaggio. By nightfall of May 7, he was camped on the heights over-looking the Golo River, with his left column in Lento and his right column in Canavaggio. Marbeuf, located to the east of Vaux, was ready to assist his commander or to enter the Casinca. With Paoli's troops now massed to the south, east, and west of Ponte-Nuovo, a major clash between the opposing forces was imminent.

The battle of Ponte-Nuovo on May 8 was to Paoli what Borgo had been to the French in the campaign of 1768. To protect the Golo River, Paoli at dawn went on the offensive, throwing part of his troops against Lento. Although they fought courageously, they were caught in a devastating cross fire from French troops coming from Canavaggio, from Vaux's left wing, supported by some of Marbeuf's men, and from Vaux's center column. This center column counterattacked quickly. Caught in a classic military vice, the Corsicans retreated toward the bridge, where for some inexplicable reason they were fired upon by Prussian and Swiss mercenaries who had been in Genoa's pay but were now serving Paoli and were located on the right bank of the Golo River overlooking the bridge.[43] Whether the mercenaries betrayed their employer or their fire resulted from a misunderstanding has never been resolved. At Ponte-Nuovo, Paoli lost five to six hundred men, two hundred fifty of whom were killed on the bridge either by gunfire or by drowning. The French lost about fifty men. Thereafter the road to Corte was open. In addition, more and more Corsicans began to leave Paoli.[44]

After Ponte-Nuovo, Vaux began to follow Paoli as the Corsican general moved south. The mopping-up operations had begun. Marbeuf was in the Casinca, Arcambal in the Balagne, and Jean-François, comte de Narbonne-Pelet began to move east from Ajaccio in an effort to cut off Paoli's retreat. Vaux pursued the Corsican general down the center of the island

Battle of Ponte-Nuovo, May 8, 1769
(Jean Ange Galletti, *Histoire illustrée de la Corse*. Paris, 1863).

from Morosaglia to Corte to Vivario, and by June 8 he was at Bocognano. Paoli stayed just a few days ahead of Vaux's advancing forces. At Bastelica, on June 4, Paoli had thought of a campaign via Vico, Niolo, and Corte, designed to place him behind the French troops and in a position to cut them off from Bastia and Saint-Florent. Advised against such a move, Paoli continued his retreat via Levie and Quenza to Portovecchio where two English ships were waiting. On June 13 those ships left Portovecchio with Paoli, his brother Clemente, and 340 of their followers on board. Paoli's destination was first Leghorn and then England.[45]

On June 22 Vaux wrote Choiseul to inform the minister that Paoli had fled the island, which was now totally vanquished. The human cost of the conquest for France had been eleven officers and eighty soldiers killed, twenty officers and two hundred soldiers wounded. Vaux believed it necessary to leave a force of twenty-four batallions and one legion in the island until the Corsicans gave up hope of English assistance.[46]

202

Vaux's appraisal of the island's complete submission was not, however, entirely correct. In his rather rapid pursuit of Paoli, he had intentionally bypassed certain pockets of resistance, the most troublesome of which was the Balagne. The campaign there had begun early in May, led by Colonel Luker of the regiment of Bourgogne. By the end of the month the region was subdued, but it was not secured until early in August. Vaux's policy toward such pockets of resistance was one of terror. As he told Luker, when sending him into the Balagne: "Spare neither the houses, nor the vines, nor the olive trees of those who refuse to submit; this is the only way to enforce [a policy of] terror and to lead them to obedience." [47]

Vaux extended this policy to other areas in a general proclamation he issued in August. He thought it advisable to reveal to the Corsicans "the laws of war" to which they exposed themselves by resisting the king. The villages "without fortifications" that resisted would be burned and devastated, and anyone captured in them would be sent to France. Villages fortified or defended from outside would be asked to surrender. If they did not, the French would presume that followers of Paoli had not allowed the inhabitants to make their own decision. Inhabitants of occupied areas found with arms would be treated as brigands. In villages not occupied, small armed groups without orders would also be treated as brigands. Voluntary submission would mean favorable treatment.[48]

A special ordinance against carrying arms was published on August 23 to reinforce one of these laws of war. Because previous warnings had not been heeded, the ordinance declared, all Corsicans found carrying arms within fifteen days after publication of the ordinance would be punished by death, *sans rémission*. The *prévôt des maréchaux* was to examine such cases, and there was no appeal from his decision.[49]

Vaux's proclamation and ordinance gave him the kind of powers he thought he needed to combat the guerrilla-type resistance of the islanders. By mid-August communications by land were free in most of the island.[50] Throughout the rest of the year and the first months of 1770, Vaux's troops disarmed the villages, took their oaths of loyalty to Louis XV, and established the king's authority within them. Brigands, that is, small roving bands of Paoli's supporters, deserters, or actual thieves, continued to plague his efforts, and toward them his policy was brutal. He continually urged that the only way to eliminate this problem was to devastate the houses and possessions of the brigands' relatives. He also vigorously denounced the "perversity" of the religious and advised closing all the convents of Corsica except those of the Capuchins. Only in this way, Vaux believed, could he terminate the assistance given to the brigands by the religious.[51]

Like most of the French officers, Vaux wanted to leave Corsica as soon as the actual military campaign ended. Tasks like supervision of road construction bored him. Conflicts over administrative problems discouraged him. Moreover, Vaux became ill, which only intensified his other problems. Unlike most of the other officers, however, he could not escape to the continent by taking a *congé*. As early as July 1769 he requested his recall; but Choiseul stressed the necessity of the commander's continued presence on the island. Not until May 10, 1770, did he finally sail away from France's newly conquered territory, leaving Marbeuf behind him as the new commander.[52]

French conquest of Corsica naturally involved some diplomatic relationships with other powers, which kept Choiseul busy throughout the actual conquest. The power most hostile to the acquisition and conquest was England, which for years had been saying it would not allow Corsica to fall into French hands.[53] Although Choiseul faced the danger of active intervention, he had caught England at a bad moment. Not only were the English experiencing difficulties with their restive American colonies, but they also were disturbed by quarreling factions within the government.

As soon as news of the treaty began to spread, Choiseul had made plans to present England with a *fait accompli*. He never believed England would fight to keep the French out of Corsica. Naturally there was the risk he might be wrong, but he believed it was a risk worth taking. Choiseul at first stalled for time so that English pressure could not be brought to bear before fulfillment of the treaty was well underway. Therefore, when Commander Spry, the commander of the English Mediterranean fleet, began to press Genoa for information about the rumored treaty,[54] Choiseul advised the republic to send its envoy to London via Paris. "It is *très convenable,*" Choiseul wrote to Boyer, "that the minister whom Genoa sends to England use the same language we do regarding the motive and object of the engagements that we have made with Genoa. It is certain that M. Ageno will receive here the instructions which he will need in this respect."[55]

Very shortly after the treaty of cession had been signed, the English ambassador to Paris, Lord William H. Rochford, began to protest it, although its provisions were then unknown. He was directed to inform Choiseul that the possession of Corsica by France would be unacceptable.

[It is] a step totally departing from that principle so often laid down by [the French] court and observed by this, and what has been repeatedly asserted to be the guide of every measure of theirs, that the extension of territory, force, or possession of any of the great powers of Europe cannot be a matter of indifference to their neighbors, and may consequently endanger the peace of Europe.[56]

This protest was a stab in the dark, for the English ministers knew nothing definite about the treaty at that time. They had, however, discovered that it would be difficult to learn anything definite, for France and Genoa were using the same vague language in explaining the rumored treaty. Louis-Marie Florent, comte de Châtelet, the French ambassador to London, had said that French acquisition of Corsica was a defensive measure designed to protect the French coast against Corsican attacks, an explanation that fooled no one. As Lord William Shelburne, the British Secretary of State for the Northern Department, scoffed: "it is a naturally excessive and extravagant supposition that the Corsicans would ever provoke France." [57]

Shelburne nevertheless moved cautiously. He directed Rochford "to be temperate in his relations with Choiseul, allowing him opportunity to retract this measure and giving to [George III] the time to discover the reactions of other courts, who have been silent on this so far." [58]

Not until the end of June did the English Government learn the true nature of the treaty. By then, however, England had indeed been presented with a *fait accompli*. There was considerable pro-Corsican sentiment throughout England, which put pressure on the government to act on behalf of "the brave Corsicans." Even the Russian Government offered assistance if England wanted to keep Corsica out of French hands.[59] Yet Choiseul had been correct. England did not want war over the island, in part because English finances could not stand the strain and in part because it could not arouse the other powers. Another decisive factor was a cabinet controversy, which pitted Shelburne's government against the "war party" led by William Pitt. If Shelburne gave in to war sentiment, there was a strong possibility that he would lose control of the government.[60]

England did send a special agent, one Captain Dunant, to Corsica to sound out the situation; and for a time England supplied some surreptitious aid to Paoli. But it would not come out openly in Paoli's favor, which would be considered a declaration of war against France. The English Government protested, but that was all.[61] Even the protest was both late and weak, perhaps in part because Choiseul threatened to aid the American colonists if England aided the Corsicans. George III's answer to the French declaration on the annexation of Corsica was sent by Rochford to Horace Walpole, the English ambassador to Paris, on September 1, 1769. Its language was so "consistent and clear," Rochford noted, that there was no need to interpret it. The cession of Corsica was "an enterprise which could trouble the general peace, while bringing injury to the interests of the different States of Italy, which were happily established and confirmed by the last treaties of peace." The French treaty with Genoa had not calmed George III's uneasiness about this affair, Rochford added; nor had Louis XV's declarations. The latter, in fact, had only proved that George III's concern was well founded.[62] Mr. Wickham Legg has summarized the English reaction astutely: "Never perhaps was a feebler part played by a lately victorious government towards its conquered foe." [63]

In addition to raising the possibility of war with England, French acquisition of Corsica worsened Versailles' relations with the Bey of Tunis. Ever since the 1660s, when French interests in Tunis developed, French residents in northern Africa had faced harassment from Tunisian pirates, from the anti-foreigner policy adopted by Bey Hossein-bel-Ali, and from Algerian invasions in the 1750s. By the 1760s Versailles' relations with Tunis had reached a low point when the Bey declared he was powerless to stop Moroccan and Tunisian raids on the Barbary coasts and Provence. The new Bey, Ali, had already started refusing to receive French consuls when Corsica was ceded to France.[64]

In the summer of 1768 Paoli had tried to establish relations with the Bey of Tunis and had sent an agent to the Bey to treat for a truce and some provisions in grain. French agents reported that the Bey did not view Paoli's approaches very favorably, but that he envisioned some possibility that Tunisian corsairs would be able to use Corsican ports and had therefore replied favorably to Paoli's propositions. As an indication of his friendship, the Bey returned to Corsica four Corsican slaves. He also sent along some rather exotic gifts, including two Negroes, four tigers, and a lion.[65]

Versailles' reaction to Paoli's Tunisian diplomacy was mixed. The Duc de Praslin was worried, for he believed that drastic action against Tunisian corsairs in Corsican ports would break the treaties France had with Tunis and would pose great danger to French navigation of the Mediterranean. He therefore advised that if Tunisian corsairs entered Corsican ports, they should be given any aid needed and then asked to leave.[66]

Choiseul was more angry than worried over closer Corsican-Tunisian relations. Perhaps emboldened by the success of his

Corsican venture, Choiseul believed that the time had come to teach Tunis a lesson. French demands that the Bey of Tunis recognize "la réunion de la Corse" were supported by M. de Brèves' ships, which arrived before Goulette in August 1769. Even then the Bey refused to recognize the French acquisition, and his behavior exasperated the French Government and led it to resort to stronger measures. In July and August 1770, M. de Brèves bombarded Bizerte and Sousse. The Bey thereafter saw the light and in September 1770 signed a treaty with France recognizing French acquisition of Corsica.[67]

In retrospect French relations with England and Tunis concerning the acquisition and conquest of Corsica might have proved dangerous. But in reality they were mere sidelights to the main event. By July 1769, Corsica had been won for France both by treaty and by conquest. This was two months before the English Government lodged its weak protest and fourteen months before the Bey of Tunis formally recognized the acquisition.

NOTES

1. F. Girolami-Cortona (*Histoire de la Corse*, p. 387), wrote: "Il fallait au génie de Napoléon un plus vaste horizon que celui de la Corse, voilà pourquoi la Providence avait réuni cette île à la France." J.-T. Biancamaria repeated this phrase almost exactly in his recent book, *La Corse dans sa gloire ses luttes et ses souffrances* (Paris, 1963), p. 194.

2. Jean de Lenchères, aide-de-camp and brigadier de cavalerie, "Mémoire sur la Corse, principaux faits des campagnes de 1768 et 1769, établissements, militaires et civils, etc.," AG, *Mém. hist.*, 248 1, fols. 2 and 9. This memoir is a capital document, not only because of its author's intimate knowledge of the subject but also for his extensive treatment; the memoir in manuscript contains 88 folios. It was written at the end of 1771 and marginal notes bring the account up to 1775. Hereafter cited as Lenchères, "Mémoire."

3. Marbeuf to Choiseul, Feb. 25, 1766, AG, *Arch. hist.*, A1 3638.17.

4. Paulain, "Mémoire, Isle de Corse," *ibid.*, A1 3644.22.

5. *Ibid.*, A1 3647.11.

6. Marbeuf to Choiseul, June 7 and 10, 1768, *ibid.*, A1 3647.76 and 3647.80. Marbeuf received similar advice from his subordinate officials

regarding the Corsicans' attitudes toward France. On March 8, 1768, Jadart, the French *commissaire des guerres* at Ajaccio, informed him that France had nothing to fear from *tout le peuple*. On April 28, Jadart said that the Corsican "chiefs" were alarmed about news of a treaty between France and Genoa and had said that they would oppose the entry of Frenchmen into the interior of the island with all their strength. See Z. Campocasso and L. Letteron, eds., "Correspondance de M. Jadart (12 août 1767–12 mai 1768), commissaire des guerres, suivi de la correspondance (15 août 1767–19 juillet 1768) du comte de Marbeuf, commandant des troupes de S.M.T.C., en Corse," *BSHNC* (1882–1883). The letters cited are in the issues of this journal for November 1882, p. 657, and December 1882, pp. 717–718. This source contains much information on French-Genoese-Corsican relations on Corsica from Aug. 1767 to July 1768.

7. *Carteggio*, p. 595, and Tommaseo, *Lettere*, p. 130.

8. May 29, 1768, *Carteggio*, p. 594, and Tommaseo, *Lettere*, p. 131.

9. François Barrière, ed., *Mémoires du général Dumouriez*, 2 Vols. (Paris, 1862), I, 63. Although Dumouriez's judgment of Chauvelin turned out to be correct, it was based on hindsight. At the time, Chauvelin's appointment was favorably received, especially in Genoa. See Boyer to Choiseul, [July] 29, 1768, AE–CP, *Gênes*, Vol. 152, fol. 221. Other officers chosen for the troops in Corsica were: Marbeuf, Grandmaison, and Narbonne-Pelet, maréchal de camp; the Chevalier de Fontette, maréchal général des logis, with Lenchères and the Chevalier de Bethisy as aides; Pujol, major général, with Lavarenne and the Chevalier de Bufavant as aides. AG, *Arch. hist.*, A¹ 3660.9.

10. Vaux to Choiseul, March 30, 1768, *ibid.*, A¹ 3647.12. Choiseul's order is found in *ibid.*, A¹ 3647.17.

11. Barrière, *Mémoires du Dumouriez*, I, 61.

12. AG, *Mém. hist.*, 1098.34 and 1098.37.

13. Lenchères, "Mémoire sur la Corse," May 4, 1768, *ibid.*, 1098.41.

14. "Instruction à M. le chevalier de Fabry, major de la marine," June 6, 1768, AM, B² 389, fols. 305–306.

15. Buttafuoco to Choiseul, April 14, 1768, AG, *Arch. hist.*, A¹ 3647.14.

16. Lenchères, "Mémoire," fol. 3.

17. Paoli to Raimondo Cocchi, April 18 and May 3, 1768, in Giovanni Livi, ed., "Lettere inedite di Pasquale de'Paoli," *ASI*, CXVIII (1890), 106, 229.

18. AG, *Arch, hist.*, A¹ 3648.212–.213, 3648.217–.218, 3655.24, 3646.139.

19. Marbeuf to Choiseul, May 30 and June 16, 1768, *ibid.*, A¹ 3647.62, 3647.85; *Ragguagli dell'Isola di Corsica*, No. III, *ibid.*, A¹ 3647.89. *Ragguagli dell'Isola di Corsica* was the official journal of Paoli's national government and was published from May 1762 to May 1769. See H. Yvia-Croce, "Panorama de la presse Corse au XVIIIme et XIXme siècles (1762–1852)," *Corse Historique*, Nos. 23–24 (1966), 5–9.

20. See his letters to Choiseul on May 30 and June 7, 10, 18, and 25, AG, *Arch. hist.,* A¹ 3647.62,–.76,–.80,–.85,–.94.
21. *Ragguagli dell'Isola di Corsica,"* No. III, and Marbeuf to Choiseul, June 17, 1768, *ibid.,* A¹ 3647.88,-.84.
22. *Ibid.,* A¹ 3647.92.
23. Lenchères ("Mémoire," fol. 9) suggested some reluctance on Marbeuf's part, indicating that he was forced ". . . par des ordres réitérés de marcher. . . ." Marbeuf apparently still believed, at the end of July, that Paoli would not resort to open hostilities.
24. J.-M. Jacobi, *Histoire générale,* II, 316–317; Charles-Pierre-Victor, comte de Pajol, *Les guerres sous Louis XV,* VI, 78–83.
25. *Code Corse. Recueil des Édits, Déclarations, Lettres Patentes, Arrêts et Règlements publiés dans l'Isle de Corse depuis sa soumission à l'obéissance du Roi, avec la traduction en Italien. Imprimé par ordre de Sa Majesté,* 3 Vols. (Paris, 1778), I, 128–130.
26. Chauvelin to Choiseul, Aug. 30, 1768, AG, *Arch. hist.,* A¹ 3647.188.
27. Lenchères, "Mémoire," fols. 8–9.
28. AG, *Arch. hist.,* A¹ 3647.183.
29. AG, *Mém. hist..* 907.
30. *Ibid.,* 907. This letter to Istria is one of several pieces sent by a Corsican historian, Antoine Friess, to the Minister of Public Instruction in 1844.
31. Chauvelin to Choiseul, June 3, 1768, *ibid.,* 1098.41a.
32. Principal primary sources for the campaign of 1768 are: Lenchères, "Mémoire," fols. 9–14; Barrière, *Mémoires du Dumouriez,* I, 63–77; Tommaseo, *Lettere,* pp. 137–143, 162–168. See also Giovanni Arena, "Della cose di Corsica dal 1730 al 1768," *ASI,* XI (1846), 268–237. Biancamaria, *op. cit.,* pp. 185–188, is a particularly helpful secondary account of the military action. The author is a Lieutenant-Colonel and presents an able discussion of military matters. Also helpful are Marius Peyre, "L'Établissement des français en Corse (1768–1769)," *Revue des Questions Historiques,* XCIX (1923), 38–61, and Pajol, *op. cit.,* VI, 77–103.
33. François-Claude, marquis de Chauvelin, "Mémoire sur la Corse; moyens de la réduire," Sept. 30, 1768. AG, *Mém. hist.,* 1098.41b; Biancamaria, *op. cit.,* p. 187.
34. Chauvelin to Choiseul, Sept. 7, 1768, AG, *Arch. hist.,* A¹ 3648.17; [Sept. 21, 1768], AG, *Mém. hist.,* 1098.41d; see also the letters written by Costa de Castellana (an officer in the regiment Royal-Corse), Sept. 14, 1768, AG, *Arch. hist.,* A¹ 3648.37,-.38.
35. Chauvelin to Choiseul, Sept. 19, 1768, *ibid.,* A¹ 3648.43; AG, *Mém. hist.,* 1098.41d; Buttafuoco to Choiseul, Oct. 18, 1768, AG, *Arch. hist.,* A¹ 3642.102.
36. "Délibérations de la Consulte provinciale de Balagne . . . ," Dec. 1, 1768, *ibid.,* A¹ 3648.171.

37. Lenchères, "Mémoire," fol. 18. The expenses for subsistence of the troops and "extraordinary expenses" for the 1768 campaign were over two and one-half million livres. See AG, *Arch. hist.*, A[1] 3654 bis.

38. Vaux to Choiseul, March 30, 1768, *ibid.*, A[1] 3647.12.

39. Gustave Baguenault de Puchesse, "La Conquête de la Corse et le maréchal de Vaux, 1769," *Revue des Questions Historiques*, XXVIII (1880), p. 157. Lenchères ("Mémoire," fol. 19) reported that the Corsican command was first offered to the Prince de Beauveau, who refused. The Maréchal d'Armentières convinced Choiseul that Vaux was the best possible man for the position.

40. Feb. 14, 1769, AG, *Arch. hist.*, A[1] 3651.46–.47. Choiseul's comment on the lack of plans for great troop movements gives additional support to the judgment that the 1768 campaign was not designed to be a campaign of conquest. It is a judgment further supported by the words of a French officer reporting on the war in Corsica: "On avait envisagé cette enterprise plutôt comme un objet de négociation que de guerre; c'est ce qui fut cause des petites désastres que nous éprouvames que firent une si grande sensation en Europe, et donnerent une si haute idée de Paoli et de sa nation." M. de Wimpfen, maréchal de camp, to an officer of the Empire, Sept. 1, 1768, AG, *Mém. hist.*, 248 [1].

41. Puchesse, *op. cit.*, pp. 159–164; Tommaseo, *Lettere*, pp. 168–172.

42. Primary sources for the 1769 campaign are Puchesse, *op. cit.*, pp. 165–183; Louis de la Trémoille, *Mon grand-père à la cour de Louis XVI* (Paris, 1904), *passim;* Lenchères, "Mémoire," *passim;* the Abbé L. Letteron, ed., "Pontenovo; 8 mai 1769," *BSHNC* (April–June 1913), 27–43; and Barrière *Mémoires du Dumouriez*, I, 78–92. Dumouriez's discussion of the 1769 campaign is primarily a discussion of Dumouriez, so it is not as informative as his treatment of the earlier campaign. See also Biancamaria, *op. cit.*, pp. 188–195, and Pajol, *op. cit.*, VI, 103–122.

43. Biancamaria (*op. cit.*, p. 192) has drawn up, in military fashion, an extremely helpful battle map of the battle of Ponte-Nuovo.

44. The best discussion of the battle is in Letteron, "Pontenovo," especially pp. 30–39.

45. On Paoli's retreat, see Puchesse, *op. cit.*, pp. 169–175.

46. Quoted in *ibid.*, pp. 176–177.

47. Quoted in *ibid.*, pp. 189–190.

48. AG, *Arch. hist.*, A[1] 3655.47.

49. *Code Corse*, I, 181–182.

50. Choiseul to Chardon, Aug. 26, 1769, AG, *Arch. hist.*, A[1] 3652.36.

51. Puchesse, *op. cit.*, pp. 200–205.

52. *Ibid.*, pp. 183, 210.

53. See the concise summary of England's frequently reiterated position in Lord Fitzmaurice, *Life of William, Earl of Shelburne, afterwards*

First Marquis of Lansdowne, 2nd. rev. ed., 2 Vols. (London, 1912), I, 362–363.

54. For Spry's insistent questioning and the vague replies he received from Genoese officials, see his letters to the Earl of Shelburn, June 3, 17, and 28, 1768, *Calendar of Home Office Papers of the Reign of George III, 1766–1769,* 5 Vols. (London, 1879), II, 346, 349–351.

55. June 14, 1768, AE–CP, *Gênes,* Vol. 152, fol. 151. Ageno, the Genoese minister to London, was not in regular residence often enough to conduct an effective diplomacy. For example, when the treaty of 1768 was signed, he was not in London. See comments on him and on the "crisis of recruitment" in Genoese diplomacy in the eighteenth century in René Boudard, *Gênes et la France,* pp. 111–112.

56. Shelburne to Rochford, May 27, 1768, in L. G. Wickham Legg, ed., *British Diplomatic Instructions, 1689–1789,* Vol. VII, *France, Part IV, 1745–1789* (London, 1934), pp. 101–102. Royal Historical Society Publications, Series 3, Vol. 49.

57. *Ibid.,* p. 102.

58. *Ibid.,* p. 103. In April English officials began a series of efforts to discover the nature of Versailles' agreements with Genoa concerning Corsica. For these efforts, and the way that Choiseul stalled them, see Paul Vaucher, ed., *Recueil des instructions données aux ambassadeurs et ministres de France . . . ,* pp. 450–453.

59. See the lengthy discussions of Corsica in *The London Magazine, or Gentleman's Monthly Intelligencer,* Vols. 46–47, and in *The Universal Magazine of Knowledge and Pleasure,* Vols. 42–43. On the Russian offer, see Lord Cathcart to Lord Viscount Weymouth, Oct. 12 (23), 1768, *I Russkoe istoricheskoe obshchestvo [Diplomatic Dispatches from English Ambassadors at the Court of Russia, 1762–1769]* (St. Petersburg, 1837), pp. 338–339. Count Nikita Panin, the Russian chief minister, said that if King George III wanted to keep Corsica from the French, Russia would furnish cannon and munitions for 7,000 men; but if the English were not interested, then neither were the Russians. Paoli somehow knew about the Russian offer, and as late as March 1769 he hoped that some results might come from it. See Tommaseo, *Lettere,* p. 173.

60. John F. Ramsey, *Anglo-French Relations, 1763–1770,* pp. 189–190.

61. See the correspondence between the Duke of Grafton and George III, Aug. 14, 16, and Sept. 14, 1768, in Sir John Fortesque, ed., *The Correspondence of King George III from 1760 to December 1783,* 6 Vols. (London, 1927), II, 38–39, 43–44.

62. Legg, *op. cit.,* pp. 109–110. Choiseul's threat is found in the same source, pp. 108–109.

63. *Ibid.,* pp. xviii–xix. The confusion among British officials over French acquisition of Corsica is described by Ramon E. Abarca, "Bourbon

'Revanche' against England: The Balance of Power, 1763–1770" (Unpublished Ph.D. dissertation, University of Notre Dame, 1965), pp. 301ff.

64. Alfred Spont, "Les Français à Tunis de 1600 à 1789," *Revue des Questions Historiques,* LXVII (1900), 103–139.

65. Praslin to Choiseul, July 16, 1768, and Boyer to Choiseul, July 16, 1768, AE–CP, *Gênes,* Vol. 152, fols. 191–192.

66. Praslin to Choiseul, Aug. 8, 1768, *ibid.,* Vol. 152, fol. 230.

67. Spont, *op. cit.,* pp. 150–141; V. Brun, *Guerres maritimes de la France: Port de Toulon,* 2 Vols. (Paris, 1861), I, 496–497.

Conclusion

A study of French efforts to resolve the Corsican question might well end with a sampling of the varied reactions among Frenchmen to the manner in which it was finally accomplished. Many Frenchmen frankly approved of Choiseul's policy and praised the Duc for successfully bringing to an end a problem that had gradually become an economic and military burden and a prestige risk. Others remained largely indifferent to the acquisition and conquest of the island, just as they had been indifferent to the entire Corsican question. Still others were ambivalent in their judgments. Perhaps they realized the strategic importance of the island, but they could not forget how much its conquest had cost in terms of lives, money, and prestige. Some of this group apparently had definite objections to the conquest and yet assumed the appearance of ambivalence because forthright criticism of an official government policy would be risky. Finally, an articulate minority of Frenchmen disapproved of Choiseul's Corsican policy and more or less severely condemned him for it.

It is not at all surprising that a large number of Frenchmen heartily approved Choiseul's acquisition of Corsica. For decades the island had been a topographical cannon pointed at the southern coasts of France, a cannon that became less figurative and more ominous when Pasquale Paoli appeared ready to invite the English into Corsica and thus give the British gunboats protected harbors for the real cannons that could blockade and bombard French ports, cut communications by sea with the Bourbon powers of Spain and the Two-Sicilies, and disrupt, perhaps stop entirely, French trade with the Levant. For decades Corsica had absorbed part of France's diplomatic, economic, and military energies and resources— and for decades Frenchmen had speculated about the eventual fate of the island. Choiseul brought the Corsican problem to a conclusion favorable to French interests. Moreover, acquisition of the island lessened the sting of the renunciation of Minorca as stipulated by the Peace of Paris of 1763, a peace for which Choiseul had to bear the responsibility. His Corsican policy therefore increased his reputation as a minister and statesman whose efforts had restored French power and prestige after the disasters of the Seven Year's War. As an anonymous officer of the regiment of Picardie wrote during the 1770s, "the *calcul* of the Duc de Choiseul was . . . that of a statesman, who collected under one point of view an infinite number of reasons which made [Corsica] necessary to France."[1]

Not many of Choiseul's contemporaries went so far as one French memoirist who saw great humanitarianism in his Corsican policy. This writer praised Choiseul because the minister's "love of peace and humanity" caused him to hold out a helping hand to the Corsicans. If left to themselves, the islanders would continue to destroy each other; but under French protection they could be saved from themselves.[2] More often those who approved Choiseul's policy did so because they were relieved that the seemingly interminable and potentially dangerous controversy over Corsica had finally been ended.[3] Thus *raison d'état* had triumphed, and Choiseul's final resolution of the Corsican problem added to his stature in the eyes of many of his countrymen. When he neared the end of his ministry in 1770, he was more highly regarded and more widely praised than any other minister of foreign affairs during the long reign of Louis XV.

Indeed, Choiseul's disgrace and dismissal from power in December 1770 brought a startling outburst of public opinion in his favor. One of his biographers indicated that a French minister's dismissal generally "left the public quite indifferent." But Choiseul's dismissal was not like this. The marks of public sympathy for him "took the proportions of a national manifestation and each day became more wounding and more injurious to King Louis XV and to the triumphant party" that caused his downfall. Choiseul's biographer wrote that the movement in the minister's favor was "an irresistible movement of public opinion," and that Choiseul's departure from Versailles was a "veritable triumph." The greatest figures of Paris came to see him before he left for exile at Chanteloupe. In fact, the streets near his residence were so crowded with carriages that traffic stopped. Portraits were painted, busts were made, and medals were struck in Choiseul's honor. Above all, Choiseul was praised and his enemies were attacked in epigrams and verse.[4]

A second reaction to Choiseul's Corsican policy was indifference or ambivalence. Jean le Rond d'Alembert's reaction to the conquest of Corsica suggested indifference. To Alembert, the Corsican affair was like "the fable of the frog and the rat [being] carried away by the kite." Indifferent also was Charles de Brosses, *président à mortier* in the parlement of Bourgogne. Writing to his cousin on November 18, 1768, Brosses observed: "I will speak to you neither about Corsica, nor about grains, nor about [the] controller [general]. I am persuaded that all of these objects and others are as well as can be and will always be the same." [5] Voltaire was ambivalent in his judgment of Choiseul's Corsican policy. Voltaire thought that Corsica was "a very miserable country," which would cost more to keep than it cost to conquer. Perhaps, he wrote, it would have been better for France simply to declare itself the protector of the island and to exact a tribute from it. Yet Voltaire did not explicitly criticize Choiseul's Corsican policy, possibly because he considered Choiseul a friend of the *philosophes*. Those who govern, Voltaire wrote, have insights that common individuals do not have. It may be that Corsica will become important if future troubles develop in Italy. In any case, "the ministers are able to see what the rest of the world does not see. Moreover, this enterprise, having once been started, can hardly be renounced without shame." [6]

What Voltaire said about the Corsican venture depended largely upon the person to whom he was writing at any given moment. To the Duchesse de Choiseul, he wrote that the Corsican affair brought "much honor" to her husband, whom Voltaire began to call "la corsique." But to the Comte de Schomberg, he wrote in a lighter vein: Through his Corsican policy, Choiseul "wins a kingdom with one hand and he builds a city with the other. He could say, like Lulli to a page, while he opened a beer-barrel, 'My friend make the sign of the cross because, as you can easily see, I have both my hands occupied'." [7]

Like Voltaire's judgment of Choiseul's Corsican policy, the later judgment made by the wily Talleyrand reflected ambivalence. Writing in 1811, Talleyrand cast his eyes back upon Choiseul's ministry, and he did not like what he saw. Included in his critique was an evaluation of the acquisition of Corsica. Talleyrand thought the conquest of the island was too costly in men and money. Moreover, he wrote, the advantages expected from Corsica for the French navy had been nil. Yet his final judgment of Choiseul's Corsican policy was not entirely negative. He realized that Corsica formed a French province in the Mediterranean, a province much envied by the English. Finally, he wrote, "there is a possibility that this possession may yet be of use to us in the future." [8]

Although Choiseul's popularity suggests that a majority of his contemporaries either approved of his Corsican policy or were ambivalent in their judgments, there is evidence that a large number of Frenchmen vigorously criticized French acquisition of the island—for a variety of reasons. Some critics believed that the cost of conquest was far too great. Reflecting this criticism was the Abbé Joseph-Alphonse Véri, admirer of the *philosophes,* friend of Turgot, and a member of the physiocratic school of economic thinking. Véri thought that the acquisition of Corsica was one of Choiseul's worst mistakes. Corsica, he said, is "an acquisition useless in time of peace and troublesome in time of war." Véri was certain that if Choiseul had anticipated "the men and millions he would have to bury" in Corsica, he would not have acquired the island for France.[9]

The Duc de Croy suggested that criticism of Choiseul's expensive Corsican policy was widespread, and that this criticism was damaging to the minister's position at court. Croy feared for the health of Louis XV throughout the end of 1768 and the beginning of 1769. He also had fears, he said, because the condition of the finances seemed very bad. Although he said the new controller general, Maynon d'Invault, appeared to be doing very well, there was the intolerable burden of Corsican expenses, which severely hurt the kingdom. Croy concluded that "Corsica makes many inveigh against Choiseul," and thus added to the dangers posed by his unfriendly relations with Mme du Barry. Yet Croy claimed to believe that Choiseul seemed to be bearing it all with dignity.[10]

E. A. Vignerod du Plessis de Richelieu, duc d'Aiguillon, also reflected a growing criticism of Choiseul's ministry among the members of the du Barry party at Versailles. Aiguillon was a member of that party, which eventually brought about Choiseul's dismissal. Moreover, Aiguillon profited personally from Choiseul's downfall by becoming secretary of state for foreign affairs. In the Corsican affair, Aiguillon found something that he thought would discredit Choiseul's ministry and he made the most of it, vigorously denouncing the acquisition of Corsica. The island, he said, was "a kingdom of misery" and was of little value to France.[11]

Finally, Choiseul's Corsican policy was severely criticized by the *philosophes.* They were far from unanimous in opposing the acquisition, as the comments by Alembert and Voltaire suggest, but even those who favored Choiseul's policy recogized that the *philosophes* reproved him for his treatment of

Paoli and the Corsicans. Colonel Jacques-Antoine-Hippolyte Guibert, commander of the Corsican legion, noted the widespread disapprobation among the *philosophes*. These "pretended philosophers," wrote Guibert, "judge only through the unfaithful prism of their petty opinions," and they claim that "the war [Choiseul] has just made is an outrage against the vigor of a happy and free nation." [12]

Though the Abbé Vatar of Rennes disagreed with these criticisms of Choiseul, he too recognized the widespread disapproval of the latter's policy. Writing to Choiseul on June 27, 1770, Vatar said that the French *savants* and *profonds nouvellistes* had asked "one hundred times" what good this island was to France. It was mountainous, unproductive, and unhealthy; its conquest had cost more than its value; and its upkeep would now add new expenses. France would have nothing but trouble from Corsica, for its people would never be pacified. Moreover, Vatar noted, Choiseul's critics believed that the English would cause trouble whenever they found an opportunity. Vatar thought such reasoning could be excused because it was based on ignorance and not on spite and envy. [13]

The Abbé Vatar was not entirely fair to those he judged when he commented that the *savants* and *profonds nouvellistes* based their criticisms of Choiseul's Corsican policy on ignorance. They judged that policy harshly because they realized that, in both human and financial terms, the costs of conquest for France had been great. They also realized that the costs had been even greater for the islanders, who lost not only men and money but also their one real chance to become an independent nation. It is possible to disparage the Corsican hopes for independence. Alone they had little chance of nationhood. As a part of France they could become something more than a rustic, primitive society. Yet their desire for liberty, however restricted it may have been, and for independence, however rustic the result, gave birth to noble visions before the American and French revolutionists tried to realize similar visions. The same desires resulted in a modern patriotism and nationalism before those forces became a mainstream of western civilization. Such visions and desires, and the forces that resulted from them, placed Corsica in the mainstream of the eighteenth century, despite its lack of culture, literature, and, in general, its lack of participation in the stream of west-European civilization.

Yet the Corsicans' noble visions, their patriotism, and their nationalism counted but little in the diplomacy of the eighteenth century. As Voltaire wrote, after discussing the treaty of 1768 that ceded Corsica to France, "it remains to be known if men have the right to sell other men: but this is a question that will never be discussed in any treaty." [14] The anonymous officer of the regiment of Picardie who was cited earlier did deal with Voltaire's question. Was it not legitimate, he observed, for the Corsicans to ask by what title the Genoese practiced their tyranny in Corsica? Could the islanders not say that they had never unanimously submitted to Genoa, and whenever they did accept the republic's rule they did so under certain conditions? But these conditions had never been fulfilled, which nullified "le pacte." "And what right have [the Genoese] therefore to sell us to France without our consent?" [15]

Another writer who discussed the question that Voltaire posed was Moufle d'Angerville, author of the celebrated *Vie privée de Louis XV*. Even if the Genoese rights to Corsica were valid, Angerville wrote, were not "the constant demands of an entire people, who for almost a half-century have freed themselves from Genoa's tyrannical yoke, much more legitimate?" And even supposing the justice of Genoa's rights, could one nation be transferred to another nation without its "explicit consent?" In the end, Angerville concluded, Choiseul paid no attention to these questions and to "the ineffectual treatises on the rights of nature and of men." Instead, Choiseul used "the only law of sovereigns, the law of the strongest." [16] Corsica was not the first, nor would it be the last, small state to suffer this fate. Internal unrest within a country recognized as having a strategic position seems to invite intervention by great powers seeking security, endeavoring to protect and further their interests of state, and hoping to maintain and perhaps to strengthen their respective positions in the balance of power.

But the treatises on the rights of nature and of men were perhaps not as ineffectual as Angerville contended. Opposition to Choiseul's policy, however ineffective it was in terms of high politics, illustrates the effect of those treatises. Choiseul himself was influenced by them. After strategic and military priorities had won over all other considerations and Choiseul had acquired Corsica for France, he turned with vigor, enthusiasm, and insight to the problem he had signaled as early as 1760 when he commented that the troubles in Corsica would never be overcome until the Genoese established a new and totally different form of government in the island. Even before the Genoese were gone and French troops had conquered the island, Choiseul began the task of reconstruction and regeneration that the Genoese had been unable to accomplish. He not only attempted to establish a form of government different from that of Genoa; he attempted to found in Corsica a form of government different from that in France, a government more suitable to the particular needs and circumstances of the Corsican people. His efforts were to a large extent inspired by those treatises on the rights of nature and of men, or, in broader terms, by the reforming spirit and ideas of the Enlightenment.[17]

The influence of the Enlightenment's treatises, ideals, and principles can also be traced in the writings of the anonymous officer of the regiment of Picardie who was cited earlier both for his approbation of Choiseul's statesmanship in acquiring Corsica and for raising the question whether Genoa had the right to determine the fate of the Corsican people without their consent. As a military officer this writer clearly realized the strategic importance of Corsica to France; thus the acquisition was necessary. He also realized that Paoli's resistance had compromised Choiseul to the point that the conquest became necessary. Yet, as the following quotation indicates, he was also warmly sympathetic to the Corsicans and appreciative of their struggle:

> To overthrow the tyrant, only a single well-determined will is necessary. The history of despots is filled with such examples. But to destroy tyranny, general cooperation, the union of individual wills, is necessary, and this unanimity can only be the product of strong, vigorous, and virtuous spirits. Although these examples are perhaps no longer rare, . . . the Corsican people furnish a quite living one to all Europe, which is a certain guarantee that, in every case, a handful of courageous men, well united, virtuous, and incorruptible, will always be a check, which, sooner or later, will hinder the effects of despotism, if they do not destroy it. There is the aspect that speaks to me in favor of these people.

The examples of history, this officer continued,

> teach us that the greatest examples of virtue, of grandeur of spirit and of courage, have been given only by free peoples, because liberty alone makes us capable of exercising our faculties to the full. . . . Posterity alone can pronounce this equitable judgment on the conduct of this people, on its attachment to its liberty, and on the means that it has put to use in order to obtain it.[18]

Thus the Corsican question and its resolution by Choiseul and French troops posed to Europe a number of highly charged questions a decade before the American Revolution posed similar questions. One of the ironies of history is that France was the great power that suppressed the Corsicans' liberty and denied them independence; it was also the great power that militarily and morally helped the American colonists achieve liberty and independence. Yet both facts can be explained more fully by invoking *raison d'état* rather than irony.

NOTES

1. V. de Caraffa, ed., "Mémoires par un officier du régiment de Picardie," p. 88.
2. Anonymous, "Mémoire sur l'ile de Corse, événements principaux de 1731 à 1769," [April, 1770], AG, *Mém. hist.*, 248 [1], pp. 28–29.
3. Examples of those who approved Choiseul's Corsican policy are numerous. See, for example, M. Guibert, "Mémoire sur la Corse," June 26, 1769, *ibid.*, 1098.48; the Abbé Vatar to [Choiseul], June 27, 1770, AE, *France*, 1536, fol. 82; Abbé de Germanes, *Révolutions de Corse*, III, 38.
4. Gaston Maugras, *La disgrace du duc et de la duchesse de Choiseul* (Paris, 1903), pp. 3–12.
5. Alembert to Voltaire, Sept. 14, 1768, in *Oeuvres complètes de d'Alembert*, 5 Vols. (Paris, 1821–1822), V, 179; Yvonne Bezard, ed., *Lettres du président de Brosses à Ch.-C. Loppin de Gemeaux* (Paris, 1929), p. 311.
6. Voltaire to the Comte de Wargemont, Jan. 16, 1769, in Theodore Besterman, ed., *Voltaire's Correspondence*, 107 Vols. (Geneva, 1953–1965), LXXI, 43.
7. Voltaire to Mme de Choiseul, July 3, 1769, and to the Comte de Schomberg, Sept. 22, 1769, in *ibid.*, LXXII, 121, and LXXIII, 72.
8. Duc de Broglie, ed., *Memoirs of the Prince of Talleyrand*, Mrs. Angus Hall, trans. 5 Vols. (New York, 1892), V, 383. Of course, Talleyrand's judgment may have been influenced by the fact that Corsica was the birthplace of his master.
9. Baron Jean de Witte, ed., *Journal de l'abbé de Véri*, 2 Vols. (Paris, 1935), I, 54.
10. Vicomte de Grouchy and Paul Cottin, eds., *Journal inédite du duc de Croÿ, 1718–1784*, 2 Vols. (Paris, 1906), II, 364.
11. Cesari-Rocca and Louis Villat, *Histoire de la Corse*, pp. 220–221. On the intrigues of Choiseul's enemies against him, see Gaston Maugras, *Le duc et la duchesse de Choiseul; Leur vie intime, leurs amis et leurs temps* (Paris, 1902), pp. 379–467.
12. M. Guibert, "Mémoire sur la Corse," June 26, 1769, AG, *Mém. hist.*, 1098.48.
13. The Abbé Vatar to [Choiseul], June 27, 1770, AE, *France*, 1536, fol. 82. It would perhaps be of some value to know something more about this person, if for no other reason than that he sounds interesting. His letter mentions projects that he had submitted to the minister on the following subjects: the navy; Sardinia; cultivation of tobacco and fabrication of woolen goods; interception of English ships trading with Italy and Turkey; Portugal; and turning Prussian ambitions toward commerce and navigation to cause the English trouble. These

projects, Vatar reported, constituted less than one-twentieth of his views, some of which had been adopted without giving him credit. Naturally, he had also presented a project on Corsica.

14. *Précis du siècle de Louis XV*, in Adrien Beuchot, ed., *Oeuvres complètes de Voltaire*, XV, 415.
15. V. de Caraffa, ed., *op. cit.*, pp. 238–239.
16. "Extrait de la vie privée de Louis XV," AN, T 1169 [1].
17. Choiseul played a key role in efforts to regenerate Corsica after the conquest, as I have suggested in an article on "Thought and Practice of Enlightened Government in French Corsica," *The American Historical Review*, LXXIV (Feb. 1969), 880–905.
18. V. de Caraffa, ed., *op. cit.*, pp. 236–237, 240.

Sources

I. MANUSCRIPT SOURCES

The manuscript sources for this study are widely scattered through several major French archival repositories in Paris and in two French departments. Those repositories include the *Archives Nationales,* the Archives of the Ministries of Foreign Affairs, War, and the Navy, the Departmental Archives of Corsica and of Bouches-du-Rhône, and the Manuscript Division of the *Bibliothèque Nationale.* In general, the classification systems adopted by the various archives have been admirably established to provide easy access to documents dealing with a great variety of subject matter. Yet the researcher can never be certain that he will find all the material properly classified under the series or subseries dealing with the subject indicated by their titles. Indeed, important manuscripts are often found classified under a series title that appears irrelevant to the subject pursued. The researcher's task is like looking for a missing person. He has a few leads to assist him in the search, some of which are cited in the bibliography under the heading "Bibliography and Special Aids." At other times the researcher must resort to calculated guesses in an effort to discover those leads for himself. In the section on manuscript sources that follows, only those cases in which the present search has produced important results are cited.

A. *Archives Nationales:* Paris

Information on Corsican affairs in this repository is widely scattered throughout several series. For this study, the following *laisses* (bundles of loose documents held together by a ribbon) were important:

Series K; *Monuments historiques*
    K 1225
    K 1226
    K 1229

Series Q; *Titres Domaniaux*
    Q^1 291
    Q^1 295
    Q^1 298^1

Series T; *Séquestre*
    T 1169^{1-3}
    T 1527

B. *Archives du Ministère des Affaires Étrangères:* Paris

There are two principal series of manuscripts in this archival deposit: *Mémoires et documents* and *Correspondance politique*. The following volumes in these series have particular bearing on the subject of the eighteenth-century Corsica:

Mémoires et documents
    Corse, 1536 (1769–1789)
    Corse, 1541 (1681–1779)

    France, 540

Correspondance politique
    Corse,   I (1732–1738)
    Corse,   II (1739–1742)
    Corse, III (1749–1750)
    Corse, IV (1751–1752)
    Corse,   V (1752–1757)
    Corse, VI (1709–1780)
    Corse, VII (1737–1780)
    Corse, VIII (1739–1768)
    Corse, IX (1730–1757)

C. *Archives du Ministère de la Guerre:* Château de Vincennes

Because of the frequent intervention by the French army in eighteenth-century Corsican affairs, the manuscripts of this archival deposit were of special importance for this study. The two series in which pertinent sources were found are *Mémoires historiques* and *Archives historiques.* The latter series contains correspondence of various officials with the *Ministère de la Guerre.* Also useful was the personal dossier, *Valcroissant,* and the record books of the series *Pensions de la Trésorerie Royale,* which list pensions accorded to military personnel. The following volumes and *laisses* were of particular importance:

Mémoires historiques

145	907	1098
206[3]	907[1]	1099
248[1]	952	

Archives historiques

A[1] 2871	A[1] 3332	A[1] 3653
A[1] 2885	A[1] 3539	A[1] 3654 bis
A[1] 3234	A[1] 3635	A[1] 3655
A[1] 3248	A[1] 3638	A[1] 3659
A[1] 3300	A[1] 3644	A[1] 3660
A[1] 3305	A[1] 3646	A[1] 3661
A[1] 3306	A[1] 3647	A[1] 3662
A[1] 3307	A[1] 3648	A[1] 3666
A[1] 3330	A[1] 3651	A[1] 3669
A[1] 3331	A[1] 3652	

Y[a] 194

D. *Archives du Ministère de la Marine:* Paris

Because the various French occupations and the French conquest of Corsica were primarily the work of the army, the naval archives were not as important for this study as the *Archives de la Guerre.* However, there is much information on Corsica scattered throughout the many volumes of the B Series of the *Archives de la Marine.* This information deals with the following subjects: transportation of troops to Corsica and problems of supply; ships and ordnance for Corsica; exploitation of the forests of

Corsica; early economic and administrative organization of the island during the conquest; and miscellaneous news from the island. Special attention is called to the following subdivisions of Series B and to the volumes contained in each subdivision that have important bearing on the subject of this study.

B¹ *Travail du roi et travail du ministère*
Vols. 60 (1738–1739)
       61 (1740–1742)
       66 (1751)
       69 (1764)
       73 (1768)
       75 (1770)

B² *Ordres et dépêches du roi*
Vols. 340 (1750)
       342 (1751)
       389 (1768)
       392 (1768)
       393 (1770)
       395 (1770)

B³ *Lettres reçues*
Vols. 564 (1764)
       567 (1765)
       571 (1766)
       579 (1768)
       586 (1769)
       590 (1770)

E. *Archives départmentales de la Corse:* Ajaccio

In general, this archival deposit did not furnish important information for this study of the French policy toward the Corsican question, although it is a rich source of information for local history. One register in Series C, *Intendance,* should be noted: C 126, register of letters from the intendant Chardon to Choiseul and others. There are a few *laisses* that deal with problems on the island during the conquest and immediately thereafter. These *laisses* include C 48, C 543, and C 549.

F. *Archives départmentales des Bouches-du-Rhòne:* Aix-en-Provence

This archival deposit provided information for the present study because troop movements to Corsica originated in Antibes, Toulon, and Marseille. The important series was Series C, *Intendance,* manuscripts in which provided information on transportation of troops and dependents to the island; problems of supply for troops; engineers sent to Corsica; recruits for the regiment *Royal-Corse;* evacuation of men and materials when French troops left the island; interministerial controversy over jurisdiction while the French forces were on Corsica; illness among the troops; Post-boats; Jesuits; and miscellaneous news from the island. Special attention is called to the following *laisses:*

Series C: *Intendance.*

C 2306 (1737–1738)	C 2925 (1768–1770)
C 2307 (1739–1741)	C 2926 (1767–1769)
C 2920 (1753)	C 2927 (1768–1770)
C 2924 (1765–1770)	

G. *Bibliothèque Nationale,* MSS Division: Paris

The *Bibliothèque Nationale* does not have many manuscripts that deal with the eighteenth-century Corsican question. Those it does hold are widely scattered and are not of primary value. However, attention should be called to the following:

Fonds français, 6433. "Histoire [des guerres]," by the Abbé Guillaume Thomas Raynal. This is a seven-volume work, Volume V of which makes several references to Corsica during the 1730s and 1740s. It is useful for military events and for the author's comments on the Corsican character.

Fonds français, 8965. "Recueil des mémoires sur l'histoire, l'administration, les mines, les bois et forêts de l'île de Corse, avec cartes et plans levés XVIIIe siècle," 102 *feuillets.* This collection of memoirs pertains mostly to the period after 1768. However, it does contain information about Paoli's efforts to develop his island's natural resources.

Fonds français, 10661. *Correspondance diplomatique diverses.* This volume contains copies of Noailles' letters on Spanish affairs.

Fonds français, 13791. *Tableau historiques de l'isle de Corse,* by the Abbé Halma, librarian to the Empress Josephine. This document is essentially in the rare-book category—a curious piece of work, beautifully done, but otherwise of little historical value.

Fonds français, 14608. "Mémoires historiques et critiques contenant les opérations des troops . . . en Corse . . . , par Guyot de Puymorin," MS Original, eighteenth century, 88 *feuillets.* This manuscript is a very personal account of the author's service in the regiment of Flanders which served in Corsica in 1739. The document refers to military action on Corsica, the nature of the Genoese Government, the Corsican character, and advantages the island holds for France. There are frequent references to the author's state of mind, health, and *coeur.*

Nouvelles acquisitions françaises, 9400. This volume is part of a larger collection related to the French navy under Louis XV. It bears the title "Événements de Corse (1736–1750)." The volume contains 351 *feuillets.*

Nouvelles acquisitions françaises, 13505. "Choiseul, duc de Stainville, madame de Pompadour, et le cardinal de Bernis (1719–1758)," by Pierre Muret.

II. A SELECTED BIBLIOGRAPHY

A. BIBLIOGRAPHY AND SPECIAL AIDS

Aimes, Paul and Pierre Lamotte. *Les Archives de la Corse; source essentielle pour la connaissance de l'île.* Ajaccio, 1954.

R. Benson, *Sketches of Corsica.* London, 1825.

Berthelot, André and F. Ceccaldi. *Les cartes de la Corse, de Ptolémée au XIX siècle.* Paris, 1939.

Busquet, J. *Le Droit de la vendetta de les paci corses.* Paris, 1920.

Cesari-Rocca, Colonna de. *Histoire de la Corse.* Paris, 1907.

Giardelli, Renato. *Saggio di una bibliografia generale sulla Corsica.* Genoa, 1938.

Mémoires pour servir à l'histoire de la Corse. Printed for S. Hooper. London, 1768.

Michel, Ersilio. "I manoscritti della Biblioteca Nazionale di Parigi relativi alla storia di Corsica," *Archivio Storico di Corsica,* V (1929), 152–168.

———. *I manoscritti dell'Archivio Nazionale di Parigi relativi alla storia di Corsica.* Leghorn, 1935.

Ministère de la Guerre. *Inventaire sommaire des Archives Historiques (Archives Anciennes-Correspondance).* 7 Vols. Paris, 1930.

Ministère des Affaires Étrangères. *Inventaire sommaire des Archives du Département des Affaires Étrangères: Correspondance Politique.* 2 Vols. Paris, 1908.

Roncière, Chevalier [Charles] de la. *Catalogue général des manuscrits des bibliothèques publiques de France: Bibliothèques de la Marine.* Paris, 1907.

Starace, Carmine. *Bibliografia della Corsica*. Isola del Liri, 1943.

Tuetey, Louis. *Catalogue général des manuscrits des bibliotheques publiques de France: Archives de la Guerre*. 3 Vols. Paris, 1912.

Villat, Louis. *La Corse de 1768 à 1789: Thèse complémentaire; Essai de bibliographie critique*. Besançon, 1925.

B. PRINTED PRIMARY SOURCES

"L'administration municipale de Bastia sous la domination gênoise." *Corse Historiques*, No. 1 (1953), 54–67.

Alembert, Jean Le Rond, *dit d'*. *Oeuvres complètes de d'Alembert*. 5 Vols. Paris, 1821–1822.

Argenson, René-Louis Voyer. Marquis d'. *Journal et mémoires du marquis d'Argenson*. E. J. Rathery, ed., 9 Vols. Paris, 1859.

Avenel, J. L. M., ed., *Lettres, instructions diplomatiques et papiers d'état du Cardinal Richelieu*. 8 Vols. Paris, 1853–1877.

Barbier, Edmond-Jean-François. *Chronique de la régence et du règne de Louis XV (1718–1763), ou Journal de Barbier*. 8 Vols. Paris, 1857.

Bellin, Jacques Nicolas. *Description géographique et historique de l'isle de Corse, pour joindre aux cartes et plans de cette isle*. Paris, 1769.

Bezard, Yvonne, ed. *Lettres du président de Brosses à Ch.-C. Loppin de Gemeaux*. Paris, 1929.

Boswell, James. *The Journal of a Tour to Corsica; and Memoirs of Pascal Paoli*. Morchard Bishop, ed. London, 1951.

Bréguigny, Felix de. *Histoire des révolutions de Gênes, depuis son établissement jusqu'à la conclusion de la paix de 1748*. 2nd ed., 2 Vols. Paris, 1752.

Campocasso, Z. and the Abbé L. Letteron, eds. "Correspondance de M. Jadart (12 août 1767–12 mai 1768), commissaire des guerres, suivi de la correspondance (12 août 1767–19 juillet 1768) du comte de Marbeuf, commandant des troupes de S.M.T.C. en Corse," *Bulletin de la Société des Sciences historiques et naturelles de la Corse* (numerous numbers, 1882–1883).

Caraffa, P., ed. "Memorie per servire alla storia delle rivoluzioni di Corsica dal 1729 al 1764, del Padre Bonfiglio Guelfucci, di Belgodere," *Bulletin de la Société des Sciences historiques et naturelles de la Corse* (June and Aug. 1882), 1–235.

Caraffa, V. de, ed. "Mémoires historiques sur la Corse par un officier du régiment de Picardie (1774–1777)." *Bulletin de la Société des Sciences historiques et naturelles de la Corse* (Apr.–June 1889).

Cervoni, Baron, ed. "La première intervention français en Corse en 1738," *Bulletin de la Société des Sciences historiques et naturelles de la Corse* (Feb. 1882), 367–412.

Choiseul, Étienne-François, Duc de. *Choiseul à Rome; Lettres et mémoires inédites (1754–1757).* Maurice Boutry, ed. Paris, 1895.

———. *Choiseul et Voltaire, d'après les lettres inédites de Choiseul à Voltaire.* Pierre Calmettes, ed. Paris, 1902.

———. *Mémoires dè duc de Choiseul.* Pierre Calmettes, ed. Paris, 1904.

Clercq, A. de, ed. *Recueil des traites de la France.* 15 Vols. Paris, 1844–1888.

Code Corse. Recueil des Édits, Déclarations, Lettres Patentes, Arrêts et Reglèments publiés dans l'Isle de Corse depuis sa soumission à l'obéissance du Roi, avec la traduction en italien. Imprimé par ordre de Sa Majesté. 3 Vols. Paris, 1778.

Croÿ, Auguste-Philippe-Louis-Emmanuel, Duc de. *Journal inédit du Duc de Croÿ, 1718–1784.* Vicomte de Grouchy and Paul Cottin, eds. 2 Vols. Paris, 1906.

Deffand, Marie de Vichy, Marquise du. *Lettres de la marquise du Deffand à Horace Walpole.* Mrs. Paget Toynbee, ed. 3 Vols. London, 1912.

Driault, Édouard, ed. *Recueil des instructions données aux ambassadeurs et ministres de France.* Vol. XIX, *Florence, Modène, Gênes.* Paris, 1912.

Dufort, J. N. (Comte de Cheverny). *Mémoires sur les règnes de Louis XV et Louis XVI et sur la Révolution par J. N. Dufort, comte de Cheverny, 1731–1802.* Robert de Crèvecoeur, ed. 2 Vols. Paris, 1886.

Dumouriez, Charles-François. *Mémoires du général Dumouriez.* François Barrière, ed. 2 Vols. Paris, 1862.

Farges, Louis, ed. *Recueil des instructions données aux ambassadeurs et ministres de France,* Vols. IV and V, *Pologne.* 2 Vols. Paris, 1884–1888.

Faur, Louis-François [or de Laborde, Jean-Benjamin]. *Vie privée du maréchal de Richelieu, contenant ses amours et intrigues.* Fernand Mitton, ed. Paris, 1912.

Flammermont, Jules F. *Les correspondances des agents diplomatiques étrangères en France avant la Révolution.* Paris, 1896.

Fortesque, Sir John, ed. *The Correspondence of King George III from 1760 to December, 1783.* 6 Vols. London, 1927.

Gaudin, the Abbé Jacques Maurice. *Voyage en Corse, et vues politiques sur l'amélioration de cette isle.* Paris, 1787.

Germanes, M. the Abbé de, Vicaire général de Rennes. *Histoire des révolutions de Corse, depuis ses premiers habitans jusqu'à nos jours.* 3 Vols. Paris, 1771–1776.

Great Britain, Public Record Office. *Calendar of Home Office Papers of the Reign of George III, 1766–1769.* 5 Vols. London, 1879.

Guerri, Francesco. *La conquista francese della Corsica da un giornale dell' epoca.* Leghorn, 1932.

Hanotaux, Gabriel and Jean Hanoteau, eds. *Recueil des instructions données aux ambassadeurs et ministres de France,* Vols. VI, XVII, and XX, *Rome.* 3 Vols. Paris, 1888–1913.

235

Lamotte, Pierre, ed. "La formation du premier gouvernement Corse autonome," *Corse Historique,* No. 2 (1953), 12–23.

———. "L'intervention de l'Empereur en Corse en 1731–1732," *Corse Historique,* No. 3 (1953), 16–19.

Legg, L. G. Wickham, ed., *British Diplomatic Instruction, 1689–1789,* Vol. VII, France, Part IV, 1745–1789. London, Royal Historical Publications, Series 3, Vol. 49, 1934.

Letteron, the Abbé L., ed. "Carteggio fra Sua Eccellenza Pasquale de Paoli . . . e il Signor duca di Choiseul . . . , *Bulletin de la Société des Sciences historiques et naturelles de la Corse* (Sept. 1886), 443–596.

———. "Correspondance des agents de France avec le ministère," *Bulletin de la Société des Sciences historiques et naturelles de la Corse* (numerous numbers, 1902 and 1913).

———. "Journal d'Antonio Buttafoco," *Bulletin de la Société des Sciences historiques et naturelles de la Corse* (July–Sept. 1913), 2–72.

———. "Mémoire sur l'expédition des troupes allemandes en 1731–1733," *Bulletin de la Société des Sciences historiques et naturelles de la Corse* (Jan.–Feb. 1884), 243–283.

———. "Mémoires de Rostini, *Bulletin de la Société des Sciences historiques et naturelles de la Corse* (numerous numbers, 1882–1883).

———. "Osservazioni storiche sopra la Corsica dell'abbate Ambrogio Rossi," [1705–1810], *Bulletin de la Société des Sciences historiques et naturelles de la Corse* (numerous numbers, 1895–1909).

———. "Pièces diverses concernant l'insurrection de Domenico Rivarola et le siège de Bastia en 1747," *Bulletin de la Société des Sciences historiques et naturelles de la Corse* (March 1883), 48–70.

———. "Pontenovo; 8 mai 1769," *Bulletin de la Société des Sciences historiques et naturelles de la Corse* (Apr.–June 1913), 27–43.

London Magazine, or Gentleman's Monthly Intelligencer, The. London, 1768–1769, Vols. 36–37.

Luynes, Louis-Joseph-Charles-Amable d'Albert, Duc de. *Mémoires du duc de Luynes sur la cour de Louis XV (1735–1785).* L. Dussieux and E. Soulie, eds. 17 Vols. Paris, 1860–1865.

Maurepas, Jean-Frédéric Phélypeaux, Comte de. *Mémoires du comte de Maurepas, ministre de la marine.* 4 Vols. Paris, 1792.

Mémoire historique sur la négociation de la France et de l'Angleterre, depuis le 26 mars 1761 jusqu'au 20 septembre de la même année, avec les pièces justificatives. Paris, 1761.

Mercure de France, Le. Paris, 1672–1820.

Montesquieu, Charles-Louis de Secondat, Baron de la Brède et de. *Montesquieu: Cahiers (1716–1755).* Bernard Grasset, ed. Paris, 1941.

———. *Montesquieu: Oeuvres complètes.* Daniel Oster, ed. Paris, 1964.

"Notes prises pendant la campagne de 1739 en Corse," *Révue Rétrospective,* new series, V (1892), 217–237.

Ozanam, Didier, and Michel Antoine, eds. *Correspondance secrète du comte de Broglie avec Louis XV (1756–1774)*. 2 Vols. Paris, 1956 and 1961.

Paoli, Pasquale. "Lettere di Pasquale de'Paoli." N. Tommaseo, ed. *Archivio Storico Italiano*, XI (1846), 1–246.

———. "Lettere inedite di Pasquale de'Paoli." Giovanni Livi, ed. *Archivio Storico Italiano*, 5th series, V (1890), 61–107, 228–274; VI (1890), 267–306.

Pommereul, François-René-Jean. *Histoire de l'isle de Corse*. 2 Vols. Berne, 1779.

Richelieu, Louis-François-Armond du Plessis, Maréchal de. *Mémoires authentiques du maréchal de Richelieu*. A. de Boislisle, ed. Paris, 1981.

Rousseau, Jean-Jacques. *Correspondance générale de J.-J. Rousseau*. Theophile Dufour, ed. 20 Vols. Paris, 1824–1834.

———. *Oeuvres de J.-J. Rousseau*. M. Mussay-Pathay, ed. 20 Vols.; Paris, 1827.

———. *Oeuvres et correspondance inédites de J.-J. Rousseau*. G. Streckeisen-Moulton, ed. Paris, 1861.

Rousset, Camille, ed. *Correspondance de Louis XV et maréchal de Noailles*. 2 Vols. Paris, 1869.

I Russkoe istoricheskoe obshchestvo [Diplomatic Dispatches from English Ambassadors at the Court of Russia, 1762–1769]. St. Petersburg, 1837.

Schoell, Friedrich. *Archives historiques et politiques . . . relatifs à l'his-

Stefanini, François Marie. "L'Administration municipale de Bastia sous la *toire des* xviiie *et* xixe *siècles*. . . . 3 Vols. Paris, 1819.

domination gênoise (June 20, 1770)," *Corse Historique*, No. 1 (1953), 54–67.

Talleyrand, Charles Maurice, Prince de. *Memoirs of the Prince of Talleyrand*. Mrs. Angus Hall, trans. 5 Vols. New York, 1892.

Tourneaux, Maurice, ed. *Correspondance littéraire, philosophique et critique, par Grimm, Diderot, Raynal, Meister, etc.* 16 Vols. Paris, 1877–1882.

Trémoille, Louis de la. *Mon grand-père à la cour de Louis XVI*. Paris, 1904.

Universal Magazine of Knowledge and Pleasure, The. London, 1768–1769, Vols. 42–43.

Vaucher, Paul, ed. *Recueil des instructions données aux ambassadeurs et ministres de France*. Vol. XXV–2, *Angleterre, Tome 3, 1689–1791*. Paris, 1965.

Véri, Joseph-Alphonse. *Journal de l'abbé de Véri*, Baron Jehan de Witte, ed. 2 Vols. Paris, 1935.

Voltaire [François-Marie Arouet]. *Oeuvres complètes de Voltaire*. Adrien Beuchot, ed. New ed., 52 Vols. Paris, 1877–1885.

————. *Voltaire's Correspondence.* Theodore Besterman, ed. 107 Vols. Geneva, 1952–1965.

C. SECONDARY WORKS: BOOKS

Acton, Harold. *The Bourbons of Naples, 1734–1825.* London, 1956.

Albertini, Paul-Louis. *Pourquoi la Corse est française.* Paris, 1939.

———— and Georges Rivollet. *La Corse militaire, ses généraux: Monarchie, Révolution, 1er Empire.* Paris. 1958.

Albitreccia, Antoine. *Histoire de la Corse.* Paris, 1947. (*Que Sais-je* Series.)

————. *La Corse dans l'histoire.* Paris, 1939.

Ambrosi, Christian. *La Corse insurgée et la seconde intervention française au xviiie siècle, 1743–1753.* Paris, 1950.

Ambrosi-Rostino, Ambroise. *Corses et français; leurs rapports à travers l'histoire.* Nîmes, 1940.

————. *Histoire des Corses et de leurs civilisation.* Bastia, 1914.

Andreani, Pierre. *Le Fascisme et la Corse.* Marseille, 1939.

Arrighi, Arrigo. *Histoire de Pascal Paoli, ou la dernière guerre de l'indépendance, 1755–1807.* 2 Vols. Paris, 1843.

Arrighi, Paul. *Histoire de la Corse.* Paris, 1966.

Aubertin, Charles. *L'Esprit publique au xviiie siècle: Étude sur les mémoires et les correspondances politiques des contemporains, 1715 à 1789.* Paris, 1873.

Bamford, Paul W. *Forests and French Sea Power, 1660–1789.* Toronto, 1956.

Bartoli, the Abbé A. F. *Histoire de la Corse, des origines à la conquête romaine. Description, production, moeurs, curiosités.* Paris, 1898.

Baudrillart, Alfred. *Philippe V et la cour de France.* 5 Vols. Paris, 1890–1901.

Biancamaria, J.-T. *La Corse dans sa gloire ses luttes et ses souffrances.* Paris, 1963.

Blart, Louis. *Les rapports de la France et de l'Espagne après le pacte de famille, jusqu'à la fin du ministère du duc de Choiseul.* Paris, 1915.

Bonardi, Pierre. *L'Ile tragique.* Paris, 1937.

Borlandi, Franco. *Per la storia della popolazione della Corsica.* Rome, 1942.

Boudard, René. *Gênes et la France dans la deuxième moitié du xviiie siècle, 1748–1797.* Paris, 1962.

Bourguet, Alfred. *Le duc de Choiseul et l'alliance espagnole.* Paris, 1906.

————. *Études sur la politique étrangère du duc de Choiseul.* Paris, 1909.

Bradi, Lorenzi de. *La Corse inconnue.* Paris, 1927.

Broche, Gaston E. *La république de Gênes et la France pendant la guerre de la succession d'Autriche (1740–1748).* 3 Vols. Paris, 1935.

Brun, V. *Guerres maritimes de la France: Port de Toulon*. 2 Vols. Paris, 1861.

Busquet, J. *Le Droit de la vendetta et les paci corses*. Paris, 1920.

Caird, L. N. *The History of Corsica*. London, 1899.

Campi, Louis. *Histoire-biographie-bibliographie. Observations critiques sur la polemique internationale survenue entre Gênes et la Corse à propos de la justification de la révolution de 1729*. Ajaccio, 1901.

Cantù, Cesare. *Storia degli Italiana*. 15 Vols. Turin, 1877.

Carré, H. *Le Règne de Louis XV (1715–1774)*, Vol. VIII, Pt. 2, of Ernest Lavisse, ed., *Histoire de France depuis les origines jusqu'à la Révolution*. Paris, 1909.

Casanova, S.-B. *Histoire de l'église corse*. 2 Vols. Ajaccio, 1931.

Castries, Duc de. *Le Maréchal de Castries, 1727–1800*. Paris, 1956.

Cesari-Rocca, Colonna de. *Histoire de la Corse*. Paris, 1907.

————, and Louis Villat. *Histoire de Corse*. Paris, 1916.

Corbett, Julian S. *England in the Seven Years' War: A Study in Combined Strategy*. 2 Vols. London, 1907.

Dalzeto, Sebastien. *La Corse et Gênes devant l'histoire, étude de critique historique*. Paris, 1950.

Dedeck-Héry, Ernestine. *Jean-Jacques Rousseau et le projet de constitution pour la Corse*. Philadelphia, 1932.

Dimier, Louis. *Histoire de Savoie*. Paris, 1913.

Dorn, Walter L. *Competition for Empire, 1740–1763*. New York, 1940.

Fitzmaurice, Lord. *Life of William, Earl of Shelburne, afterwards First Marquis of Lansdowne*. 2nd rev. ed., 2 Vols. London, 1912.

Flassan, Gaeton de Raxis de. *Histoire générale et raisonée de la diplomatie française*, 2nd ed., 7 Vols. Paris, 1811.

Fontana, Matthieu. *La Constitution du généralat de Pascal Paoli en Corse, 1755–1769*. Paris, 1907.

Francastel, Pierre, ed. *Utopie et institutions au XVIIIe siècle: Le pragmatisme des Lumières*. Paris, 1963.

Fumarali, D. *Discourse sur l'histoire de la Corse, depuis son origine jusqu'à nos jours*. Marseille, 1930.

Gabrielli, Thadee. *La Corse. Ses luttes pour l'indépendance. Son annexion à la France*. Paris, 1937.

Gaï, Dom Jean-Baptiste. *La Tragique histoire des Corses*. 4th ed. Paris, 1962.

Galletti, Jean Ange. *Histoire illustrée de la Corse*. (Paris, 1863).

Garelli, P. *Les institutions démocratiques de la Corse jusqu'à la conquête française*. Paris, 1905.

Gay, Peter. *Voltaire's Politics: The Poet as Realist*. New York, 1965.

Gipson, Lawrence Henry. *The British Empire before the American Revolution*. Vol. XII, *The Triumphant Empire: Britain Sails into the Storm 1770–1776*. New York, 1965.

Girolami-Cortona, F. *Histoire de la Corse*. Bastia, 1906.

Goebel, Julius, Jr. *The Struggle for the Falkland Islands. A Study in Legal and Diplomatic History*. New Haven, 1927.

Grégori, Jacques. *Nouvelle histoire de la Corse*. Paris, 1967.

Jacobi, J.-M. *Histoire générale de la Corse*. 2 Vols. Paris, 1835.

James, G. ?. R. *Eminent Foreign Statesmen*. 5 Vols. London, 1832–1838.

Joly, Henry. *La Corse française au* xvıᵉ *siècle: La 1ère occupation, 1553–1559*. Lyon, 1942.

Le Glay, André. *Histoire de la conquête de la Corse par la françaises: La Corse pendant la guerre de la succession d'Autriche*. Paris, 1912.

―――. *Théodore de Neuhoff, roi de Corse*. Paris, 1907.

Lindsay, J. O., ed. *The New Cambridge Modern History*, Vol. VII, *The Old Regime, 1713–1763*. Cambridge, Eng., 1957.

Lodge, Sir Richard. *Studies in Eighteenth Century Diplomacy, 1740–1748*. London, 1930.

Lusinchi, Bertzardin. *La Corse et le problème des revendications italiennes* [Conférence faite le 4 janvier 1939 à Casablanca]. N.p., n.d.

Mahon, A. T. *The Influence of Sea Power Upon History, 1660–1783*. 12th ed. Boston, 1918.

Maquard, Georges. *Mémoire sur la crise économique de la Corse. . . .* Paris, 1908.

Maugras, Gaston. *La disgrace du duc et de la duchesse de Choiseul*. Paris, 1903.

―――. *Le duc et la duchesse de Choiseul; Leur vie intime, leurs amis et leurs temps*. Paris, 1902.

Maurel, Paul. *Histoire de Toulon*. Toulon, 1943.

Mornet, Daniel. *French Thought in the Eighteenth Century*. Laurance M. Levin, trans. New York, 1929.

Muret, Pierre. *Peuples et civilisations:* Vol. XI, *La prépondérance anglaise (1715–1763)*. Paris, 1937.

Pajol, Charles-Pierre-Victor, comte de. *Les guerres sous Louis XV*. 7 Vols. Paris, 1888.

Perkins, James Breck. *France under Louis XV*. 2 Vols. Boston and New York, 1899.

Picard, Roger. *Les salons littéraires et la société française, 1610–1789*. New York, 1943.

Piccioni, Camille. *Histoire du Cap Corse*. Paris, 1923.

Pirie, Valerie. *His Majesty of Corsica: The True Story of the Adventurous Life of Theodore Ist*. New York, 1959.

Poli, Xavier. *Histoire militaire des Corses au service de la France*. 2 Vols. Ajaccio, 1899–1900.

Rain, Pierre. *La Diplomatie française d'Henri IV à Vergennes*. Paris, 1945.

Ramsey, John F. *Anglo-French Relations, 1763–1700: A Study of Choiseul's Foreign Policy*. Berkeley, 1939.

Roberts, Penfield. *The Quest for Security, 1715–1740*. New York, 1963.

Robiquet, Felix. *Recherches historiques et statistiques sur la Corse*. Paris, 1835.

Rocca, Petru. *Un peu d'histoire . . . relatifs à l'occupation française de la Corse*. Ajaccio, 1938.

Roger, G. *L'âme de la Corse à travers la littérature française (Anthologie)*. Algiers, 1947.

Rousseau, François. *Règne de Charles III d'Espagne, 1759–1788*. 2 Vols. Paris, 1907.

Sagnac, Philippe. *Peuples et civilisations:* Vol. XII, *La fin de l'ancien régime et la révolution americaine (1763–1789)*. Paris, 1952.

Saluces, Alexandre. *Histoire militaire du Piémont*. 2nd ed., 5 Vols. Turin, 1859.

Sédillot, René. *La Grande aventure des Corses*. Paris, 1969.

Sismondi, J. C. L. Simone de. *Histoire des français*. 31 Vols. Paris, 1842.

Soltau, Roger H. *The Duke de Choiseul: The Lothian Essay, 1908*. London, 1909.

Surier, Albert. *Notre Corse: Études et souvenirs*. Paris, 1934.

Thompson, J. W., and Saul K. Padover. *Secret Diplomacy: A Record of Espionage and Double-Dealing: 1500–1815*. London, 1937.

Tinker, Chauncy Brewster. *Nature's Simple Plan: A Phase of Radical Thought in the Mid-Eighteenth Century*. London, 1929.

Tommasi, Camille. *L'administration de la Corse sous la domination génoise, 1300–1768*. Paris, 1912.

Vallance, Aylmer. *The Summer King: Variations by an Adventurer on an Eighteenth Century Air*. London, 1956.

Villat, Louis. *La Corse de 1768 à 1789*. 2 Vols. Besançon, 1924–1925.

Vitale, Vito. *Breviario della storia de Genova*. 2 Vols. Genoa, 1955.

Waddington, Richard. *Louis XV et le renversement des alliances: Préliminaires de la guerre de sept ans, 1754–1756*. Paris, 1896.

Wasserman, Earl R., ed. *Aspects of the Eighteenth Century*. Baltimore, 1965.

Winstanley, D. A. *Lord Chatham and the Whig Opposition*. Cambridge, Eng., 1912.

Wilson, Arthur M. *French Foreign Policy during the Administration of Cardinal Fleury, 1726–1743: A Study in Diplomacy and Commercial Development*. Cambridge, Mass., 1936.

Wolf, John B. *Louis XIV*. New York, 1968.

D. SECONDARY WORKS: ARTICLES

Ambrosi-Rostino, Ambroise. "La Banque Saint-Georges et la Corse de 1453 à 1562," *Bulletin de la Société des Sciences historiques et naturelles de la Corse* (Apr.–June 1912), pp. 209–245.

————. "La conquête de la Corse par les française," *Bulletin de la Société des Sciences historiques et naturelles de la Corse* (Apr.–June 1913), pp. 123–128.

————. "Théodore de Neuhoff," *Bulletin de la Société des Sciences historiques et naturelles de la Corse* (Apr.–June 1913), pp. 115–122.

Arena, Giovanni, "Delle cose di Corsica dal 1730 al 1768," *Archivio Storico Italiano*, XI (1846), 248–279.

Battesti, Juliette. "L'arrivée de Pascal Paoli en Corse," *Revue de la Corse*, No. 108 (1938), 28–44.

————. "Le développement économique de la Corse sous le généralat de Paoli," *Revue de la Corse*, No. 112 (1938), 274–280.

————. "Le généralat de Pascal Paoli: L'organisation financière," *Revue de la Corse*, No. 110 (1938), 130–143.

Bourgeois, Émile. "Un nouvelle édition des mémoires de Choiseul," *Revue Historique*, LXXXVIII (May–Aug. 1905), 83–91.

Casanova, S.-B. "Concession de la nationalité française aux Corse," *Revue de la Corse* (July–Aug. 1935), pp. 233–237.

Combi, Piera. "La cessione di Corsica alla Francia da parte della Repubblica di Genova," *Archivio Storico di Corsica*, II (1926), 22–106.

Courtillier, Gaston. "La Corse et l'opinion publique au xviiie siècle," *Bulletin de la Société des Sciences historiques et naturelles de la Corse* (Oct.–Dec. 1911), pp. 5–53.

Dumay, Raymond. "Quand Figero 1er régnait sur la Corse," *Les Oeuvres Libres*, CLXVIII (1960), 77–102.

Giovellina, Colonna de. "Les Buttafoco: Mathieu Battafoco," *Revue de la Corse*, No. 75 (1932), 114–120.

Grassi, Alexandre. "La prise de Capraia (1767)," *Revue de la Corse*, No. 4 (1923), 129–133, 177–183.

Hall, Thadd E. "The Development of Enlightenment Interest in Eighteenth-Century Corsica," *Studies on Voltaire and the Eighteenth Century*, LXIV (1968), 165–185.

————. "Thought and Practice of Enlightened Government in French Corsica," *The American Historical Review*, LXXIV (Feb. 1969), 880–905.

Hauser, Henri. "En Corse: une terre qui meurt," *Revue du Mois*, No. 47 (Nov. 1909), 539–569.

Letteron, the Abbé L. "Pascal Paoli avant son généralat, 1749–1755," *Bulletin de la Société des Sciences Historiques et naturelles de la Corse* (Oct.–Dec. 1913), pp. 1–47.

Lossky, Andrew. Review of *Louis XIV*, by John B. Wolf, *The Journal of Modern History*, XLII (March 1970), 98–104.

Marini, Philippe. "La Consulte de Caccia et l'élection de Pascal Paoli, 1752–1755," *Bulletin de la Société des Sciences historiques et naturelles de la Corse* (Apr.–June 1913), pp. 65–112.

Oreste, G. "La prima insurrezione còrsa del secolo xvIII (1730–1733)," *Archivio Storico di Corsica,* XVI (1940), 1–12, 147–164, 292–315, 393–430; XVII (1941), 32–79, 159–209.

Petti-Rossu, M. de. "Use Antichi," *U. Fucone: Revue de littérature et d'études corses.* 3rd year, No. 4 (June 1928), 55–61.

Peyre, Marius. "L'établissement des français en Corse (1768–1769)," *Revue des Questions Historiques,* XCIX (1923), 38–61.

Puchesse, Gustave Baguenault de. "Le conquête de la Corse et la maréchal de Vaux, 1769," *Revue des Questions Historiques,* XXVIII (1880), 152–213.

Rispoli, Rosalia. "La seconda insurrezione còrsa del sec. xvIII (1733–1737)," *Archivio Storico di Corsica,* XVII (1941), 289–330, 433–459; XVIII (1942), 37–48, 161–178, 257–277.

Roberti, Giuseppi, "Carlo Emmanuele III e la Corsica al tempo della guerra de successione austriaca," *Rivista Storica Italiana,* VI (1889), 685–698.

Spont, Alfred. "Les français à Tunis de 1660 à 1789," *Revue des Questions Historiques,* LXVII (1900), 88–147.

Tommaseo, N. "Cronachetta delle cose di Corsica dal 1737 al 1741," *Archivio Storico Italiano,* XI (1846), 595–626.

Villat, Louis. "La Corse napoléonienne," *Revue des Étuces Napoléoniennes,* III (1913), 436–460.

———."La Question corse au xvIIIe siècle," *Bulletin de la Société des Sciences historiques et naturelles de la Corse* (Oct.–Dec. 1912), pp. 335–373.

Yvia-Croce, H. "Panorama de la Presse Corse au xvIIIme et xIxme siècles, (1762–1850)," *Corse Historique,* Nos. 23–24 (1966), 5–84.

E. UNPUBLISHED SECONDARY SOURCES

Abarca, Ramon E. "Bourbon 'Revanche' against England: The Balance of Power, 1763–1770" (unpublished Ph.D. dissertation, University of Notre Dame, 1965).

Lambert, Francis X. "The Foreign Policy of the Duc de Choiseul, 1763–1770" (unpublished Ph.D. dissertation, Harvard University, 1952).

Index

settlement, 5-6; sends troops to Corsica (1731-1733), 15-16; and Treaty of Vienna (1738), 48-49; seeks alliance with Piedmont-Sardinia, 59; and Treaty of Worms, 60-61; revives claims to Genoese lands, 100-101; turns away from Italy, 123; as ally of France, 123. *See also* Charles VI, Emperor, Maria-Theresa.

Austrian Succession, War of the, 46, 48, 57-81 *passim,* 102, 104, 112

Balagne, 14, 187, 197, 200-201, 203
Balance of Power, xix, 5, 16, 19, 48
Bank of Amsterdam, 32
Bank of Saint-George, 1-2
Barbary coasts, 207
Barbary powers, 144, 174
Barbary trade, 4
Barbier, Edmond-Jean-François, 37, 53 n. 37, 94-95
Bastelica, 202
Bastia, 11-14, 18, 25, 36, 40, 48, 67-68, 72-74, 105, 130, 135-136, 147, 160, 165-166, 168-170, 173, 177, 184, 187-188, 190-191, 194, 198, 202
Bath, William Pulteney, Earl of, 64
Battle of Borgo (Oct. 5-9, 1768), 196-197
Battle of Ponte-Nuovo (May 8, 1769), 201-202
Belgium (Austrian Netherlands), 73
Bellay, Cardinal Jean de, 3
Belle-Isle, Charles-Louis-Auguste Fouquet, maréchal de, 70-71, 77, 85, 87, 91, 102, 105-106, 119
Benedict XIV, Pope, 63
Bernis, François-Joachim de Pierre de, 119
Bevinco, 195
Biguglia, 194
Bizerte, 208
Bocognano, 202
Boissieux, Alphonse, comte de, 36-41, 49, 67, 97
Bonifacio, 67, 143, 147, 171

Borgo, 40, 195-198, 200
Boscawen, Vice-Admiral, 102
Boswell, James, viii, 153 n. 51
Botta-Adorno, General Antoniotto, 70
Boudard, René, xxi, 6, 125-126
Boufflers, Joseph-Marie, duc de, 71-73
Boufflers, Louis-François, maréchal de, 71-72
Bougainville, Louis Antoine de, 149
Bourbon, House of, 60, 63, 65-66, 168
Bourgogne, *parlement* of, 217
Boyer de Fonscolombe, Joseph, 109-112, 125, 132-134, 143-145, 157, 160-162, 166-167, 173-174
Bozzio, 11, 63
Brandenburg-Prussia, 37, 106, 136
Brandone, 63
Brèves, M. de, 208
Brosses, Charles de, 217
Burns, James MacGregor, xxiv
Buttafuoco, Matteo de, 162, 165, 168, 170-171, 186

Calvi, 8, 46, 48, 67-68, 103, 105-107, 120, 128, 135, 147, 156, 159-161, 173
Camera (Genoa), 7
Campile, 200
Campo Fregoso, Galeazzo, 1
Campo Fregoso, Giano de (doge), 1
Campo Fregoso, Ludovico de (doge), 1
Campo-Freddo, 100
Campredon, Jacques de, 16-17, 27-35, 38, 42-43, 46
Canavaggio, 200-201
Cap Corse, 14, 67, 164-167, 169, 171, 177, 184, 187, 191-192, 198
Capraja, 143-144, 159, 161, 171, 174, 191
Capuchins, 204
Carlos, Don, 14, 17-18, 48. *See also* Charles III, Naples, Spain.
Carteret, Lord John, 62

Casinca, 107, 137, 141, 147-148, 170, 195, 199, 200-201
Castries, Charles-Gabriel de la Croix, marquis de, 104-105
Cateau-Cambrésis, Treaty of (1559), 3
Cauro, 192
Ceccaldi, Andrea Colonna, 11, 13, 15, 24
Celavo, 192
Centurione, Tommaso, 35
Cervione, 8
Cesari-Rocca, Colonna, xviii-xix, 103
Chambrier, Jean de, 37
Chanteloupe, 217
Chardon, Daniel-Marc-Antoine, 186-187, 191-192, 199
Charles, King of the Two Sicilies, 99. See also Don Carlos, Charles III, Naples, Spain.
Charles III, 155-157. See also Don Carlos, Naples, Spain.
Charles VI, 5, 15-19, 24, 26-27, 36, 38, 40, 43, 45-46, 58, 61, 96. See also Austria, Emperor.
Charles VII, 66
Charles-Emmanuel III, 49, 58-61, 64, 66, 68-69, 71, 73. See also Piedmont-Sardinia, Sardinia, Savoy.
Châtelet, Louis-Marie Florent, comte de, 205
Chauvelin, François-Claude de, 77, 85, 89-90, 92, 95, 127-128, 186, 190-191, 193-196, 198
Chauvelin, Germain-Louis, xxi, 30-31
Choiseul, Duchesse de, 218. See also Crozat.
Choiseul, Étienne-François, duc de, xxi-xxv, 106, 112-113, 119-154, 155-182, 183-213, 215-224, passim. See also Corsica, France, Genoa, Paoli.
Choiseul-Beaupré, Colonel, 73
Ciurlino, Étang of, 195
Clement XII, Pope, 15, 96

Clement XIII, Pope, 108, 155
Clergy, role in Corsican rebellion, 14, 204
Col de San-Giacomo, 200
Colbert, Jean Baptiste, 4
Comité, 171-173, 180 n. 26
Compiègne, First Treaty of (Aug. 14, 1756), 103-104, 135
Compiègne, Second Treaty of (Aug. 6, 1764), 135
Conspiracy theory of history, xxiv
Contract theory of government, 192, 221
Controller-General, 217, 219
Convention of Saint-Florent (Sept. 6, 1752), 94
Corsica, passim; powers that have dominated, 1; Genoa's claim to, 1-2; and the Bank of Saint-George, 1-2; and Treaty of Cateau-Cambrésis, 3; offers itself to Louis XIV, 4-5; as part of Mediterranean balance of power, 5-6; local leadership in, 7-8; Genoese government in, 7-10; poor harvests in 1729, 11; rebellion of 1729, 10-11; successes of rebels in 1730-1731, 13; rumors of pretentions to, 14-15; seeks aid from European powers, 14-15, 26; Imperial intervention in, 15; and Peace of Corte (1732), 15-16; establishes "Magistrato Supremo del Regno," 24; declares its independence, 25-26; receives aid from England, 31-32; and Neuhoff's government, 31-32; appeals to France for aid, 38-39; and Convention of Fontainebleau (1738), 41; and regency government, 63-67; and Consulate government, 67; internal divisions in, 72-73; intervention in by Piedmont-Sardinia, 68 ff.; and Treaty of Aix-la-Chapelle, 77; and Convention of Saint-Florent (1752), 93-94; rejects Convention of Saint-Florent, 95; and govern-

ment of Supreme Directory, 95; reaction to Gaffori's assassination, 95-96; and "Council of Regency" government, 96; justifies the rebellion to Europe, 96; under Paoli's leadership, 99 ff.; elects Paoli General-in-Chief, 99; and Paoli's constitution, 99-100; reaction to First Treaty of Compiègne, 104-105; rejects Genoa's conciliation efforts, 107-108; its principles for negotiating peace, 108; growing support for Paoli in, 108; and ecclesiastical reform, 108-109; parallels with Minorca, 123-124; appeals to England for aid, 124; reaction to French intervention (1764), 136-137; begins correspondence with Choiseul, 137; refuses Choiseul's offers, 138-139; sends Choiseul a plan for peace, 139-140; limitations imposed by *Consulte* of Casinca, 141; view of Corsican-French-Genoese relations, 142; appeals to European opinion, 142; takes military action against Genoa, 143; replies to Choiseul's alternatives, 147; negotiations with Choiseul deadlocked, 147; reaction to Jesuits, 156; refuses Choiseul's propositions, 162-170; plans for treaty with France, 168; ceded to France, 174-175; differences between Minorca and, 177-178; decides to resist France, 183-184; makes preparations to resist, 188-190; and victory at Borgo, 195-196; proposes armistice with France, 197-198; action against opposition to Paoli, 197-198; suffers defeat at Ponte-Nuovo, 201-202; seeks aid from Bey of Tunis, 207-208; Paoli's flight from, 201-202. *See also* Choiseul, France, Genoa, Paoli.
Corsican *junte de guerre ou inquisition*, 197

Corsican *junte d'observation*, 192
Corsican legion, 220
Corsican *levée en masse*, 199
Corsican nationalism, xxvi, 25, 67, 170-171, 200, 221
Corsican patriotism, xxvii, 189, 220-221
Corsican Question, *passim;* historiography of, xvii ff.; responsibility of Genoa for, xix; effect of on Genoa, xix, xxvi; interpretations of Choiseul's approach toward, xxiii-xxv; modernity of issues involved in, xxv-xxvii
Corsican roads, 187-188, 190, 199, 204
Corte, 8, 18, 25, 63, 67, 95-96, 99, 187-188, 195, 198, 200-201
Corte, Peace of (May 13, 1732), 15-16, 23-25
Council (France), 84, 198
Council of Orezza (April 20, 1731), 14
Courcy, Colonel de, 88, 94
Coutlet, François, 27
Croce, 194
Croÿ, Duc de, 219
Crozat, Louise-Honorine, 119. *See also* Choiseul, Duchesse de.
Cursay, Marie Rioult de Douilly de, 74, 86-94, 96

Denmark, 136
Doge (Genoa), xxvi, 1, 7, 172
Doria, Andrea, 4
Doria, Camillo, 12-13
Dresden, Peace of (Dec. 1745), 69
Driault, Édouard, xx-xxii, 31, 43, 72, 103, 111
Du Barry, Madame, xxv, 219
Dumouriez, Charles-François, 186-187, 194
Dunant, Captain (English agent), 206
Dunkirk, 102
Durazzo, Carlo-Emmanuele, 45
Durazzo, Marcello di, 172

portance in French policy, 49-51, 61; seeks English guarantee, 57-63; and neutrality, 5, 57, 61, 69, 100, 110; and Treaty of Worms, 60-65; offers concessions to Corsica (1742-1743), 61-64, 72; receives papal emissary, 63; seeks arrangements with Vienna and Turin, 64; and Treaty of Aranjuez, 66-67; returns to repression in Corsica, 67-68; appeals to France for aid (1745), 68; occupied by Austrian troops, 70; receives French aid in Corsica, 71 ff.; and Treaty of Aix-la-Chapelle, 77; requests continued French aid, 84-85; requests recall of Cursay and French troops, 89-93; requests new aid from France, 101; and "First Treaty of Compiègne" (1756), 102-104; conflicts with French troops in Corsica, 106-107; requests increased subsidies from France, 107; attempts to suppress Corsican rebels alone, 107; attempts conciliation, 107-108; hostility to apostolic visitor, 108-109; failure to undermine Paoli's power, 131-132; seeks new aid from France (1762), 132-133; internal division in, 132-133; and "Second Treaty of Compiègne" (1764), 134-136; outrage on learning Paoli's plan, 140-141; willingness to make an agreement with France, 141; proposes a treaty with France, 144; concern over withdrawal of French troops, 157, 161; seeks Spanish aid, 157; proposes cession of Corsica to France, 172; cedes Corsica to France, 174-175. *See also* Choiseul, Corsica, Doge, France, Paoli, Senate, Spain.
Genovesi, Antonio, 97
George III, 206-207
Gherardi, Gerolamo, 143-145, 161-162, 174

Giafferi, Luigi, 11, 13, 15, 24
Gibraltar, 5, 123
Giuliani, Gian Tommaso, 63, 73
Giustiniani, Pietro Maria, 62-63, 67
Golo River, 97, 195, 201
Goulette, 208
Grandmaison, Maréchal de camp, 194
Great Council *(Maggior Consiglio)*, 6-7, 12
Grimaldi, Doctor, 96
Grimaldi, Don Filippo, 107
Grimaldi, Gian Battista, 45
Gropallo, Francesco, 13
Guadeloupe, 124
Guastalla, 94
Guerrilla war, xxvi, 15, 203
Guibert, Colonel Jacques-Antoine-Hippolyte, 220
Guise, Charles (Cardinal of Lorraine), 3
Guise, François (Duc de Lorraine), 3
Guymont, Pierre-Paul, 69, 73, 76, 85, 90

Hapsburg-Valois Wars, 2, 15
Henry II, 2
Holland, 18, 32, 58, 73, 92, 108
Hossein-bel-Ali, Bey of Tunis, 207

Ile Rousse, 61
Instructions, xx, xxii, *passim;* to French envoys to Genoa (1685-1715), 5, 19 n. 8; to Campredon, 16-18, 30-31, 34, 42; to Boissieux, 36, 39; to Maillebois, 41, 69; to A.-M. Pignon, 37-39; to Jonville, 42-45; to Guymont, 69-70, 76; to Boufflers, 71-72; to Richelieu, 72-74, 78; to Fontette, 74; to Cursay, 74, 86-88; to Rouveret, 88; to Courcy, 88; to Chauvelin, 90; to Neuilly, 100; to Pujol, 101; to Castries, 105; to Vaux, 107; to Régny, 123-124; to Valcroissant, 129; to Boyer, 109-110, 132-134,

Neuhoff, Baron Theodore von, 31-32, 35, 37, 43, 52 n. 21, 58, 61-62, 64, 68, 90

Neuilly, Jacques-Philippe Fyot de la Marche, comte de, 100-101, 106, 109, 121

Newcastle, Thomas Pelham-Holles, Duke of, 58, 62-63

Nicholas V, Pope, 1

Niolo, 202

Noailles, Maurice, maréchal de, 70, 102, 112

Oletta, 191, 195-196

Olmeta, 195-196

Orano, convent of, 24

Orezza, 14, 27, 67

Orezza, *piève* of, 196

Ornano, 192

Orticoni, Canon Erasmo, 14-15, 26, 38, 40

Pacte de famille, 110-111, 156-157, 170

Pallavicino, Gerolamo, 35

Pallavicino, Paolo, 24-25

Paoli, Antonio-Filippo-Pasquale, 24, 97-101, 104-105, 107-109, 124, 128-131, 134-149, 156-160, 162-172, 176-179, 183-186, 188-189, 191-196, 198, 200-204, 206-207, 216, 220. *See also* Choiseul, Corsica, France, Genoa.

Paoli, Clemente, 96-97, 99, 138, 202

Paoli, Giacinto, 24-25, 96-97

Papacy, 108, 111

Parlement, 193

Parma, 5, 17-18, 28, 48, 60, 66, 94, 111

Paulain, Sieur, 184

Paulmy, Antoine-René de Voyer, marquis de, 105

Pavi, 66

Peace of Paris (1763), 124, 176, 216

Penta, 195

Pentremole, 111

Pères du commune, 8, 26

Petit Council *(Minor Consiglio),* 6-7, 35, 132-133, 140, 172

Philip II, 92

Philip V, 5, 26, 73

Philippe, Don, 37, 71, 94, 111, 125

Philisophes, 119, 155, 187, 218-220

Physiocratic school, 219

Piacenza, 17, 48, 60

Piedmont mountains, 59

Piedmont-Sardinia, 49, 58-59, 65-66, 125. *See also* Charles-Emmanuel III, Sardinia.

Pignon, A.-M., 37-39

Pinelli (Genoese Senator), 161

Pinello, Felice, 11-12

Pinet, Michel de, 132-133

Pitt, William, 177, 206

Plaisance, 60, 66, 94, 111, 125, 126

Po River, 60

Podestats, 9, 62

Poitou, 86

Polish Succession, War of the, 25, 48

Pombal, Sebastian Joseph Carvalho, marquis de, 155

Pommereul, François-René-Jean, 12

Pompadour, Madame de, 91-92, 119

Ponte-Nuovo, 201-202

Port Mahon, 102, 147, 177

Porto Maurizio, Father Leonardo da, 63

Portovecchio, 202

Portugal, 136, 155

Praslin, César-Gabriel, duc de, 124-125, 132-134, 151 n. 10, 207

Présides, xxiii-xxiv, 48, 67, 95, 104, 106, 126-129, 131, 134, 136, 139, 141, 146, 148, 156-157, 160, 162, 166-167, 169-170, 174, 176-178, 185, 188, 198

Provence, 70, 75, 121, 164, 207

Puget (Provence), 70

Pujol, M. de, 101

Puysieulx, Louis-Philoxène Brulart, marquis de, 74-77, 80 n. 38, 83-85, 87-91, 93-94

Quenza, 202